Provincial Geographies of India

General Editor
Sir T. H. HOLLAND, K.C.I.E., D.Sc., F.R.S.

THE MADRAS PRESIDENCY
WITH MYSORE, COORG AND
THE ASSOCIATED STATES

THE MADRAS PRESIDENCY
WITH MYSORE, COORG AND
THE ASSOCIATED STATES

BY

EDGAR THURSTON, C.I.E.

SOMETIME SUPERINTENDENT OF THE MADRAS GOVERNMENT MUSEUM

Cambridge :
at the University Press
1913

CAMBRIDGE UNIVERSITY PRESS
Cambridge, New York, Melbourne, Madrid, Cape Town,
Singapore, São Paulo, Delhi, Tokyo, Mexico City

Cambridge University Press
The Edinburgh Building, Cambridge CB2 8RU, UK

Published in the United States of America by
Cambridge University Press, New York

www.cambridge.org
Information on this title: www.cambridge.org/9781107600683

© Cambridge University Press 1913

First published 1913
First paperback edition 2011

A catalogue record for this publication is available from the British Library

ISBN 978-1-107-60068-3 Paperback

EDITOR'S PREFACE

THE casual visitor to India, who limits his observations of the country to the all-too-short cool season, is so impressed by the contrast between Indian life and that with which he has been previously acquainted that he seldom realises the great local diversity of language and ethnology. This local variety, however, receives expression even in the forms of administration ; for the success of the British rule in India is largely due to the fact that the early ad ministrators adopted the local systems of government and moulded them gradually according to the lessons of experience. And this was because the British occupation was that of a trading company of which the present Government of India is a lineal descendant—a fact too often apparently overlooked in the modern administration of the country.

The recent enlargement of the functions of the Local Governments, and more complete management of local affairs, with the formation of Executive, and extension of the Legislative, Councils, all tend to direct more intensely the people's thoughts to the affairs of their own provinces. It is hoped that these Provincial Geographies will in some way reflect this growing tendency to develop special provincial atmospheres, and with this object in view endeavours

have been made to select as authors those who, besides
having an accurate and detailed knowledge of each area
treated, are able to give a broad view of its features with
a personal touch that is beyond the power of the mere
compiler.

Among the "provinces" the Madras Presidency has
above all developed an individuality of its own—advanced
in education through early missionary effort, free of frontier
worries, comparatively homogeneous in ethnic composition,
and sufficiently unknown to the Central Government to
escape undue interference, its officials and its people are
distinctly "Madrassi," and are rightly proud to be so. No
geographical unit could more appropriately be selected to
initiate this series, and everyone who knows the Senior Presidency will recognise the pre-eminent fitness of Mr Edgar
Thurston to give a true picture of South India. As
Superintendent of the Madras Museum for 25 years, he
sampled every form of natural product in the south. As
Superintendent for many years of the Ethnographic Survey,
he travelled through every district and obtained an intimate
acquaintance with the people, his numerous publications
on Ethnography being summed up in his encyclopaedic
work on the *Castes and Tribes of Southern India*. Old
friends, whose number cannot be counted, will recognise
Mr Thurston's touch throughout the book : no one else
could so readily recall an appropriate story or legend to
add to the human interest of nearly every place mentioned ;
many of those whose interests are more human than geographical will read the book merely because of the Author's
personality. Nothing better could be said of it, and no

better recommendation could be offered to those who have
not had the privilege of knowing Mr Thurston personally.

The Author has had the willing help of several friends,
among whom might specially be mentioned Mr J. S. Gamble,
C.I.E., F.R.S., who, as an old official of the Indian Forest
Department, has dealt authoritatively with the chapter on
the Flora and Forests.   Mr E. B. Havell, who is well
known by his charming books on Indian Art, has con-
tributed the chapter on Architecture, a subject which he
had an opportunity of specially studying when for many
years he was Principal of the Madras School of Art, while
Mr George Romilly, who, as the representative for many
years of the planters' community on the Legislative Council,
has given the benefit of his personal knowledge of, and successful commercial experience with, the planting industries.
For the shortcomings of the chapter on Geology I am
mainly responsible.

We are indebted to various friends, official and private,
for permission to use photographs and maps, and the source
of each illustration is acknowledged in the list.

T. H. H.

May 1913.

CONTENTS

LIST OF ILLUSTRATIONS AND MAPS

Figs. 3, 4, 5, 9, 10, 17, 18, 29, 30, 31, 36, 37, 38, 39, 40, 42, 54, 62, 64, 65, 66, 67, 68, 70, 74, 75, 76, 77, 78, 88, 90, 91, 93, 95, 96, 98, 99, 100, are reproduced from photographs by Messrs Wiele and Klein, photographers, Madras.

Figs. 23 and 94 are from photographs by Messrs Barton, Son and Co., photographers, Bangalore.

CHAPTER I

AREA ; BOUNDARIES ; DIVISIONS

THE large tract of country dealt with in the present volume includes: (*a*) the **Madras Presidency**, or Presidency of Fort St George, so named after the patron saint of England ; (*b*) the States of **Travancore** and **Cochin**, and the smaller States of **Pudukkottai**, **Banganapalle**, and **Sandur**, which have political relations with the Government of Madras ; (*c*) the State of **Mysore**, and the small British Province of Kodagu or **Coorg**, which have direct political relations with the Government of India ; (*d*) the **French Possessions**, all of which, with the exception of Chandernagore in Bengal, are situated in the south of the Peninsula.

The title of Presidency, as applied to Madras, which has been called in disparagement the Benighted Presidency or the Cinderella of the Indian Provinces, and more happily Clive's Province, had its origin in the seventeenth century, when the Agent of the East India Company was raised to the rank of President, independent of Bantam in Java. The city of Madras is still known in official parlance as the Presidency, in contra-distinction to the outlying and up-country districts and stations, which are known as the mofussil (mufassal, provincial).

The etymology of the name **Madras** has been the subject of much speculation. It has, for example, been connected with a legend concerning a fictitious fisherman named

T.   I

Madarasen. The suggestion has been made that it is a corruption of Manda-rājya, meaning realm of the stupid, or of the Portuguese Madre de Dios. A further suggestion is that it is derived from a Telugu ruler named Mandaradzu.

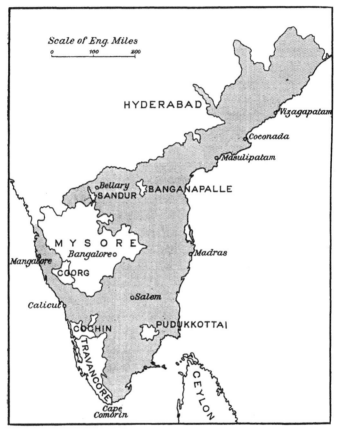

Fig. 1. Madras Presidency, Coorg, and associated States.

The firman from the Nāyak or chief, from whom Mr Francis Day acquired permission, in 1639, to settle at Madras, and build a fort, refers to " our port of Madraspatam " (Madras city). In a seventeenth century print, Madirass is shown on the north of Fort St George. The authors of *Hobson-Jobson* point out that the earliest maps show Madraspatanam as the Muhammadan settlement, and suggest that the name is probably of Muhammadan origin, and connected with Madrasa, a college. The name now applied by Indians to the city of Madras is Chinnapatanam, which is commonly said to be derived from that of Chennappa, the father of the Nāyak from whom permission to build Fort St George was obtained. The name Chīnāpatan occurs on coins of the Moghul Emperors Aurangzīb and Farrukh-siyar struck at Madras. It would seem improbable that the name is, as has been suggested, connected with the intercourse of the Chinese with South India, though Mendoza, in his book on China published in 1585, refers to

Fig. 2. Chīnāpatan Rupee of Aurangzīb.

a town on the Coromandel coast "called unto this day the Soile of the Chinos, for that they did reedifie and make the same." Chinese coins are, it may be noted, occasionally picked up on the sea-shore at Mahābalipuram (Seven Pagodas), 35 miles south of Madras.

The **Travancore State** is situated in the extreme south-west of the Peninsula, and extends southward to Cape Comorin. It is bounded on the north by the Cochin State, on the east by the western ghāts or ghauts, and on the west by the Arabian Sea, which has been defined as the name applied to the portion of the Indian Ocean bounded east by India, north by Baluchistan and part of the southern Persian littoral, west by Arabia, and south, approximately, by a line between Cape Guardafui, the north-east point of Somaliland, and Cape Comorin. The State has its own currency, the coins being minted at the capital Trivandrum or Tiru-ananthapuram, the holy city of Anantha, in whose name coins called Ananthan cash, and Ananthan varāhas or pagodas, have been struck. At the religious ceremony called tulabhāram or tulupurushadānam (tulu, scales; purusha, man; dānam, gift), the Mahārāja is weighed in scales against gold coins called tulabhāra kāsu, specially struck for the occasion, which are subsequently distributed among the priests and Brahmans.

The **Cochin State** is, for the most part, bounded on the north by the district of Malabar; on the east by the Malabar and Coimbatore districts, and Travancore; on the west by Malabar and the Arabian Sea; and on the south by Travancore. The isolated tāluk (subdivision) of Chittūr is entirely surrounded by the districts of Malabar and Coimbatore. Coins, called puthans, were formerly current in the State, but, owing to the large number of forgeries that had found their way into circulation, and the difficulty of handling the puthans in Treasury transactions, they were withdrawn from circulation, and, since 1900, the British Indian coins have been the sole currency.

Both Travancore and Cochin were principalities before the supremacy of the British, and are held under treaties made originally with the East India Company. They pay subsidies which were originally payments for military protection by the British. The troops were ultimately withdrawn, and the military protection is now by troops outside the territories of the States.

The **State of Pudukkottai** (new fort), which has an area of 1,100 square miles, is surrounded by the districts of Tanjore, Madura and Trichinopoly, and occupies the territory formerly known as Tondaimandalam (the Tondimān country) after the family name of the ruling chief. The State was given to a former Tondimān as a reward for faithful services to the British during the military operations against the French, Haidar Ali, and the poligars or feudal chiefs of Madura and Tinnevelly, in the eighteenth century. Copper coins called Amman kāsu (goddess cash) are still current within the State, and their greatest circulation is during the Navaratri or Dusserah festival, when they are distributed along with a dole of rice.

The **Banganapalle State** (255 square miles) is situated on the Deccan table-land within the Kurnool district. A title-deed, dated 1761, records that the Nizam appointed a certain Muhammadan as Kiladar (commandant) and Faujdar (magistrate) of Banganapalle. When the Nizam handed over the Ceded Districts, including Kurnool, to the British in 1800, the control was transferred to the British Government. In 1871, the Muhammadan head of the State received the hereditary title of Nawāb.

The **Sandur State** (161 square miles), which is bounded by the Bellary district and a corner of Mysore, is situated in a valley shut in between two ranges of hills. The sanitarium of Rāmandrūg, called after a celebrated poligar or feudal chief named Komāra Rāma, is situated on a plateau 3256 feet above the sea. The State was originally feudatory to the Marāthas, and was handed over to an ancestor of the present Marātha Rāja by a sanad or deed of grant. The family name of the Rājas, Ghorpade, is connected with a legend, according to which one of them scaled a precipitous fort by clinging to a big lizard (ghorpade), which was crawling up it.

The **Mysore State**, which has been described as a rocky triangle, is situated on a table-land or plateau, where the eastern and western ghāts converge towards the Nīlgiri hills. It is surrounded by the Madras Presidency except in parts of the west and north, where Coorg and the

Bombay Presidency form the boundaries. It naturally divides itself into the malnād or hill country on the west, and the maidān or open country to the east. For administrative purposes, it is divided into eight districts, viz. Bangalore, Kolar, Tumkur, Mysore, Hassan, Kadur, Shimoga, and Chitaldroog. The State is best known in history in connection with the Muhammadan usurpers Haidar Ali and his son Tīpu (or Tippoo) Sultan in the latter part of the eighteenth century. On the death of Tīpu, Krishna Rāja Wodeyar, the representative of the Hindu (Wodeyar) dynasty was placed on the throne, but deposed by the British Government some years later. The rendition of the State, in connection with which the Mahārāja was placed on the throne by the Governor of Madras, took place in 1881. The mint was abolished in 1843. Many specimens of the coins of Tīpu Sultan and Krishna Rāja Wodeyar can still be obtained in the bazars of Bangalore, Mysore, Seringapatam, etc.

Coorg is a mountainous province, situated to the west of Mysore on the summit and slopes of the western ghāts, with Mercāra as its principal town. The reigning Rāja, who had shown marked signs of disaffection, was deposed in 1834, and the Commissioner of Mysore was appointed Commissioner of the new British province. The deposed Rāja visited England in 1852 with his young daughter, to whom Queen Victoria stood sponsor through the Archbishop of Canterbury at her baptism. The Kodagas or Coorgs, who form 20 per cent. of the population, are a stalwart race, among whom many ceremonies still take the form of indicating physical fitness. They wear a picturesque full-dress consisting of dark cloth coat showing the arms of a white shirt, with a red or blue girdle, in which a war-knife with an ivory or silver hilt is stuck.

The **French Possessions** consist of Pondicherry, Kārikāl,

and Yanam or Yanaon on the east coast, and Mahē on the west. The settlement of **Pondicherry** (115 square miles), which includes the town of the same name, is surrounded by the South Arcot district, except on the east, where it faces the Bay of Bengal. The name Pondicherry, which has sometimes been spelt Pont de Cheree, is a corruption of Puduchchēri (new town). In early records reference is made to Phoolcheri, and silver coins struck by the French Company bear the name Phulcheri in Persian characters. **Kārikāl** (53 square miles) is surrounded on three sides by the Tanjore district, and bounded on the east by the Bay of Bengal. Many coolies emigrate thence to the French colonies. The little settlement of **Yanam** (5 square miles) is situated on the banks of the Gautami Godāvari and Coringa rivers, and surrounded by the Godāvari district. **Mahē** (26 square miles), named after the distinguished Frenchman, Mahé de la Bourdonnais, is picturesquely situated at the mouth of a river on the Malabar coast, about four miles south of Tellicherry. The French have also a loge, consisting of about six acres on the sea-shore, about half a mile north of the lighthouse at Calicut in Malabar. In the town of Masulipatam, on the east coast, the quarters of several European nationalities, which have carried on trade there, are recognised. These are known as the English pālem, Valanda (Hollander) pālem, and French pettah, the ownership of which is still vested in the French Government.

It is recorded by Sir Mountstuart Grant Duff, a former Governor of Madras, that "when I was passing through Rome, Biancheri, the speaker of the Italian Parliament, said to me, 'What is the size of this country you have been governing?' 'It is,' I said, 'larger than Italy, including all the Italian islands.' 'Good heavens,' he replied, 'what an empire is that, in which such a country is only a province!'" The **area and population** of the British territories and Native States, as recorded at the census, 1901, were as follows :—

	Area sq. miles	Population
Madras Presidency and Feudatory States	143,221	38,623,066
Mysore	29,444	5,539,399
Travancore	7,091	2,952,157
Cochin	1,361	512,025
Coorg	1,582	180,607

The **area** under consideration is situated within the Tropic of Cancer between 8° 5'—20° 26' N. latitude, and 74° 34'— 85° 12' E. longitude. It embraces the whole of the southern portion of the Indian peninsula, which narrows southward to the extreme point at Cape Comorin or Kanniyakumāri— the *Komaria akron* of Ptolemy—where stands a temple dedicated to Kanniyāmbāl, the virgin goddess, which is a favourite resort of Hindu pilgrims, who bathe in the sea. The irregular northern boundary, due to the accident of history, and not to ethnic or physical considerations, is formed from east to west by Orissa, the Central Provinces, the Native State of Hyderabad or the Nizam's Dominions, and the southern districts of the Bombay Presidency. The west and east coasts are washed respectively by the waters of the Arabian Sea, and those of the Bay of Bengal and Gulf of Manaar. This gulf, which is named after the island of Manaar off the coast of Ceylon, separates the Rāmnād and Tinnevelly districts of the Madras Presidency from the island of Ceylon. It is bounded on the north by the chain of rocks called Adam's Bridge, concerning which the legend runs that the common striped or palm-squirrel (*Sciurus palmarum*) was employed by Rāma to assist the army of monkeys in the construction of the bridge to connect Pāmban island with Ceylon, whither Rāvana had carried off his wife Sīta. The squirrel helped the monkeys by rolling in the sand on the shore, so as to collect it in its hairy coat, and then deposited it between the piled-up

stones, so as to cement them together. Seeing it fatigued
by its labours, Rāma sympathetically stroked its back with
the three middle fingers of his right hand, the marks of
which still persist in the squirrels at the present day.
According to tradition, the temple at Rāmēsvaram was
founded by Rāma as a thank-offering for the success of
the expedition against Rāvana. The possibility of making
an artificial union between South India and Ceylon by
means of a railway across Adam's Bridge is at the present
time under consideration.

North of the Gulf of Manaar are Palk's Straits and Bay,
named after Mr Robert Palk, Governor of Madras, 1763—
1767. The name "Palk's Streights" appears in a survey
chart dated 1764. The Bay is bounded on the west by the
coast of the Tanjore and Rāmnād districts, and the pro-
montory of Point Calimere, which is 40 miles distant from
Point Pedro in Ceylon. The reserved forest of Point
Calimere is noted for its black-buck (antelope), spotted
deer, and wild pigs.

The Madras Presidency has been roughly divided into
five natural divisions, viz. (1) the strip facing the Arabian
Sea, which is commonly known as the west coast; (2) the
central table-land, or Deccan; (3) the Agencies; (4) the
east coast division, extending from Ganjam in the north as
far south as the Nellore district; (5) the southern division,
including the whole of the Tamil country, which is spread
over the districts of North Arcot, Madras, Chingleput,
Salem, Coimbatore, South Arcot, Tanjore, Trichinopoly,
Madura, Rāmnād, and Tinnevelly.

The **west coast**, which is bounded on the west by the
Arabian Sea, and on the east by the western ghāts, com-
prises the districts of South Canara and Malabar or
Malayālam (the hill country), and the Native States of
Travancore and Cochin, all of which are included in the
ancient kingdom of Kērala. According to the legend,

Parasu Rāma (Rāma of the axe), an incarnation of Vishnu, secured from the gods permission to reclaim some land from Varuna the sea-god.   Accordingly, he threw his axe from Cape Comorin as far as Gokarnam in South Canara, and immediately the sea receded, and there was dry land between these places as far as the western ghāts.   To people this land, he brought the Nambutiri Brahmans from the north, gave them peculiar customs, such as the marumakkatāyam law of succession (descent in the female line), and located them in sixty-four grāmams (Brahman villages).   To rule over the people, an individual named Kēya Perumal was selected, who was the first king of Malabar.   The name Kērala is at the present day per-petuated in the masonic lodge called Lodge Kērala at Calicut.

The name **Deccan** (dakhan, the south) has been applied by some writers to the whole of the Peninsula south of the Nerbudda river, but is more properly restricted to the table-land between the eastern and western ghāts.   It includes the Cuddapah, Kurnool, Bellary, and Anantapur districts, which are also known as the Ceded Districts, as they were ceded to the British in 1800, after the death of Tīpu Sultan.

The **Agencies** include the mountainous western portions of the Ganjam, Vizagapatam, and Godāvari districts in the north-east of the Presidency, which are inhabited by various wild tribes, e.g. the Kondhs, Savaras, and Koyis, who "differ in religion, language, customs, and ethnic characters, from the dwellers in the plains below them.   Within these tracts, the ordinary law of the land is in force only to a limited extent.   Collectors (or chief administrative officials) have extended and unusual judicial authority, both civil and criminal, which they exercise under the special title of Agents to the Governor."

The name **Northern Circars** or Sirkars (divisions of

territory) has been applied to the territory to the north of the Coromandel coast, which includes the districts of Ganjam, Vizagapatam, Godāvari, Kistna, and Guntur. The original Circars of Chicacole, Rajahmundry, Ellore, Konda-pille, and Guntur, were the subject of a grant obtained by Clive from the Great Moghul in 1765. The tract of country known as the Northern Circars corresponds approximately with that which, in early times, formed the kingdom of Kalinga. The port of Calingapatam in Ganjam, and the Oriya Kalinji and Telugu Kalingi castes, still preserve the ancient name. Kling (a corruption of Kalinga) is applied in the Malay countries, including the Straits Settlements, to the people of Peninsular India who trade thither or are settled in those regions. The phrase Orang Kling Islam, i.e. a Muhammadan from the Madras coast, which occurs in Patani Malay, refers to the Labbai and Marakkāyar Muhammadans, who go to the Straits Settlements for the purpose of trade.

The name **Coromandel** was formerly applied to the east coast of the Madras Presidency, extending northward from Point Calimere to the mouth of the Kistna river, or even further. The origin of the name has given rise to much discussion. Thus it has been derived by different authorities from Kuru-mandala, the realm of the Kurus, kuru-manal, black sand, chola-mandalam, the country of the cholam millet, and khara-mandalam, the hot country. It seems most probable that the name is a corruption of Chora-mandala or Chola-mandala, i.e. the kingdom of the Cholas, who, in the tenth century, had their capital at Tanjore.

Ma'bar, which must not be confused with Malabar, is said by Ibn Batuta, the Arab traveller, who visited South India in the fourteenth century, to be the name which the Arabs gave to the coast of Coromandel. In Marsden's edition of *The Travels of Marco Polo*, Maâbar is defined as an appellation, signifying passage or ferry, given by the

Muhammadans to Tinnevelly, Madura, and perhaps the Tanjore country, from their vicinity to Adam's Bridge. Viceroys were appointed by the Sultans of Delhi to govern this country. Copper coins are found in the bazars, bearing the names of the Sultans Muhammad Taghlak, Kutb-ud-din, etc., and of the usurping Viceroy Jalāl-ad-din Ahsan Shāh, who struck coins in his own name.

The name **Carnatic**, meaning Canarese country, has been loosely applied to the Tamil country of Madras, and the Telugu district of Nellore. According to one definition, " the province known as the Carnatic, in which Madras was situated, extended from the Kistna to the Coleroon river, and was bounded on the west by Cuddapah, Salem, and Dindigul, all of which formed part of the State of Mysore. The northern portion was known as the Moghal Carnatic, the southern the Mahratta Carnatic." In discussing the modern misapplication of the name, Bishop Caldwell writes that " when the Muhammadans arrived in Southern India, they found that part of it with which they first became acquainted—the country above the ghāts, including Mysore and part of Telingāna (the Telugu country)—called the Karnātaka country. In course of time, by a misapplication of terms, they applied the same name Karnātaka or Carnatic to designate the country below the ghāts, as well as that which was above. The English have carried the misapplication a step further, and restricted the name to the country below the ghāts, which never had any right to it whatever, and what is now geographically termed the 'Carnatic' is exclusively the country below the ghāts on the Coromandel coast." The line of Nawābs of the Carnatic, which commenced with Zu-l-Fikar Khān in 1692, terminated with Ghulam Muhammad Ghaus Khan, who died in 1855. In 1883 a masonic lodge, called Lodge Carnatic, was founded in Madras for Indian freemasons.

CHAPTER II

THE two main mountain systems of Southern India are called respectively the **eastern** and **western ghāts**, which include between them the great table-land of the Deccan and Mysore, and meet at an angle in the Nīlgiri Hills. The word **ghāt**, in its proper application, means a path of descent or steps leading to a river, such as the celebrated bathing-ghāt at Benares, or a mountain pass. In the latter sense, it is correctly used by Sir Walter Scott in *The Surgeon's Daughter*, which deals with Madras and Mysore in the time of Haidar Ali. The word is now generally applied to the mountain ranges or ghāts, through which the passes lead. The best known of such passes is the Coonoor ghāt on the Nīlgiris, which can be ascended either by the ghāt road, or by the mountain railway. The road, cut through the hill-side, is protected by a stone parapet, to prevent vehicles from falling down the precipitous hill-side or khud. The steep bluff called Hulikal Drūg (tiger-stone fort), or more commonly the Drūg, at the south end of the ravine which forms the Coonoor ghāt, is surmounted by an old fort, and derives its name from a legend relating to a man-eating tiger which once infested the neighbourhood. Other ghāts on the Nīlgiris are the Sigūr, Gudalūr, Karkūr, Sispāra and Kotagiri ghāts, which lead to the Mysore and Wynaad table-lands and the plains of Malabar and Coimbatore.

The name **Nīlgiris** or Blue Mountains (nīla-giri) is probably derived from the blue haze which hangs over the

Fig. 4. Toda buffaloes

hills when viewed from the distant plains, and not, as has
been suggested, to the periodical diffused flowering of the
blue *Strobilanthes*.   The Nīlgiri plateau, which has an
average altitude of about 6,500 feet above the sea, consists
largely of open grassy "downs" dotted with wooded sholas
(glades), in the vicinity of which a Toda mand or mad
(settlement), composed of half-barrel-shaped dwelling-huts
and dairy, and cattle-pen, may be seen here and there.
The highest point on the Nīlgiris is the summit of Dodabetta (big hill) rising to a height of 8,760 feet above the
sea, on which cinchona, jalap, and ipecacuanha, have been
successfully cultivated.   Ootacamund, the hot-weather
headquarters of the Madras Government, lies in an amphitheatre surrounded by Dodabetta, Snowdon (8,299 feet),
Elk hill (8,090 feet), and Club hill (8,030 feet).   The name
elk, it may be noted, has been wrongly applied by sportsmen to the sāmbar deer.   A conspicuous feature of the
landscape, as one looks westward from Ootacamund, is the
Kundah range, which rises precipitously from Malabar,
with the triangular hill called Mūkarti (cut nose) peak
(8,403 feet).   Further west, beyond Naduvatam, where
the Government cinchona factory is situated, is the beautiful Ouchterlony valley, named after Mr James Ouchterlony,
a pioneer of coffee cultivation on the Nīlgiris, which has
been extensively opened up for planters' estates.   At the
east end of the plateau is the sacred hill called **Rangaswāmi peak**, with the isolated pillar rock named Rangaswāmi pillar.   Of the indigenous people who inhabit the
plateau, the best known are the pastoral and polyandrous
Todas, who maintain a large-horned race of buffaloes, on
whose milk, and the products thereof, they depend largely
for existence.   The agricultural element is represented by
the Badagas, and the artisan by the Kotas.   The Badagas
live in villages, often situated on the summit of low hillocks,
and surrounded by the fields which yield the crops.   Their

Fig. 4. Toda buffaloes

number was returned at the census, 1901, as 34,178, against
1,267 Kotas, and 807 Todas. The Kotas inhabit seven
villages, of which six are on the plateau, and one is on
the western slopes at Gudalur. They are the blacksmiths
and goldsmiths, carpenters, rope-makers, and potters of the
hills, and are also employed in cultivation. They are,
further, the musicians at Toda and Badaga funerals, for
which they provide the band. The jungles on the slopes
of the hills are inhabited by the primitive Kurumbas and
Irulas, some of whom work for the forest department or on
planters' estates.

The **Wynaad table-land**, situated at an average height
of 3,000 feet above the sea, stretches from the foot of the
northern slopes of the Nīlgiris into Malabar and the
Mysore plateau. The dense jungles have been opened
up by planters for the cultivation of coffee, tea, and pepper,
which gives employment to a large number of Canarese
and Tamil coolies (hired labourers). In the middle of the
last century, when planters first began to settle in the
Wynaad, they purchased the land with the Paniyans living
on it, who were practically slaves (*adscripti glebæ*) of the
land-owners.

The **Western Ghāts**, which commence in the Bombay
Presidency, extend southward through South Canara
(which they separate from Mysore), Coorg, Malabar, Cochin,
and Travancore, and terminate near Cape Comorin in the
extreme south of the Peninsula. The range is continuous
and unbroken, except for the natural break, 16 miles
wide, formed by the Palghāt Gap between the districts of
Coimbatore and Malabar, by means of which, even before
the days of the railway, communication between the Tamil
and Malabar countries was easy. The difference in the
appearance and customs of the indigenous population,
cultivation, and scenery, eastward and westward of the
Palghāt Gap, is very marked. The Western Ghāts range

T.   2

from about 3,000 to 8,000 feet above the sea, and, in
Ānaimudi (elephant forehead) peak in the High Range
of Travancore, possess the highest point (8,837 feet) in
Southern India. A conspicuous peak in South Canara
called Kudremukh (horse's face), which is resorted to by
officials as a hot-weather sanitarium, reaches a height of
6,215 feet above the sea. South of the Palghāt Gap are
a series of hill ranges, which have received a variety of
names. The **Ānaimalais**, or elephant hills, which extend
from the Coimbatore district southward into Travancore,
are inhabited by Kādirs, Muduvars, Malasars, and other
hill tribes. An important forest station is situated, in the
midst of a dense bamboo jungle, at Mount Stuart, playfully
named after Sir Mountstuart Grant Duff, who visited the
spot when Governor of Madras. On the Ānaimalais, elephants are caught in pits—made with hands and covered
over with bamboo and earth for the purpose of securing
them—and tamed. The forests of the **Nelliampathis**
(1,500 to 5,000 feet) in the Cochin State have been opened
up in recent years by the Cochin Forest Department for
the sake of their timber. Further south, in Travancore,
are the **Cardamom** and Pīrmed hills (3,000 to 3,500 feet),
with the hill-station of Pīrmed. In the southern portion
of the ghāts is the conical peak called Agastyamalai (6,200
feet), where the sage Agastya Maharshi, who is regarded
as the pioneer of Aryan civilisation in Southern India, is
supposed still to live as a Yōgi in pious seclusion. The
Palni hills, which run out from the main line of the ghāts
in a north-easterly direction in the Madura district, derive
their name from the town of Palni. Thither devotees flock
from Malabar and other places to worship at the shrine of
Subramaniya, some with silver mouth-locks, others with
a skewer piercing the cheeks, or carrying a kāvadi (portable
shrine) containing milk or fish. The Palnis are divided
into the Eastern Lower Palnis (3,000 to 4,000 feet), and

Fig. 5. General view of Kodaikānal, with the lake.

the Western Palnis with a mean elevation of 7,000 feet, rising in Vembādi Shola hill to 8,218 feet above the sea. In the central portion of the range is the popular hill-station of Kodaikānal (7,200 feet), which is reached by a ghāt road from the town of Periyakulam near the foot of the hills. The crow has not yet found its way to Kodai-kānal, and it is on record that a Brahman who had to perform the srādh or anniversary ceremony for his dead father, in which crows play an important part, telegraphed to Periyakulam for a pair of these birds, which duly arrived in a cage. The Palnis are inhabited, among others, by the Kunnuvans, and by the Paliyans, who are also found further south near the foot of the Tinnevelly hills.

The **Eastern Ghāts** have been described as "a disjointed line of small confused ranges which begin in Orissa, pass into Ganjam, the northernmost district of the Madras Presidency, and run through a greater or less extent of all the districts which lie between Ganjam and the Nīlgiri plateau. They are about 2,000 feet in elevation on an average, and their highest peaks are less than 6,000 feet. In Ganjam and Vizagapatam they run close to the shore of the Bay of Bengal, but, as they travel southwards, they recede further inland, and leave a stretch of low country from 100 to 150 miles wide between their easternmost spurs and the sea." In the three northern districts of Ganjam, Vizagapatam and Godāvari, the hill country is included in the Agencies (p. 10). The **Māliahs** or high-lands of Ganjam, composed of a series of undulating pla-teaux, contain the highest peaks, named Singarāzu and Mahendragiri, which rise to a height of nearly 5,000 feet above the sea. Many passes lead into these hills, and include the Kalingia ghāt from Russellkonda, the Muni-singhi ghāt from Parlākimedi, and the Taptapāni or hot-spring ghāt, so named from its containing a hot sulphur

spring. The Māliahs are inhabited, among others, by
Kondhs, Savaras, Gonds, and Pāno hill weavers. The
Kondhs formerly performed human or meriah sacrifices,
and the Madras Museum possesses a wooden post from
Balligūda, roughly hewn into the shape of an elephant's
head, on which the sacrificial victim was tied. In the
Vizagapatam district the **Jeypore hills** form a series of
plateaux, with an average elevation of 3,000 feet above the
sea. In the Agency tracts of the Godāvari district is the
Rampa country, which was the scene of many disturbances,
commencing at the end of the eighteenth century, and
culminating in the Rampa rebellion of 1879. During one
of these disturbances, in 1834, the body of one Pāyaka
Rao, who was hanged by the British, was suspended in an
iron cage on a gibbet. In the jungles of Anantapur there
was formerly a gibbet, now in the Madras Museum, from
which two iron cages were suspended by iron hooks. According to local tradition, the two ringleaders of a band of
dacoits (robbers) were put alive into the cages, and starved
to death. On a stone near the gibbet was an inscription
recording that two men were hung in 1837 for killing a
man by throwing a noose. In the Kurnool district are
two ranges of hills called the **Erramalas** (red hills), about
600 feet above the sea, and the **Nallamalais** (black hills)
with Bhairani Konda (3,048 feet) as the highest point.
The latter are inhabited by the jungle Chenchus, who are
said to levy a toll in return for protecting pilgrims on their
way to the shrine of Mallikarjuna (Siva) at Srīsailam.
The **Pālkonda** or milk hills, which are said to derive their
name from the excellent grazing they afford, commence at
the sacred hill of Tirumala or Tirupati, and run through
the Cuddapah district into Anantapur at an average elevation of 2,000 feet above the sea. In the **Nagari** hills of the
North Arcot district are a peak called Nagari Nose (2,824
feet), and a plateau called Kettle Bottom, which serve as

landmarks for ships making the port of Madras. The
Javādi hills of North Arcot, the Kalrāyan, Kollaimalai,
and Shevaroy hills of Salem, and the Pachaimalais of Trichinopoly, are all inhabited by Malayālis (= hill people),
who, according to tradition, originally belonged to the
Vellāla caste of cultivators, and emigrated from the sacred
city of Kānchipuram (Conjeeveram) to the hills when
Muhammadan rule was dominant in Southern India. The
Shevaroy hills contain the small hill-station of Yercaud or
Erkād (4,500 feet). The Malayālis hold an annual festival
on the summit of the Shēvarāyan hill, where the temple
of the god Servarāyan is situated in the midst of a sacred
grove.

The most mountainous region of the Mysore State,
situated in the Kadur district, is bordered on the west by
the Western Ghāts. It has been said to rise into some of
the loftiest peaks between the Nīlgiris and the Himālayas,
supporting on its centre the stupendous barrier of the Bāba
Buden chain, which rises, in Mulainagiri, to 6,317 feet
above the sea. The god of the temple at Bēlur is believed
to make occasional trips to the Bāba Buden hills to visit
the goddess, wearing a huge pair of slippers kept for him
at the temple, which are renewed by leather-workers when
they become worn out, and presented at the shrine. In
the Mysore district, the Biligirirangan range reaches a
height of 5,091 feet, and, in the Hassan district, the
Subrahmanya or Pushpagiri mountain rises to 5,626 feet.
Further east, in the Kolar district, the hill range reaches
its highest point at Nandidrūg (4,851 feet).

CHAPTER III

RIVERS

FROM the great watershed of the western ghāts, only short rivers flow westward through the plains of South Canara, Malabar, Cochin, and Travancore, into the Arabian Sea, the main drainage making its way for the most part eastward, and emptying itself into the Bay of Bengal.

The Gersoppa Falls, formed by the **Sharāvati** river, and situated on the Bombay-Mysore frontier, derive their name from the village of Gersoppa. The name has been corrupted by Anglo-Indians into Grasshopper Falls. The falls are said to have few rivals in the world in height, volume, and beauty, the river hurling itself over a cliff 830 feet high in four cascades called the Rāja or Horse-shoe, Roarer, Rocket, and La Dame Blanche.

Of the rivers which flow westward, communicating, in many cases, with the extensive system of backwaters (p. 190), may be noted the Netrāvati and Gurpur rivers in South Canara, the Ponnāni, Beypore, and Valarpattanam in Malabar, and, further south, in Cochin and Travancore, the Alwaye, Chālakudi, and Periyar. The **Netrāvati** and Gurpur rivers have a common entrance into the sea at Mangalore. The **Beypore** river flows through the Nilambur valley, and much timber from the forests is floated down to its mouth, near which it is connected with Calicut by the Conolly canal. The **Ponnāni** forms part of the boundary

between Malabar and the Cochin State. The upper waters
of the **Periyar**, which rises on the Sivagiri hills, have been
utilised in connection with the Periyar Project (p. 203).

Of the rivers which flow eastward into the Bay of
Bengal, the most celebrated are the Godāvari, Cauvery, and
Kistna.

The **Godāvari** or Godā river (900 miles) rises on a hill
in the Nasik district of the Bombay Presidency. At its
source the water trickles from the mouth of a graven
image. The sacred nature of the river is said to have been
revealed to Rāma by the rishi Gautama. According to
tradition, it proceeds by an underground passage from the
same source as the Ganges, and reaches the sea by seven
branches, made by the seven rishis Kasyapa, Atri, Gautama, Bharadvāja, Vasishta, Visvāmitra, and Jamadagni.
The pilgrimage, called sapta sāgara yātra, or pilgrimage of
the seven confluences, is made especially by those desirous
of offspring. The Godāvari flows past the town of Nasik,
one of the most sacred places of Hindu pilgrimage, where
the banks and bed of the river are studded with bathing-
ghāts, temples, and shrines. It traverses the Hyderabad
State, and forms the boundary between it and the Godāvari
district of the Madras Presidency, being joined by the
Sabari or Saveri river. Thence it flows between the Godāvari and Kistna districts, and passes through the gorge,
where it is contracted by the eastern ghāts, through which
it passes. When the river is in flood, boatmen are said to
break a coconut to appease the demon Bīraiya, and so
save themselves from being dashed against the rocks, and
drowned in a whirlpool. Leaving the hills, the river opens
out into broad reaches dotted with islands called lunkas, on
the fertile soil of which tobacco is cultivated. After passing
Rājahmundry, it divides, at Dowlaishweram, into two
branches, the Gautami Godāvari and Vasishta Godāvari,
and so reaches the Bay of Bengal. The Gautami Godāvari

flows past the French settlement of Yanam, and enters the sea near Point Godāvari. At its mouth is the Sacramento shoal, where the United States steam frigate *Sacramento* went ashore in 1867. The Vasishta Godāvari reaches the coast at Point Narasapur. A few miles above the entrance into the sea, a branch, called the Vainatēyam, forms the island of Nagaram between itself and the Vasishta Godāvari. The Pushkaram festival, held once in twelve years, during which Telugus bathe at various spots on the banks of the Godāvari, is regarded by them as being of the same importance as the Mahāmakam festival at Kumbakonam (p. 256) is to all Hindus. The ghāt at Rajahmundry, where Hindus bathe in the river, is called Kotilingam (crore of lingams) ghāt, in connection with a legend. Pilgrims who go from the Godāvari district to Benares empty half of the contents of the pots of Ganges water, which they bring back with them, into the Godāvari, and replenish them therefrom.

The **Kistna** or Krishna river (800 miles) rises in the western ghāts, north of the hill-station of Mahābaleshwar in the Bombay Presidency, and enters the Hyderabad State, being joined by the Tungabhadra in the Raichur district of the Nizam's Dominions. On reaching the eastern ghāts, it turns sharply south-east, and, flowing between the Kistna and Guntur districts, passes the town of Bezwāda, and enters the Bay of Bengal by two mouths, one of which is at the low headland of Point Divi. The ruined stupa of Amarāvati is situated on the south bank of the river, which, in the vicinity thereof, is studded with islands or lunkas.

Between the Godāvari and Kistna districts is the **Colair** (Kolleru) lake. This, it has been said, is "the only large natural freshwater lake in the Madras Presidency. Half lake, half swamp, it is a great shallow depression, which was doubtless originally part of the old Bay of Bengal. On either side of it the Godāvari and Kistna pushed their deltas further and further out into the sea, until the south-ward extremity of the one joined the northward limit of the other, and the arm of land thus formed cut off the Colair depression from the salt-water. The streams which flow into it now keep its waters fresh, but the silt they carry is rapidly filling it up, and, in the course of time, it will inevitably disappear. During the monsoon it exceeds 100 square miles, but, in the dry weather, it shrinks con-siderably, and sometimes, as in the drought of 1900, the lake dries up altogether."

The **Tungabhadra** river (400 miles) is formed by the union of the Tunga and Bhadra, which rise together in the western ghāts at Gangāmula in Mysore, and unite at Kudali in the Shimoga district of that State. The river forms the boundary between Mysore and Bombay, Bombay and Madras, and Madras and Hyderabad, and eventually joins the Kistna river near Kurnool. In its course it passes the ruined city of Vijayanagar, amid scenery, of which enormous rocky boulders are the dominant feature. Among other affluents, it receives the Hagari or Vedavati, formed by two rivers called the Veda and Avati, which rise in the Bāba Budan hills in Mysore. In the Chitaldroog district of Mysore, the Hagari supplies the great Mari Kanave reservoir, which has an area of 34 square miles. It finally joins the Tungabhadra at Hālekota. On the Tungabhadra, as on some other rivers, coracles are used for conveying passengers from place to place. Concerning this primitive type of boat, Bishop Whitehead writes that it "corresponds exactly to my idea of the coracle of the ancient Britons. It consists of a very large, round wicker basket, about eight or nine feet in diameter, covered over with leather, and propelled by paddles. As a rule, it spins round and round, but the boatmen can keep it fairly straight, when exhorted to do so. Some straw had been placed in the bottom of the coracle, and we were allowed the luxury of chairs to sit upon, but it is safer to sit on the straw, as a coracle is generally in a state of unstable equilibrium." The French traveller Tavernier, who visited India in the seventeenth century, wrote (1676) that, on his way to Golconda, "the boats employed in crossing the river are like large baskets, at the bottom of which some faggots are placed, upon which carpets are spread."

The **Penner** river rises on Channarāyan-betta, in the Kolar district of Mysore, and enters the Anantapur district of the Madras Presidency. After passing through the Cuddapah and Nellore districts, it enters the Bay of Bengal below the town of Nellore. In Cuddapah it is joined by the Chitrāvati, and flows through the gorge of Gandikota (gorge fort), which has been described as the most splendid river pass in South India, with the exception of the wild bed of the Kistna, where it cuts its way through the Nalla-malai hills. The fort of Gandikota is situated on the top of a hill, 1,670 feet above the sea, overlooking the river. Lower down, the Penner is joined by the Pāpaghni river.

The **Pālar** river (230 miles) is supposed to rise on Nandidroog, in the Kolar district of Mysore. The Beta-mangala tank, which is supplied by it, is the source of the water-supply for the Kolar gold-fields. The river enters the North Arcot district of the Madras Presidency, and, passing Vellore, Arcot, and Chingleput, reaches the Bay of Bengal near Sadras.

The **Ponnaiyar** river (250 miles) rises on Channarāyan-betta in Mysore, and, entering the Madras Presidency, flows through the Salem and South Arcot districts. It finally reaches the coast at Cuddalore. In the Tamil month Tai, the Ganges is believed to flow into it by an underground passage, and a festival is celebrated on its banks.

The **Vellar** river (135 miles) is formed by the junction of the Vasishtanadi and Swetanadi, which rise in the Salem district, and carry off the drainage of the Pachaimalai,

Kollaimalai, and Kalrayan hills. It constitutes the boundary between the South Arcot and Trichinopoly districts, and reaches the Bay of Bengal at Porto Novo. According to tradition, it reaches the waters of the Coleroon out at sea; and, in the Tamil month Māsi, the idol from the temple at Srīmushnam is taken in procession to the shore opposite the spot, and Hindus bathe in the sea.

The **Cauvery** or Kāveri (475 miles) is sometimes called the Dakshina Ganga, or Ganges of the south. Its divine origin is set forth in the *Kāveri Mahātmya*. Among the Hindu death-rites is the sacred bath for the atonement of sins and purification of the soul, which is called kāveri or samudra snana, according as the dying person is near a river or the sea. The Cauvery rises at Tale-Kāveri on the Brahmagiri hills in Coorg. Near the Coorg frontier it flows past Fraserpet, and enters the Mysore State, passing soon afterwards through a narrow gorge, with a fall which gives rise to the rapids of Chunchankatte. The Kabbani river joins it at Tirumakudlu near Narsipur, and the confluence is regarded as a very sacred spot. In its course through Mysore, the Cauvery forms the islands of Seringapatam and Sivasamudram (sea of Siva). At the latter are the celebrated Cauvery Falls, called the Gagana Chukki (sky spray) and Bhar Chukki (heavy spray), which have been said to far surpass the falls of the Rhine at Schaffhausen in height, volume, and grandeur. In the centre of the Bhar Chukki is a hollow shaped like a horse-shoe, down which the main stream falls. In the rainy season, the Bhar Chukki is about a quarter of a mile broad. On the island of Sivasamudram is the tomb of Pīr Wali, a Muhammadan saint, which is the scene of an annual festival. Below the falls, the river narrows to form the mēke dhātu or goat's leap. At Sivasamudram the Cauvery enters the Madras Presidency, forming the boundary between the Salem and Coimbatore districts, and further on enters the Trichinopoly

Fig. 6. Cauvery Falls, utilised for the development of the hydro-electric power used on the Kolar gold-fields.

district. Near Alambādi in Coimbatore is the smoking rock, so named from a rock which throws up a cloud of spray from the middle of the river. According to native belief, there is a hole or chasm, four palm trees deep, into which the water falls. At the island of Srīrangam, near Trichino-poly, which is about nineteen miles in length, the river divides into two main delta-branches, the Coleroon or Kollidam and Cauvery, which irrigate the fertile delta called the garden of South India. The former enters the Bay of Bengal near Dēvikotta, and the latter shrinks into an insignificant stream.

The chief tributaries of the Cauvery in the Madras Presidency are the Bhavāni, Noyil, and Amarāvati. The **Bhavāni**, famous for its mahseer (*Barbus tor*) fishing, which rises in the Attapādi valley in Malabar, is joined by the Moyar, and, flowing past Mettupalaiyam, where it is crossed by the Nīlgiri railway, unites with the Cauvery near the town of Bhavāni. The **Moyar** commences as the Paikāra river, which rises on the slopes of Mūkarti peak on the Nīlgiris, and, flowing past Paikāra, forms the Paikāra falls, and so reaches the Wynaad plateau. Under the name of the Moyar it runs through the Mysore ditch, separating the Nīlgiris from Mysore, and enters the Bhavāni.

The **Vaigai** river rises by two streams, which drain the Kumbam and Varushanād valleys of the Madura district, and receives much of the water from the Palni hills. Passing the town of Madura, it enters the Bay of Bengal about 10 miles east of Rāmnād. Its water-supply has been much increased in recent years by the Periyar Project.

The **Tāmbraparni** river rises on the slopes of Agasty-amalai, a conical peak in the Travancore State, and reaches the plains of the Tinnevelly district by the falls of Pāpa-nāsam (pāpa, sin; nāsam, destruction). This is a very sacred spot, with a Saivite temple, and is visited by large numbers of pilgrims. The fish in the river are fed from the temple

funds. The river finally enters the sea in the Gulf of
Manaar. It receives, in its course, the waters of the
Chittar river, which forms the Kuttālam or Courtallum
falls in the Tenkāsi tāluk of the Tinnevelly district. Near
the falls is the temple of Kuttālanāthaswāmi, and the spot
is regarded as sacred by Hindus, who bathe there.

CHAPTER IV

ISLANDS

THE **Laccadives** (laksha dvīpa, a hundred thousand
islands) are a group of coral-reefs and islands (atolls),
situated between 10° and 12° N., and 71° 40′ and 74° E.,
at a distance of about 125 to 200 miles from the Malabar
coast. The northern group, called the Amindivi islands,
consists of five islands—Chetlat, Kiltan, Kadamat, Amini,
and Bitra—which are administered by the Collector of South
Canara. The southern group, which comes within the juris-
diction of the Collector of Malabar, is made up of Androth,
Kavaratti, Agatti or Akatti, Kalpeni, and the isolated atoll
of Minicoy, intermediate between the Laccadives and the
Maldive islands further south, which are tributary to the
Ceylon Government. For administrative purposes, Professor
Stanley Gardiner informs us, the **Maldives** are divided into
thirteen provinces, which are called Atoḷu, each with a
governor, the Atoluveri. These provinces are often con-
terminous with the atolls, whence arose this term. The
Laccadive islands are low-lying, and recognisable from the
sea by means of the coconut plantations, with which they
are covered. They are said to have emerged, in nearly all
cases, from the eastern and protected side of the reef, the
western side being completely exposed to the south-west

monsoon. The surface coral has been excavated on the principal islands (e. g. Androth and Kalpeni), according to tradition by a race of giants. In the excavations, various food-grains and vegetables are cultivated. For their livelihood, the islanders depend largely on the products of the coconut, which are taken in sailing-boats to the west coast. Great damage is done to the coconut trees by rats, for the extermination of which owls, rat-snakes, and mungooses, have been introduced from time to time. In recent times, periodical kuttams (assemblies) or rat-hunts have been organised, and it is said that the Amīn (headman) has the power of inflicting a fine for non-attendance thereat. The bulk of the population of the Laccadive islands is made up of Muhammadan Māppillas. According to tradition, these Māppillas were originally inhabitants of Malabar—Nambutiri Brahmans, Nāyars, Tiyans, etc.—who went in search of Chēramān Perumāl, king of Malabar, who was converted to the Muhammadan faith and left for Mecca, and were wrecked on the islands. They are divided into castes, of which the highest is represented by the Koyas, who own the coconut trees and boats (odams). The navigating class is represented by the Malumis (pilots), and the lowest class are the Mēlacheris, who carry out the tree-tapping, coconut-plucking, and other menial services. The Koyas are said to be descendants of Nambutiris, the Malumis of Nāyars, and the Mēlacheris of Tiyans and Mukkuvans.

Pāmban (snake) island, on the south-east coast, is said to owe its name to the tortuous, snake-like course of the narrow Pāmban Pass, 1,350 yards in width, which separates it from the mainland. It is recorded by Professor Stanley Gardiner that there are clear indications of a former land connection between India and north Ceylon, the so-called Adam's Bridge, and the islands of Manaar on the Ceylon coast and Pāmban, appearing indubitably to be the remains

of a formerly elevated limestone flat, which has been more
or less cut down by the sea to the low-tide level. Tradition
runs to the effect that, at the time of the separation of the
island from the mainland on the one side, and Ceylon on
the other, the cows became prisoners on it, took to living
on sea-weeds, and became converted into diminutive meta-
morphosed cows, which may still be seen grazing on the
shore. The legend is based on the fancied resemblance of
the horned coffer-fishes (*Ostracion cornutus*), which are
frequently caught in the fishing-nets, to cattle. The island,
which is about eleven miles long by six wide at its widest
part, narrows towards the eastern end, where a strip of

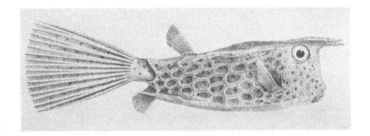

Fig. 7. *Ostracion cornutus.*

sand, with wind-blown sand-dunes, runs down to a point
towards Adam's Bridge. On the west side of the Pāmban
Pass is the Great Dam, consisting of large masses of sandstone, all having a more or less flat surface, which are said
to have once formed part of the causeway extending across
to the mainland. The remains of this causeway are still
visible on the road leading across the island from the town
of Pāmban to Rāmēsvaram. This sacred place is visited,
on account of its temple, by huge numbers of pilgrims
from all parts of India, who go through a course of
ceremonies and ablutions in the sea under the direction of

T.   3

a priest, and deposit coins and clay images therein. The population of Pāmban is largely made up of boatmen and fishermen, some of whom find employment in ferrying pilgrims from the mainland to the island. Coolies are engaged in warping vessels through the Pass, when the wind is adverse. The north coast of the island is fringed by a coral-reef. In the extension of the reef-band towards Rāmēsvaram appears a limestone, consisting entirely of calcareous algæ (*Lithothamnium*), with a few scattered

Fig. 8. Sub-fossil Coral Reef, Pāmban.

coral masses. Near Pāmban, a sub-fossil reef, largely composed of enormous blocks of *Porites*, forms a miniature cliff, several feet in height, above high-tide mark. Some years ago masses of pumice were heaped up on the shore near this reef. The pumice was no doubt discharged from the volcano of Krakatoa in the Straits of Sunda, during the great eruption of 1883, and drifted by currents across the ocean. South of the Pāmban Pass are a series of little coral islands (Pulli, Pullivausel, Coorisuddy, etc.), which form a natural breakwater, protecting the Pass and channels leading to it from the violence of the south-west winds. The South India Railway Company is at the present time building a viaduct across the Pāmban Pass, with an opening for vessels by means of a Scherzer lifting bridge. The railway line goes across the island to the extreme point at Dhanushkodi, and arrangements are being made for a steamer service to Talemanaar in Ceylon.

The low and swampy **Hope Island**, situated near one of the mouths of the Godāvari river, is covered with low jungle, and to a great extent submerged during high tides.

The coral-girt island, called **Hare Island**, outside which steamers anchor, is situated $2\frac{1}{2}$ miles from Tuticorin. Hares and partridges may be shot on it, and sluggish holothurians (bêches-de-mer) collected in abundance at low-tide.

Srīharikota is a low-lying alluvial island, 35 miles long, off the Nellore coast, bounded on the east by the Bay of Bengal, and on the west by Pulicat lake. On the north it is separated from the mainland by a narrow channel. It is covered with jungle, and affords an important source of supply of fuel for firewood, which is transported to Madras by the Buckingham Canal. The island is the head-quarters of the jungle Yānādis, who are expert sportsmen and trackers (shikāris), and collect minor forest produce for the Forest Department.

The alluvial deposit, which forms the island of **Vypeen** on the west coast, $14\frac{3}{4}$ miles in length, is bounded on the west by the Arabian Sea, and cut off from the land on the north, south, and east, by the mouths of the Cranganore and Cochin rivers, and the backwater. According to tradition, the island was thrown up in 1341 A.D., and, from that time, a new era, called the Pudu Veppu, or era of the new bank, began. The suggestion has been made that the name Pudu Veppu may commemorate the establishment of the first Christian church on the island, or the date when it first became cultivatable. The spot possesses considerable historic interest. "Cranganore (Kudangalur) has been confidently identified with the Musiris of the ancients, the greatest emporium of India according to Pliny the Elder, which stood on a river two miles from its mouth according to the *Periplus Maris Erythræi*, the river being known as the Pseudostomos or False Mouth, a correct translation of Alimukam, as the mouth of the Periyar is still called."

The island, known as **Sacrifice Rock**, situated about eight miles out at sea, to the north of Quilandi in Malabar, is probably the white island of the *Periplus Maris Erythræi*, and is still called Velliyan Kallu, or white rock, owing to the deposit of white excrement (guano) of birds on it. It is said to have received the name of Sacrifice Rock, because the Kottakkal Kunhāli Marakkar pirates slaughtered the crew of a Portuguese vessel there, or according to another version, because Haidar Ali left state prisoners and others there, to die of hunger and thirst. The naturalist Jerdon found on the island a cave, which contained a large number of nests of the edible-nest swiftlet (*Collocalia fuciphaga*), which are made of grass, moss, and feathers, cemented together by inspissated saliva.

The **Daryā Bahādurgarh island** shelters the roadstead off Malpe in South Canara. A few miles further north is **St Mary's Island**, which is so called because Vasco da Gama is said to have put up a cross on it, when he landed there in 1498. The islets opposite to the mouth of the inlet of the sea at Mulki in South Canara are known as the **Mulki Rocks**.

CHAPTER V

SEAPORTS ; MARITIME TRADE

THE most important ports from north to south are :
(a) on the east coast, Gopalpur, Calingapatam, Bimlipatam,
Vizagapatam, Cocanāda, Masulipatam, Madras, Pondicherry,
Cuddalore, Kārikāl, Negapatam, Pāmban, and Tuticorin ;
(b) on the west coast, Mangalore, Cannanore, Tellicherry,
Calicut, Cochin, Alleppey, Quilon, and Kolachel.

There is, in South India, no natural harbour to serve as
a haven for ocean-going steamers during stormy weather.
The maritime trade is mainly conducted from open road-
steads, where big ships lie at anchor, sometimes at a distance
of several miles from the shore. On the west coast, the
ports are more or less closed to shipping during the rough
weather of the south-west monsoon.

The oily **mud-banks of Alleppey and Nārakkal** on the
Travancore-Cochin coast afford smooth-water anchorage
for ships during the south-west monsoon, waves passing
over the banks being diminished in height, and lessened in
velocity. Dr W. King was of opinion that the oil in the
mud is derived from the decomposition of organisms, and
a distillation of oil in the subjacent lignitiferous deposits
belonging to the Warkilli strata. Sometimes the mud-bank
of Nārakkal is heaped against the shore, and a channel has
to be cut to enable boats to reach the sea. At times the
mud deposits appear out at sea, rising to a height of three
or four feet. It has been shown by Messrs Rohde and

Fig. 9.   The sea-front, Tuticorin.

Crawford : (*a*) that, when the backwaters of Alleppey, which open into the sea, rise, the extent of the smooth-water tract increases, and mud "volcanoes" burst into the sea ; (*b*) that the mud-bank at Alleppey is formed at intervals, and is gradually washed southward by littoral currents, and slowly dissipated by the waves. Usually, before the old `bank has disappeared, a new one starts. Sometimes, for several miles down the coast, and from the beach out to sea for a mile and a half, the sea is nothing but liquid mud, which gives rise to a heavy mortality among the fishes. It has been assumed by Mr P. Lake that, under the sand of Alleppey, is a layer of mud which crops out under the sea. When the backwater rises to any height, the pressure forces the mud out under the sea, and forms the mud-bank. The Nārakkal mud-bank is, according to Mr Lake, probably to a large extent formed of the silt carried down by the Cranganore river.

Cargo is, at many ports, conveyed from ships in light boats capable of passing through the surf which breaks on the sandy shore. The present day **masula** (or mussoola) boat of the Madras coast is of the same build now as it was several centuries ago. It was recorded by a traveller in 1673 that he "went ashore in a Mussoola, a boat wherein ten men paddle, the two aftermost of which are the Steers-men, using their paddles instead of a Rudder. The Boat is not strengthened with knee-timbers as ours are ; the bended Planks are sewed together with Rope-yarn of the Cocoe, and calked with Dammar so artificially that it yields to every ambitious surf. Otherwise it could not get ashore, the Bar knocking in pieces all that are inflexible." The archives of Madras contain repeated references to Europeans being thrown violently on shore, or drowned from the over-turning of masula boats in the surf, through which a landing had to be effected before the Madras pier was built. It is recorded in the Fort St George Consultations, 1679, that

" a mussoollee being overturned, although it was very smooth water, and no surf, and one Englishman being drowned, a Dutchman being with difficulty recovered, the boatmen were seized and put in prison, one escaping."

The screw-pile pier at **Madras** was completed in 1862. The stone commemorating the commencement of the harbour was laid by the Prince of Wales (afterwards King Edward VII) in 1875. The harbour, when completed, consisted of two parallel masonry breakwaters, each 500 yards distant from the pier, running out at right angles to the shore for 1200 yards into $7\frac{1}{2}$ fathoms of water, and bending towards each other, so as to leave an opening 500 feet wide in the centre of the east side for the ingress and egress of ships. Quite recently, a new north-east entrance has been made, and was first used, in the presence of the Viceroy, in 1909. The old east entrance, which was rapidly shallowing owing to silting of sand, has since been permanently closed.

Proposals have long been under consideration for the construction of a harbour at **Vizagapatam**, where the tidal backwater is sheltered on the south by the headland of Dolphin's Nose and the hills behind it, and on the other side by distant hills. The conclusion arrived at by an expert was that a groin from the end of Dolphin's Nose would stop the formation of the sand-bar, produced by the waves acting on the sand from the south, which stretches across the entrance to the backwater. At Vizagapatam, a Muhammadan saint is buried on the top of the hill overlooking the backwater. He is considered to have great power over the waters of the Bay of Bengal, and silver dhonis (native vessels) are offered at his shrine by Hindu shipowners after a successful voyage.

Proposals have also been under consideration to cut a ship-canal through **Pāmban island**, to obviate the necessity of large steamers, which are making for ports along the east coast, going out of their way round Ceylon. A channel,

which is used by small coasting steamers, has been artificially produced by deepening the Pāmban Pass, which
separates the island from the mainland of the Rāmnād
district.

The extensive **backwater of Cochin**, which covers an
area of several square miles, is connected with the sea by
the mouth of the Cochin river.   Along the river-banks are
ranged rows of fishing nets, called "Chinese nets," which

Fig. 10.   Dolphin's Nose, Vizagapatam.

are worked from wood and bamboo platforms or jetties.
The backwater affords safe anchorage for vessels of light
draught, but the bar, which is about a mile from the shore,
presents an obstacle to the passage of big ships.

Emigration takes place from various ports on the east
coast, e.g. Tuticorin, Negapatam, Kārikāl, Madras, and
Cocanāda, to Natal, Fiji, the Straits Settlements, the French
colonies, Ceylon, and Burma.   It is said that the mail

Fig. 11. Fishing nets, Cochin.

steamers to Rangoon carry consignments of stone and
metal idols, commissioned by the South Indian settlers in
Burma for the purpose of domestic and public worship.

Nearly half the **maritime trade** is conducted from the
port of Madras, which is followed in order of importance
by Tuticorin—the terminus of the South India Railway—
and Cochin.

Exports of the Principal Articles, 1910—11.

		Rs
Cotton, raw		4,14,18,843
Hides and Skins ...		3,75,29,684
Seeds	Castor, cotton, ground-nut, niger, gingelly, coriander, etc. ...	2,51,56,746
Grains and Pulses ...	Rice, 99 per cent.	1,42,19,442
Coffee		1,31,24,107
Tea		1,22,89,442
Cotton manufactures		1,03,98,593
Fruits	Chiefly coconut kernels or copra	92,58,731
Coir	Coconut fibre and matting ...	68,69,887
Spices	Pepper, ginger, chillies, etc. ...	52,63,729
Oils	Chiefly coconut oil, also castor, ground-nut, and lemon-grass...	41,83,505
Cotton twist and yarn		23,00,612
Drugs, medicines, and narcotics	Leaf tobacco, cigars, senna leaves, nux-vomica, etc.	17,49,569
Timber	Sandalwood, blackwood or rose-wood, teak, etc.	17,32,606
Bristles and fibres for brushes	Mainly palmyra palm fibre ...	15,22,650
Dyeing and tanning materials	Indigo, turmeric, myrabolams, etc.	12,33,574
Sugar		11,82,255
Rubber	Exports 1909—10, Rs 1,95,120 ...	8,13,435
Silk, raw		2,29,703

*Value of Exports to the principal countries outside
India,* 1910—11.

	Lakhs of Rupees
British Empire	620.82
Ceylon	358.31
France	305.41
Germany	174.47
Japan	145.43
Belgium	121.41
Straits Settlements ...	91.61
United States of America	69.98

CHAPTER VI

CLIMATE has been defined as the average condition of the atmosphere, while weather denotes a single circumstance, or event, in the series of conditions. The climate of a place is thus in a sense its average weather. Two types of climate have been described as occurring in the Indian Peninsula, viz. (*a*) continental, which prevails, except in certain coast districts, from December to May, and is characterised by the prevalence of land winds, dry air, and large diurnal range of temperature ; (*b*) oceanic, from June to December, with a smaller diurnal range of temperature, dampness of the air, and more or less frequent rain.

The climate of the southern districts of the Madras Presidency has been not inaptly summed up as being three months hot, and nine months hotter. As shown by the table, the mean temperature of the city of Madras is 89·6° F. during the hot month of May, and 76·2° F. in the "cold weather" month of January.

The chief types of weather, and the periods during which they prevail in Madras and the Carnatic, have been classified as follows :

(1) "Cold weather"—from the end of December to the end of February;

(2) Hot weather—from the beginning of March to the end of May;

(3) South-west monsoon—from the beginning of June to the first week in October;

(4) North-east monsoon—from the second week in October to the third week in December.

Temperatures recorded at ten stations.

Station	Height in feet above sea-level	Mean Temperature in Degrees Fahrenheit			
		January	May	July	November
Vizagapatam (Waltair)	226	74·9	86·7	84·8	78·5
Cocanāda	26	73·8	91·4	85·4	77·0
Nellore	71	76·6	93·9	88·6	79·1
Cuddapah	433	76·8	94·6	86·6	78·6
Madras	22	76·2	89·6	87·3	76·7
Madura	447	78·3	88·8	84·8	80·0
Coimbatore	1,348	75·6	84·3	79·4	77·6
Calicut	27	78·7	84·2	78·2	80·4
Trivandrum (Travancore)	198	77·5	81·6	77·6	77·6
Wellington	6,200	56·5	67·1	64·5	59·6

The word **monsoon** is derived from the Arabic mausim, meaning season, which was corrupted by the Portuguese into monçao, and by the Dutch into monssoyn or monssoen. The monsoons have been summed up as winds which blow alternately in opposite directions, and at opposite seasons of the year, i.e. blowing over the land from the Arabian Sea in the south-west, and from the Bay of Bengal in the north-east monsoon.

During the "**cold weather**," the hottest area is in the southern districts of Trichinopoly, Madura, and Tinnevelly, and the coolest areas in the plains are in the three northern districts, Ganjam, Vizagapatam, and Godāvari, and in Bellary, Anantapur, and Kurnool. At Ootacamund (7,000 feet above sea-level), on the Nīlgiri hills, and even at Wellington, nearly a thousand feet lower, light frosts occur in the cold months. Sometimes, in the early morning, the valleys and hollows of the hills are covered with hoar-frost.

In January, showers fall, which are called **Pongal showers**, in reference to the Pongal (boiled rice) or Sankranti festival observed by Hindus on the first day of the month of Tai, commencing approximately on the 12th January, when Hindus offer boiled rice and milk to propitiate the sun-god. The showers which fall in March and April are called **blossom showers** in the coffee-growing areas, and elsewhere mango showers, because they occur at the time when the mangoes are commencing to ripen.

During March and April, the damp and enervating **"long shore" winds** blow from the south along the Madras coast. They are said to derive some of their moisture from having to pass through miles of space filled with fine spray thrown up into the air by the heavy surf that breaks on the coast at this season. These winds have been described by the author of *Letters from Madras* (1843), as " very disagreeable—a sham sea-breeze blowing from the south, whereas the real sea-breezes blow from the east. It is a regular cheat for the new-comer, feeling damp and fresh, as if it was going to cool them." The true sea-breeze is one which blows from the cool sea towards the heated land in the afternoon and evening, whereas the land wind blows from the cooled land to the warmer sea in the morning.

During the **hot weather**, the hottest areas are the Ceded districts and the Deccan. Cuddapah takes rank as the hottest station in the Madras Presidency, with a mean temperature of 94·6° F. in May. The four Deccan districts —Cuddapah, Kurnool, Bellary, and Anantapur—which are in the dry zone, where the rainfall is slight, suffer more from famine than any others.

The hot weather is varied, especially in and near the hills, by thunderstorms, which, in the plains, are preceded by strong wind and clouds of dust. In May depressions sometimes form in the Bay of Bengal, and storms strike the coast.

With the commencement of the **south-west monsoon**—commonly called "the rains"—which, under normal conditions, "bursts" during the first fortnight in June, the temperature falls on the west coast. The monsoon current strikes the coast almost at right angles, and discharges a very large quantity of rain in the plains between the Arabian Sea and the western ghāts, and on the face of the ghāts. The amount is, however, slight as compared with that which falls at Cherrapunji in Assam, where the annual rainfall is 400—500 inches. At Karkal, in South Canara, which is near the ghāts, the average rainfall is 189 inches, and 239 inches were registered in 1897. Devāla, in the Wynaad, averages 161 inches. At Mercāra, in Coorg, the average fall is 133 inches, of which 42 inches fall in July. At Naduvatam, which is situated at the western extremity of the Nīlgiri plateau, the average fall is 102 inches. At Ootacamund, which is some miles eastward of the ghāts, and only 20 miles distant from Naduvatam by road, and much nearer as the crow flies, the rainfall averages only 49 inches. Further east, at Coonoor, which receives its share of both the south-west and north-east monsoons, the average rainfall is 63 inches. During the south-west monsoon, the periods of strong wind and heavy rain are separated by spells of fine weather, which are commonly known as breaks in the rains. In the plains of Tinnevelly, in the extreme south of the Peninsula, the south-west monsoon brings strong winds to the eastern side of the ghāts, which blow great clouds of red dust, fifty or sixty feet high, from the plains towards the sea on the east coast.

The south-west monsoon ceases towards the end of

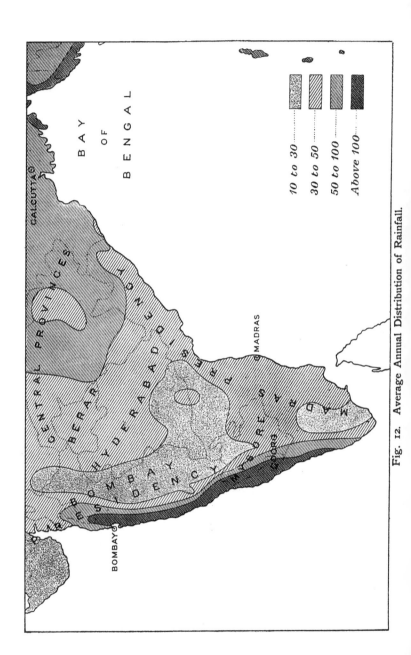

Fig. 12. Average Annual Distribution of Rainfall.

10 to 30 ....
30 to 50 ....
50 to 100 ....
Above 100 ....

September. With its cessation, humidity is high, and there is an absence of breeze on the Madras coast, until the arrival of the north-east monsoon rains, which are due about the middle of October. With the "burst" of the monsoon, the temperature drops suddenly. The rainfall is greatest along that part of the coast which lies between Pulicat lake and Point Calimere. But the annual rainfall is, as shown by the following statistics, far less on the east than on the west coast:

		Average annual rainfall, in inches
Vizagapatam,	east coast	49·27
Cocanāda	" "	40·95
Madras	" "	50·51
Calicut	west coast	118·81
Hosdrug	" "	127
Coondapoor	" "	141

The weather conditions over the Bay of Bengal during the **north-east monsoon** favours the formation of cyclones, the position and course of which determine the distribution of the rainfall. A cyclone (κυκλῶν, whirling, from κύκλος, a circle) has been defined as "an atmospheric system, where the pressure is lowest in the centre. The winds in consequence tend to blow towards the centre, but, being diverted, according to Ferrel's law, they rotate spirally inwards in a direction contrary to the movement of the hands of a watch in the northern hemisphere, and the reverse in the southern hemisphere. The whole system has a motion of translation, being usually carried forward with the great wind drifts, like eddies upon a swift stream." The northeast monsoon cyclones as a rule fill up rapidly after passing inland from the coast, and rarely cross the peninsula to the Arabian Sea. In 1886, however, a storm, after it had done so, developed again into a severe cyclone.

During a cyclone, in October 1746, when La Bourdonnais' fleet was off Madras, after the town had surrendered to the French, three of his ships and two prizes sank, and 1,200 men were drowned. In 1782, more than a hundred native craft, which had brought supplies of rice to Madras for the thousands who had taken shelter there from Haidar

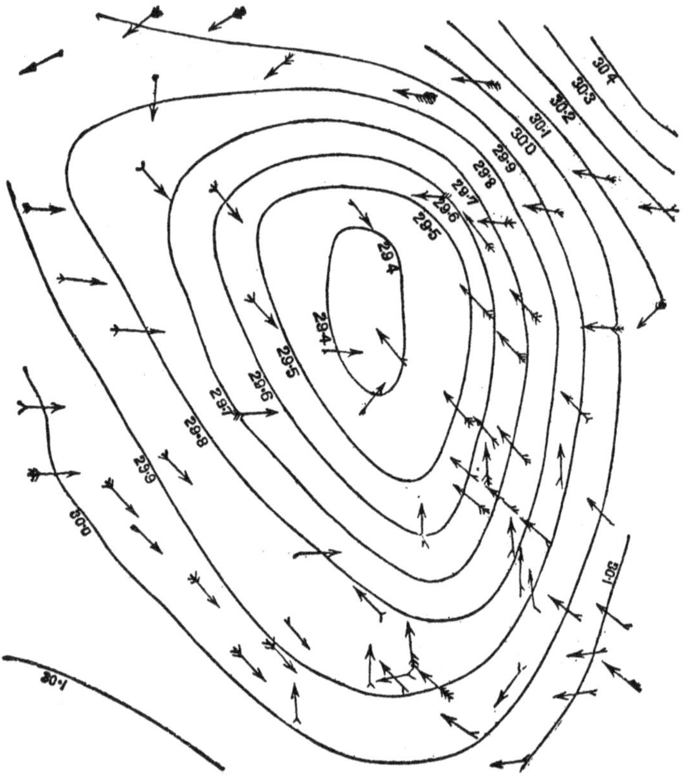

Fig. 13. Chart showing diminishing pressure from the outskirts to the centre of a cyclonic storm.

Ali's horsemen, were wrecked. During a cyclone, which struck Masulipatam in November 1864, a storm wave, thirteen feet above ordinary high-tide level, was borne inland seventeen miles from the coast. A man who clung

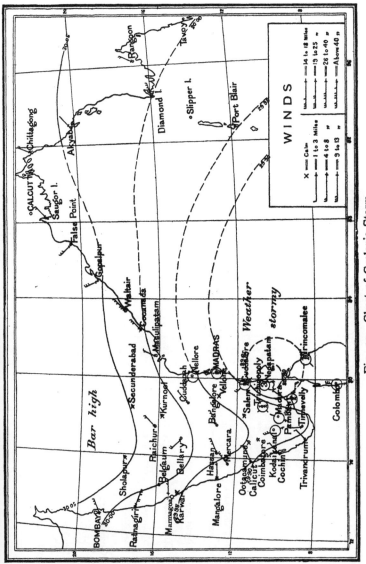

Fig. 14. Chart of Cyclonic Storm.

4—2

Rainfall recorded at ten stations.

Average rainfall in inches for 25 years, ending 1901

Station	January	February	March	April	May	June	July	August	September	October	November	December	Total of year
Waltair (Vizagapatam)	0·32	0·41	0·36	0·59	2·88	3·69	4·45	5·05	7·90	9·85	5·87	1·60	42·97
Cocanāda	0·14	0·51	0·43	0·49	1·96	4·21	5·81	5·86	6·19	8·87	5·59	0·89	40·95
Nellore	0·38	0·09	0·17	0·32	1·33	1·31	2·31	3·01	3·83	9·01	11·71	2·82	36·29
Cuddapah	0·15	0·17	0·12	0·52	1·75	3·14	4·04	5·80	6·12	5·51	3·71	1·06	32·09
Madras	0·50	0·31	0·18	0·48	1·64	2·12	3·91	5·13	4·93	11·14	13·97	6·20	50·51
Madura	0·26	0·48	0·50	2·36	2·86	1·22	1·94	3·61	5·22	8·53	4·78	2·16	33·92
Coimbatore	0·38	0·43	0·46	1·76	2·21	1·75	1·15	1·12	1·53	6·29	3·44	1·17	21·69
Calicut	0·18	0·16	0·57	4·28	9·74	35·77	27·91	16·32	7·67	10·50	4·66	1·05	118·81
Trivandrum (Travancore)	0·43	1·01	1·48	4·98	5·59	12·58	6·48	3·64	2·78	11·02	6·02	2·47	58·48
Wellington	1·05	1·44	2·39	3·59	3·66	3·47	3·48	3·97	5·71	11·06	6·89	3·94	50·65

first to a palmyra beam, and afterwards to a boat, was carried fourteen miles inland. Casks of beer and arrack from the Commissariat godown (warehouse) strewed the country for miles around. Dead bodies lay along the limit of the inundation, as sea-weed lies on a shore at high-water mark. At the crossings of the principal streets, the dead lay in heaps. Graves were dug, and the bodies thrown in —in one case ten men and a bullock in one grave. Some of the bodies were unearthed and eaten by herds of swine, and packs of marauding pariah dogs. Others were exhumed and cremated, when a supply of dry firewood was available. The loss of life was estimated at 30,000, and there was great destruction of cattle. In May 1872, nine English ships, with an aggregate tonnage of 6,700 tons, and twenty native craft, were driven ashore at Madras. During a storm at Vizagapatam, in October 1876, the new iron dome of Mr Narasinga Rao's Observatory, which had not been rivetted down, was carried 33 feet. A cyclone, which struck Madras in November 1881, knocked over two Titan cranes, which were being used in connection with the harbour works, and washed away half a mile of the breakwater.

Daily records of the atmospheric pressure, direction of the wind, temperature, humidity, and rainfall, in the southern half of the Peninsula, and round the Bay of Bengal (including Burma and the Andamans), are issued by the Government Meteorologist in Madras.

CHAPTER VII

QUITE nine-tenths of the area under consideration consists of an assemblage of crystalline rocks, similar to those which form the "basement complex" in many parts of the world. These rocks, being older than any known fossiliferous or known unaltered sedimentary rocks, are generally referred to as Archæan (*archaios*, ancient; *arche*, beginning). Resting on the weathered surface of these very ancient crystalline rocks there lie patches of unaltered sedimentary formations of different ages. The oldest of these occupy a considerable area in the Cuddapah and Kurnool districts. Similar strips of rocks very much younger than those of Cuddapah and Kurnool are preserved at different places along the Coromandel margin of the Madras Presidency, as for instance in the Trichinopoly district, near Pondicherry, around Madras, and at Rājah-mundry. There are also one or two very small patches of still younger marine rocks preserved on the Cochin-Travancore coast. Over all the formations—ancient crystalline basement, superimposed unfossiliferous sedimentary rocks, and geologically more recent fossiliferous formations—there lies a great mantle of modern laterite, with other decomposition products and cultivated soil.

The Madras Presidency is a part of the old land surface of Peninsular India, which has remained stable and undisturbed for untold geological ages. Except near the margins, there are no signs of the rocks having ever been depressed below sea-level ; no marine formations are preserved anywhere in this area, except at the places referred to above near the present sea-coast. As a consequence of this geological stability, and long-continued exposure to the erosive action of the weather, the physical inequalities which give that form of simple relief know as scenery are due merely to unequal resistance to weathering agents.

The **Archæan complex** is composed of a great variety of very ancient igneous and sedimentary rocks, which have been in many cases so altered by heat and earth movements that it is now difficult in many cases to distinguish those which were originally laid down as sediments in water from those which were injected in a molten condition into pre-existing solid parts of the Earth's crust. All the rocks of this group have been buried at some time in their history to great depths in the Earth's crust, and have since been brought to the surface by the continued erosion of the overlying cover. They show a general disposition of their constituent minerals in bands and streaks, roughly imitating the fluidal structures of semi-molten and viscous bodies, which is due to the fact that they have been moulded under enormous pressure and at high temperatures in an early stage of the Earth's history. The rocks now exposed at the surface in Madras therefore form a sample of the kind of materials that still exist at depths in the Earth's crust so great that the pressure due to the overlying masses is sufficient to mould and knead like wax the strongest rock known. There is no direct proof that these folded or banded rocks in Madras, commonly known as gneisses and schists, are similar in age to the formations described as Archæan in Europe and America. They are, however, referred to the Archæan era, because, throughout Peninsular India, as in other parts of the world, they underlie all other geological formations, and form a platform on which all later geological deposits were laid down. Among the constituents of this complex are great masses of ancient

Fig. 15. Foliation of Gneiss, Madakarai, Coimbatore district.

granites, now exposed over large areas in the Mysore State, and in the adjoining districts of Salem, North Arcot, and Bellary. These rocks, being compact and uniform in character, resist the weather more perfectly than the more complex gneisses and schists around. They consequently form conspicuous hillocks, standing up abruptly above the general level of the plains. Many of these, on account of their steep and difficultly accessible slopes, have been

Fig. 16. Characteristic hillock of Granitic Gneiss, Salem district.

utilised in past times as forts and strongholds (drūgs), such for example as that on which the old fort stands at Trichinopoly, Sankaridrūg in the Salem district, and Nandidrūg in the Mysore State.

Another prevalent type among these ancient crystalline formations is a group of rocks similar to granite in having been intruded in the igneous condition, but distinguished from all other rocks of the same class under the name

Fig. 17. The Lake, Ootacamund. An example of the artificial lakes formed on the undulating plateaux of Charnockite rocks.

charnockite series. These rocks have been so named because the material originally described was quarried for the tombstone of Job Charnock, and others of the early English settlers in Bengal. The charnockite series forms St Thomas' Mount near Madras, and other small hills further south in the Chingleput district. The same series of rocks form the Shevaroy hills, the great mountain masses known as the Nīlgiris, and the range of hills trending south from the Nīlgiris through the Malabar district, as well as the States of Cochin and Travancore, rising again above the sea-level to form the great central mass of Ceylon. The characteristic feature of these masses of charnockite is the formation of large plateau-like masses with undulating surfaces of a kind which permits, with slight artificial help, the formation of lakes, such as that near Yercaud on the Shevaroys, that of Ootacamund on the Nīlgiris, Kodaikānal on the Palnis, and at Newara-Eliya in Ceylon. Some of these plateaux stand at elevations of 7000 to 8000 feet, where the climate and the vegetation are of a kind familiar to people who live in temperate climates. Thus, on the Nīlgiri plateau, the undulating "downs" are covered with turf, and in places there occur well-developed peat-bogs, sometimes thick enough to be worked for supplies of fuel.

Among the almost endless varieties of rocks forming the rest of the crystalline complex, we have those which include the deposits of corundum, steatite, and potstone; the veins of coarse-grained granite or so-called pegmatite, which carry marketable mica, and similar veins which have yielded aquamarine in the Coimbatore district.

Associated with the crystalline complex, there occurs a group of rocks which are separately distinguished as the **Dharwar system** on account of their exposure in the district of Dharwar on the north-western border of the Mysore State. The Dharwar system is composed of an assemblage of altered rocks of various origins, some of them very

Fig. 18. Nīlgiri Downs, showing the characteristic scenery on the plateau-masses of the Charnockite series.

ancient sediments, others volcanic lava flows, and others
intrusive igneous rocks, all greatly folded by earth movements, and altered by heat and pressure. They are important, because they are sometimes traversed by veins
carrying valuable metalliferous deposits, especially of gold
and copper. The important gold mines of the Mysore
State are worked in a patch of the Dharwar formation.

The strata which cover such large areas in the Cuddapah

Fig. 19. Cuddapah limestone, Kolab river, showing the honeycomb
weathering and general flat-bedded disposition.

and Kurnool districts are utterly different in character to
those which have been grouped together under the name
Archæan. They include ordinary sandstones, shales and
limestones, which have been in places disturbed by earth
movements, and have consequently been slightly folded,
but they nowhere show signs of having been deeply buried
in the Earth's crust, and are therefore practically unaltered.
They are of a kind that might very well have been laid

down as deposits in the sea, yet they are entirely devoid of all forms of organic remains. This absence of fossils may possibly be due to the fact that the **Cuddapah** and **Kurnool formations** were laid down at a period in the Earth's history even older than that of the oldest of known fossiliferous deposits, possibly at a time when animals possessed no hard structures suitable for preservation as fossils. On account of the supposed great age of these formations in India, they have been grouped together under the name **Purāna**, a term which not only indicates the fact that they are very much older than our familiar fossiliferous formations, but also suggests that they are very much younger than the Archæan schists and gneisses on which the Cuddapah and Kurnool sediments rest; for, whilst the Purānas are reckoned as old among Hindu literature, they are in effect the reconstituted products of the still more ancient Vēdas.

There is another great gap in the geological record between the time during which the Cuddapah and Kurnool formations were laid down, and the period in which the next succeeding deposits were formed. These latter form a part of the **Gondwāna system**, which is more conspicuously developed in the northern portions of Peninsular India, where it includes the most valuable coal seams in the country. In the Madras Presidency the only representatives of the Gondwāna system are small patches of shales and sandstones preserved in the Trichinopoly district, near Madras, in various parts of the Nellore district, and near the Godāvari delta. The Gondwāna system, where fully developed in North Peninsular India, is divided into two portions, the lower of which contains the principal coal seams, while the upper division, composed largely of sandstones and shales, is practically devoid of valuable coal. It is the upper division which is mainly represented along the east coast. Most of the rocks belonging to this

system were laid down in great river valleys, but the
patches of the upper division preserved near the Coromandel coast show by the fossils they contain estuarine
and marine conditions of deposit.   The lower coal-bearing
division has been proved by borings to occur in the
Godāvari district, and is worked in the adjoining parts of
the Nizam's Dominions.   The Gondwāna system includes
rocks which range in age from those formed at about the
same time as the Coal Measures in Europe to those which
immediately preceded the English Chalk.   In the Madras
Presidency, near Pondicherry, as well as in the Trichinopoly
district, there occur small patches of marine rocks of the
Chalk period.   These marine Cretaceous rocks were formed,
not in the deep sea, but near the shore, and they, with the
small areas of marine Gondwāna rocks further north along
the Coromandel coast, form the only records of the sea
having made a serious inroad on the land in Southern
India.   Throughout a protracted geological era, India was
connected with Central and South Africa, to form a great
continent, which was separated from northern lands by an
ocean then stretching across Central Europe and Asia.
The northern shore-line of this continent, known to geologists as **Gondwānaland**, was approximately along the line
now occupied by the Central Himalayan snow-covered
peaks, while the position of the south-eastern shore-line is
indicated by the small patches of Gondwāna and Cretaceous
formations preserved along the Coromandel coast.   Whilst,
therefore, great geological changes have occurred in the
north, very little change has occurred in the shore-line of the
eastern coast, and Peninsular India, like Central and South
Africa, has remained firm, while other areas were being
profoundly altered by the crumpling of the Earth's crust.

The **Cretaceous beds** of the Trichinopoly and Pondicherry areas are specially interesting on account of the
great numbers of fossils which they contain, including

64 GEOLOGY

many species of world-wide distribution, having been found in similar rocks in Africa, Europe, Brazil, the United States, British Columbia, Japan, and Australia. Of these, mention may be made of such well-known species as *Schloenbachia inflata*, *Acanthoceras rhotomagense*, and *Pachydiscus gollevillensis*, which are forms of the extinct class of coiled-shell

Fig. 20. Cretaceous Fossils.

animals known as Ammonites; various gastropod mollusca like *Turrilites costatus*, and a gigantic form of *Cerithium* often referred to as *Nerinea*; lamellibranch molluscs, especially those related to the oyster family, like *Alectryonia carinata*, *Inoceramus labiatus*, *Trigonoarca galdrina*,

Plicatula septemcosta, and *Spondylus ariyalurensis*; different
varieties of " lamp-shells," including *Terebratula biplicata*;
and members of the star-fish family, like *Hemiaster*.

The geological record becomes broken again after the
formation of these marine Cretaceous beds, and the only
records we have of geological events during the Tertiary
period are those which formed around the coast bands of
sandstone, which have been named after the town of
Cuddalore, the head-quarters of the South Arcot district.
The exact age of these so-called Cuddalore sandstones is
not known, for they contain only fragmentary and un-
recognisable traces of organic remains.

About the most widespread geological formation in
South India is the great mantle of laterite, which is geologically recent in age. **Laterite** is of special interest to
the student of Madras Geology, because it was in this
area that the formation was first described in 1807 by
Dr Francis Buchanan-Hamilton, who gave it its name from
the Latin word *later*, a brick, in allusion to the way in
which it can be conveniently cut into brick-shaped blocks
for building purposes. The same formation has been since
found in other parts of the world more or less confined to
the humid portions of the tropical belt, and various conflicting theories have been suggested to account for its
origin. Most observers, however, agree that its peculiar
characters are due to the special conditions of weathering
which take place in a moist warm climate. Nearly all
laterites are rusty red in colour, on account of the diffused
ferruginous products, but the essential feature in which it
differs from all ordinary rock-weathering products is due to
the fact that, instead of consisting largely of ordinary clay,
which is a hydrous silicate of alumina, it contains the
alumina largely in a free state, thus resembling in constitution the material known as bauxite, which is used as
the main source of aluminium. Thus, some of the deposits

of laterite in India might ultimately prove to be of commercial value as sources of the metal aluminium. They, however, differ greatly in quality from place to place, and in many cases have been mixed up with other detrital material.

The fragmentary nature of the record of geological history in the Madras Presidency is shown by comparing the following list of formations with the table of European systems of strata.

Formation	European system	Era
Laterite and modern alluvium, beaches and coral banks	Recent	
Cuddalore sandstones and Warkalli beds ...	Pleistocene, Pliocene, Miocence, Oligocene, Eocene	Tertiary
Trichinopoly and Pondicherry formations ...	Cretaceous	Mesozoic
Gondwāna system	Jurassic, Triassic	Mesozoic
Not represented in Southern India	Permian, Carboniferous, Devonian, Silurian, Ordovician, Cambrian	Palaeozoic
Cuddapah and Kurnool formations (Purāna group)	Algonkian	
Dharwar system, Charnockite series, Granites, Gneisses, and Schists	Archæan	

CHAPTER VIII

MINERALS

In the preceding chapter, some of the minerals which are met with in the various geological formations have been mentioned. It remains to deal more in detail with the most important minerals in the area under consideration.

Asbestos, which received its name, meaning unquenchable, from the Greeks, because it is unaltered by heat, is found in abundance in the Chāmrājnagar tāluk of the Mysore State. It is a variety of hornblende, which occurs in long silky fibres, and was, in days of old, used at the cremation of the dead, so that the ashes of the corpse might be kept distinct from those of the fuel. It is at the present day used for lining iron safes, as a packing for steam-pipes and boilers, and, when short-fibred, for the manufacture of paper and cardboard.

The **Beryl** or **Aquamarine** mines at Padiyur (Pattalai) in the Dharapuram tāluk of the Coimbatore district were worked in the early part of the last century by Josiah Marshall Heath, who secured 2,196 stones valued at £1200. The discovery of coins of the Roman Emperors Augustus, Tiberius, Claudius, and others, in the neighbourhood, has been used as evidence that there was considerable commerce between the ancient inhabitants of the locality and the Roman traders. It is recorded by Pliny, in his *Natural History*, that the best beryls, which he recognised as being a variety of the emerald, are those which (like those at Padiyur) have the green colour of pure sea-water, and come from India.

Chromite has a chemical constitution analogous to magnetite (magnetic iron-ore), but differs from it in composition by the replacement of a portion of the iron oxide by chromic oxide. It is frequently found associated with the igneous rocks, such as the olivine rocks, which also contain large quantities of magnesia. In this association it is found in various parts of South India. An attempt was made by Mr Heath to work the chromite found associated with magnesite in the low hills between the town of Salem and the Shevaroy hills, the white colour of which has given

Fig. 21. Beryl crystals.

rise to the inaccurate name of the "Chalk Hills." The chromite deposits of the Mysore State first received serious consideration in 1906, when licenses were granted for their exploitation, which, however, does not appear yet to have developed into a regular industry, although the amount raised in 1907 was 11,000 tons. As in the Salem district, the chromite of Mysore is found associated with ultra-basic rocks, such as olivine rock and the product of its alteration, serpentine. The most important deposits known appear to be those situated near the village of Kadakola in the Mysore district, but other occurrences have been detected in the Hassan and Shimoga districts. Chromite is the principal natural source of chrome compounds, and the largest portion of the mineral raised is devoted to the manufacture of the salts of chromium used as dyes and pigments, and in tanning operations. A smaller fraction is devoted to the manufacture of refractory chrome bricks for lining furnaces, and of chrome steels, which are largely used for armour-plating on account of their great toughness.

Copper ore was discovered in a vein near the village of Yerrapulli in the Nellore district in 1801. Large sums of money were lost in mining operations in the first half of the last century. It is worthy of note that the ore is associated with rocks which resemble in geological relationship and lithological characters those known as the Lower Huronian in America, which are referred in India to the Dharwar system of rocks, in which the gold deposits are also found.

The **Corundum** (Sanskrit, *korund*), of which extensive deposits occur in South India, lacks the gem lustre of the rubies of Burma and blue sapphires (*nīlam*) of Kashmir, which are varieties of this mineral. Ranking in hardness next to the diamond, it is in demand as an abrading agent in metal-work and stone-cutting in India and other countries. It is the richest natural compound of the metal aluminium, but, on account of its physical characters, is not suitable to replace bauxite as a source of the metal. Its distribution in Southern India has recently been systematically surveyed, more especially in the Coimbatore and Salem districts, and in Mysore. The mineral occurs in a great variety of forms, such, for example, as lumps of a grey, greenish-grey, or flesh-colour, or purplish-brown hexagonal prisms, often found as large crystals in a matrix of finely granular felspar. In some places, e.g. at Karutapalaiyam in Coimbatore, mining or digging out of corundum is an active industry on a small scale, and the waste-lands are taken up for the purpose. At Gopichettipalaiyam, in the same district, the mineral is collected in isolated crystals in the fields, and sold to a contractor from Madras.

Diamond-mining was an important industry in the Kistna district in the days when the Kings of Golconda

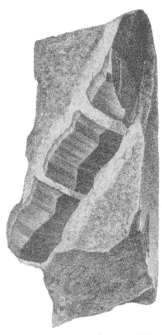

Fig. 22. Crystal of Corundum with its shell of cleared felspar forming the crystal "court" or crystal "compound."

ruled over it. The French traveller Tavernier, who visited the Kollur mines in the seventeenth century, records that 60,000 men were engaged therein. He mentions a diamond weighing 280 carats as being in the possession of the Moghul Emperor Aurangzīb. This gem was probably the Koh-i-nur (mountain of light), which is now among the

crown jewels of England, having been presented to Queen
Victoria on the annexation of the Punjab in 1849. According to tradition, this diamond was found near the Kistna
river, and worn five thousand years ago by one of the heroes
of the Mahābhārata. The Regent or Pitt diamond, purchased in 1704 when Mr Thomas Pitt was Governor of
Madras, is said to have been found at Partiāla in the Kistna
district. It was subsequently set in the hilt of the State
sword worn by Napoleon. Pitt is said to have purchased
the diamond for £20,400, and sold it to the King of France
for five times as much. Concerning the transaction,
Alexander Pope wrote the following lines in his Epistle to
Lord Bathurst :—

> " Asleep and naked as an Indian lay,
>   An honest factor stole a gem away ;
>   He pledged it to the knight, the knight had wit,
>   So kept the diamond, and the rogue was bit."

In the Chauncey MS. the last line runs,

> " So robbed the robber, and was rich as P——."

The village of Wajrakarur (*vajra*, diamond) in the Anantapur district is celebrated for its diamonds, which are said
to be frequently picked up in the fields after heavy rain by
villagers, who sell them to brokers. In 1881, a diamond,
facetiously called the Gor-do-norr after Mr Gordon Orr
the Madras jeweller, of which the original weight was
$67\frac{1}{8}$ carats, was found by a villager, and sold to the Nizam
of Hyderabad for Rs 1,65,000. Diamond mines were
worked in former days at Banganapalle, Munimadugu, and
Rāmallakota in Kurnool.

By far the largest output of Indian **Gold** is obtained
from the mines in the Kolar district of Mysore. The
metal is derived from a single free-milling vein or reef of
blue quartz, which averages only some four feet in thick-
ness, and yields gold in paying quantities for a little more

Fig. 23. Kolar gold-field.

than four miles. The attention of Europeans was called to the vein by the existence of numerous old native workings. A shaft was sunk by Mr Lavelle as far back as 1875, but it was not till 1883 that Captain Plummer struck the Champion lode, the discovery of which laid the foundation of the ultimate success of the Kolar gold-field, on which numerous Companies, including Champion Reef, Mysore, Nundidroog, and Ooregum, have been established. By 1903, the deepest working was more than 3,000 feet below the surface. The gold is extracted from the quartz by a combination of amalgamation and treatment with potassium cyanide. The tailings, or powdered refuse of the stamped ore, are heaped up in big mounds, and are sometimes treated a second time, to secure such gold as still remains in them. The mines have, since 1902, been supplied with electric power from the Cauvery falls, which are 92 miles distant. An attempt to establish a gold-mining industry in the Nīlgiri Wynaad between 1880 and 1884 ended in financial disaster. The machinery sent out from England may still be seen, covered by jungle, or lying on the roadside. A slender living is made in various localities by a class of people called Jalagadugu (*jala*, water ; *gadugu*, wash), who extract gold from the bed of rivers or nullahs (watercourses). The Kurumbas of the Nīlgiris also obtain small quantities of gold by alluvial washing. In the city of Madras, gold-washers search for gold in the drains near jewellers' shops.

Graphite, plumbago, or blacklead, which, like the diamond, is a form of carbon, is worked on a commercial scale in the Nedumangād and Neyyāttinkara tāluks of Travancore, and in the Bhadrāchalam tāluk of the Godā-vari district. Graphite of good quality further occurs in the Singampatti zamindari of Tinnevelly. In its purest form, the mineral is the material from which lead pencils are made, and it is also used for polishing grates and pottery, for the manufacture of crucibles, and as a lubricant for machinery.

The smelting of **Iron** by primitive methods has been carried out by Indians from very early times, and old-fashioned furnaces may still be found at work in remote places, where imported iron and steel are not available. An interesting fact is that the earthen crucibles used at the present day correspond both in size and shape with those

Fig. 24. Pariahs smelting small "blooms" of wrought iron, Salem district.

which were discovered during the excavations at the ancient burial-place at Aditanallur. The wootz steel, made in the Trichinopoly district and other localities, has long been celebrated, and it has been conjectured that the famous Damascus sword-blades were manufactured from it. In 1830, an Iron Company was established by Mr Heath at Porto Novo in the South Arcot district, with a view to manufacture bar iron from the indigenous ores, but the

enterprise ended in failure, after a struggle extending over
many years. Quartz-iron-ore schists form thick bands of
considerable dimensions in the Salem district, the Mysore
State, etc., but it has not as yet been found possible to
work them on a large commercial scale. And, for the
present, the iron industry remains confined to native
" bloomeries."

Magnesite (carbonate of magnesium) occurs in the form
of white veins in the olivine rocks in the " Chalk Hills " of
the Salem district. The white deposit is believed to be
made up of the bones of the mythological bird Jatayu,
which fought with Rāvana to rescue Sīta from his clutches.
During the last few years the average production of the
mineral has been 2,254 tons per annum. As it is of unusual
purity, it is likely to be useful for the manufacture of
plaster, tiles, etc., and also in refractory linings for furnaces,
and as a dephosphorising agent in the steel industry.

Of the various ores of **Manganese**, psilomelane and
braunite form the bulk of the ores exported from India.
A rapid development in the mining or quarrying of these
ores has taken place within the last few years. The
industry in the Vizagapatam district had its origin in
1891, when Mr H. G. Turner, the Collector of the district,
noticed that railway contractors were breaking up blocks
of manganese-ore for ballast. As a result, the Vizianagram
Mining Company was floated. In 1905, the deposit of
manganese-ore at Rāmandrūg in the Sandur State was
opened up, and a monopoly of the manganese and iron
ores of the State secured by the General Sandur Mining
Company. In the following year, the Mysore Manganese
Company was formed, to take over concessions in the
Shimoga district, and its success led to a rush for manganese concessions in several districts of the Mysore State.
When in hard, compact masses, the ore is hand-drilled,
and blasted. Otherwise it is simply prized out with

crowbars. The huge blocks thus detached are broken up with sledge-hammers, and carried up the hill, or out of the quarry, on the heads of coolies. The ore, which is exported to England, the United States, and Germany, is utilised

Fig. 25. Manganese quarry, Kodur, Vizagapatam district.

in the manufacture of iron and steel. The ore has been used in India, from remote times, for colouring glass and enamels. At the present day it is also used for imparting a dark colour to tiles and biscuit-ware.

Mica, which is obtained in large quantities from the Nellore mines, occurs in the form called muscovite (*vitrium muscoviticum* or Muscovy glass), owing to its use in Russia in place of glass for windows. The ancient Hindu writers recognised four classes of mica, corresponding to the four castes of Manu, viz., Brahman, white; Kshatriya, red-tinted (ruby mica); Vaisya, yellow; Sūdra, black. The

Fig. 26.   Mica crystals in the rock.   Inikurti quarry, Nellore district.

mineral in Nellore, which is characterised by a greenish tinge, forms a constituent of the granite pegmatites, mainly composed, like ordinary granite, of quartz, felspar, and mica, in which the crystals have developed on a gigantic scale Crystals or " books " of mica have, in fact, been obtained from the Nellore mines, measuring 10 feet across the basal plane, and rectangular sheets, free from cracks and flaws, sometimes measure as much as 30 × 24 inches. The mineral is worked in wide, open quarries, distributed among the four mining zones of Gudur, Rapur, Atmakur, and Kavali, and bearing, in some cases, the name of a Hindu deity, e.g. Venkatēswara and Mahālakshmi. Mica commands a special price in the commercial market, because it is a non-conductor of electricity, is able to stand great heat and rapid changes of temperature, is transparent to light, almost opaque to radiant heat, and is tough and elastic. This combination of features is not obtained in any other natural substance, and cannot be readily imitated artificially. Consequently, mica is used in covering the armatures of dynamos, as lamp chimneys, as coverings for the peep-holes of high temperature furnaces, for photographic films, and for window-panes in places exposed to great changes of temperature or violent vibrations. In India there is a demand for mica at the Muhammadan Mohurram festival for the decoration of taziahs or taboots, processional lamps, banners, etc. Waste scrap and pulverised mica are used for a variety of purposes, such as non-conducting packings and jackets for boilers and steam-pipes, the manufacture of lubricants for machinery, and as a base for soap. The invention of micanite has created an opening for the use of the smaller grades of mica, which were formerly discarded as waste. Of the world's total supply of mica, over 60 per cent. by value is obtained from India, more than a quarter of the Indian production being from the Madras Presidency. Over 7,000 workers are employed on an average daily at the Madras mica mines.

Since 1908, considerable attention has been paid to certain beach sands on the Travancore coast, which have been found to contain considerable proportions of **Monazite**, samples of which have yielded, on analysis, 12 per cent. of thoria, the substance that gives it its commercial value on account of its highly incandescent properties. The deposits are still being prospected, and 2 cwt. of the material have been sent for analysis to the Tata Institute, Bangalore.

Salt or "common salt" (chloride of sodium), the production of which is a Government monopoly, is manufactured, under the supervision of the Salt Department, in factories on the shores of the Bay of Bengal and Gulf of Manaar by concentrating sea-water in shallow evaporating pans formed by levelling and embanking the ground. In the Ceded Districts, and especially in Bellary, mounds of earth, called modas, survive as memorials of the days when the Upparas (salt-workers) manufactured earth-salt from saline soils, for consumption by the poorer classes and cattle.

Saltpetre or nitre (nitrate of potassium) is manufactured, under license from the Salt Department, by lixiviating the nitrous efflorescence in the soil, and subsequently refining it, to free it from sodium chloride and other impurities. The greater part of the refined mineral is produced in the Coimbatore and Trichinopoly districts.

Samarskite, the chief importance of which lies in the fact that it contains radium, has recently been discovered in the Nellore mica area.

Steatite (hydrous silicate of magnesium), or soapstone, as it is called owing to its greasy feel, occurs of good quality near the village of Mudvaram, seven miles from Betamcherla in the Kurnool district, where there are excavations in the dolomite (carbonate of magnesium and calcium) rock containing thin layers of the mineral. Articles for domestic use, and carved idols, are made from it in various districts. The mineral is used commercially for making gas-burners, electrical insulators, lining for stoves, etc.

Of the **Crystalline rocks** which are used for building purposes, the most beautiful are the porphyries from Chāmundi hill, Seringapatam, and other localities, which have been used as ornamental stones in the new palace of the

Mahārāja at Mysore. At Bangalore, the quarrying of the rock which is largely used as a building stone, for walls, posts for huts, etc., by means of a wood fire, which detaches large plates, has been carried to great perfection. Attention has recently been paid to the possibilities of the purple norite, which forms large masses in the hills of south-west Coorg, as an ornamental stone. The pink **sandstone** from Rāmapuram, about 40 miles north of Madras, has been used with excellent effect in the building of the Victoria Memorial Hall, Madras. The white, grey, and flesh-coloured **limestones** from the Madukarai beds near Coimbatore are eminently adapted for ornamental purposes, and have been utilised in the church at Coimbatore. The white variety is used for drinking-troughs for animals. The so-called Trichinopoly **marble**, which is largely made up of fossil univalve and bivalve shells, takes a fine polish, and is valuable as a decorative stone. White limestone from the Kistna district, out of which the sculptured railing of the Amarāvati stupa was carved, and the dark limestone from the Narji quarries, which provides the building-stones known as Cuddapah slabs, are largely used for mosaic floorings. The limestones of the Kistna and Kurnool districts have been used as lithographic stones. **Chunam** (lime), made of calcined shells, when specially prepared, produces a fine plaster, known as polished chunam, which has a shining white surface like polished marble.

On the west coast, **laterite**, cut into big bricks, is largely used in the construction of houses.

A fine **clay**, which is found in various places in South Canara, especially along the Netrāvati river, supplies the material from which the well-known Mangalore tiles are made. Clays, and kaolin (china-clay) produced by the decomposition of the felspar of granite, occur in many districts, and are used in the manufacture of pottery and earthenware.

Fig. 27. Bridge made of slabs of gneiss split by fire.

Lapidary work is carried on at Settipālaiyam, a village near Tiruppur in the Coimbatore district, where rock-crystal (quartz) spectacles, beads, lingas, figures of the elephant god Ganēsa, etc., are made. The crystals are ground on emery discs made with powdered corundum. At Vallam in the Tanjore district, rock-crystals are collected by lapidaries, and cut into a variety of articles, such as brooch-stones, watch-glasses, and double-convex spectacles. The purple amethyst crystals found at Vallam are sent to Settipālaiyam to be polished.

Quantity and Value of the principal minerals produced in Southern India, 1906—10.

Gold (Mysore).

Year	Quantity Ounces	Value £
1906	565,208	2,167,636
1907	535,085	2,041,130
1908	535,653	2,055,567
1909	545,309	2,092,605
1910	550,279[1]	2,116,064[1]
Average	546,307	2,094,600

[1] Including 2,532 ounces, valued at £10,120, produced in the Anantapur district of Madras.

Graphite (Travancore).

Year	Quantity Tons	Value £
1906	2,596	9,998
1907	2,429	7,387
1908	2,873	14,365
1909	2,132	12,529
1910	3,992	19,960
Average	3,004	12,848

Magnesite (Madras).

Year	Quantity Tons	Value £
1906	1,832	488
1907	186	50
1908	7,534	2,009
1909	737	196
1910	5,182	1,382
Average	3,094	825

Manganese Ore (Madras and Mysore).

Year	Madras Tons	Mysore Tons	Total Tons
1906	114,710	46,312	161,022
1907	162,455	113,307	275,762
1908	118,089	68,624	186,713
1909	138,454	39,895	178,349
1910	120,607	42,518	163,125
Average ...	130,863	62,131	191,994

Mica (Madras).

Year	Quantity Cwts.
1906	24,420
1907	15,865
1908	11,249
1909	8,948
1910	3,586
Average	12,814

Salt (Madras).

Year	Quantity Tons
1906	412,717
1907	353,271
1908	435,120
1909	309,583
1910	464,607
Average	395,060

CHAPTER IX

METEORITES

THE mineral kingdom, it has been said, includes not only the mineral products belonging to our own earth, but also those, called meteorites, which belong to outer space, and have fallen from the sky. About a dozen or more meteorite falls have been recorded in Southern India, and in this area, as in the rest of India, a very small proportion

Fig. 28. Parnallee meteorite.

are meteoric irons, two only of this kind having been detected, namely those which fell at Nedagolla (4,280 grams), and at Kodaikānal (2,355 grams). There is no record of the actual fall of the Kodaikānal meteorite. But a large meteor was seen to burst over the Pillar Rocks near that place a few years prior to the discovery of the meteorite, and it is possible that it fell at that time. Of the stony meteorites, the largest recorded is that which fell at Parnallee in 1857, and weighs 60,941 grams. Two meteorites, large and small, fell within a few seconds of, and about three miles apart from each other. The noise, which appears to have been heard at Tuticorin forty miles off, sounded like two claps of thunder. Many of the villagers worshipped the stones, some supposing that they were gods, or had been brought from the sea by the incantations of a Brahman, others that they had been shot from cannon on a ship.

CHAPTER X

FAUNA

(MAMMALS, BIRDS, REPTILES, FISHES, INSECTS)

ACCORDING to the classification of Wallace, South India is united with the island of Ceylon in the same zoo-geographical province—the sub-region of Ceylon and South India; and, among Mammals which are peculiar thereto, are the loris, several members of the genus *Presbytis* (*Semnopithecus*: langurs), the Malayan genus *Tupaia* (tree-shrews), and *Platacanthomys* (Malabar spiny-mouse).

The Mammals range in size from the elephant (*Elephas maximus*) to the Indian pigmy shrew (*Crocidura perotteti*), one of the smallest existing Mammals.

Excluding man (*Homo sapiens*), the **Primates** are represented by various monkeys, and one of the lemurs—the tailless slender loris, whose eyes are used in the preparation of a potent charm. The monkeys include the wanderoo, which has a ruff of long hairs encircling the head; the bonnet-monkey, which is trained to do tricks, and is frequently exhibited about the streets; the langur or sacred Hanumān monkey; and the Malabar and Nīlgiri langurs.

The **Carnivora**, or flesh-eaters, are divided into three sections, viz., Æluroidea (cats), Cynoidea (dogs), and Arctoidea (bears).

Of the Æluroidea, the largest are the tiger, leopard or panther (*Felis pardus*), hunting leopard (*Cynælurus jubatus*: chīta or cheeta), and the striped hyæna. Black leopards, in which the spots are clearly visible if the skin is viewed in the proper light, are not uncommon. They have been regarded by some writers as a distinct species, but the occurrence of black and ordinary cubs in the same litter has been repeatedly recorded. The hunting leopard is easily tamed, and trained to hunt antelopes. The fishing cat is so named, because it haunts the banks of rivers and tidal creeks, and feeds partly on fish. The Malabar civet-cat is kept in confinement, and reared for the sake of its odorous secretion, which is used for perfume and medicinal purposes. The palm-civet or toddy-cat receives its name from its liking, real or imaginary, for palm juice or toddy. The jungle-cat (*Felis chaus*) is often seen in the neighbourhood of villages, and sometimes in towns. Of the mungooses, the best known is the common mungoose, which is carried about by jugglers, to have combats with cobras. The caracal or red lynx is now a rare animal.

The Cynoidea, or dogs, include the Indian wild dog (*Cyon dukhunensis*), which hunts in packs, and lives on deer, and wild pigs; the wolf; the little Indian fox; and the jackals, who make night hideous with what Baldæus called their "hellish concert." The jackal performs useful duties as a scavenger, and affords sport to the members of the Ootacamund and Madras hunts.

The Arctoidea, or bears, comprise the Indian marten; the ratel or honey-badger, which is called the grave-digger, because, like the jackal, it has the reputation of digging into graves, and feeding on the corpses; the various otters, which live on the banks of rivers and backwaters; and the black sloth bear.

The small order of **Insectivora**, or insect-eaters, includes the hedgehog, the Madras tree-shrew, and several species of shrew, of which the best known is the grey musk-shrew, commonly called the musk-rat. The musk-shrew diffuses a strong musky odour, and used to be supposed to affect bottled beer by running over the bottles in the cellar.

The **Chiroptera**, or bats, have the forelimbs modified into wings, formed by a membranous expansion of skin between the elongated fingers. They are divided into two classes, viz., fruit-eaters and insect-eaters. The former are represented by the flying-foxes or fox-bats, which roost in colonies head downwards on trees, to the branches of which they hook themselves. They may be seen in thousands near the Jain quarters at Mudabidire in South Canara, having, it is said, discovered that the Jains do not harm any animals. Among the insect-eaters are the large-eared vampire bats, and the pretty painted bat, which hides itself in the folded leaf of the plantain.

The **Rodents**, or gnawing animals, are represented by the porcupines, which are very destructive to crops, vegetables, and rubber plantations; hares; rats; mice; and squirrels, which include the beautiful Malabar squirrel, and the common striped or palm-squirrel, whose irritating shrill voice is familiar to those who live in the plains. A campaign has been organised, in recent years, against rats, as they harbour the tropical rat-flea (*Xenopsylla cheopis*), which is an active disseminator of plague. The size of the bandicoot or pig rat, which prowls about houses, was greatly exaggerated by early travellers. Thus Friar Jordanus wrote, about 1330 A.D., that "there be some rats as big as foxes and venomous exceedingly."

The **Ungulata**, or hoofed animals, are represented by two sub-orders, viz., (*a*) the proboscidea, or animals with

Fig. 29.　Elephant with baby.

a big trunk or proboscis; (*b*) artiodactyla, or even-toed ungulates, which have the two central hoofs of each foot equal in size, and are divided into the pigs, and ruminants, or animals which chew the cud (oxen, deer, etc.).

The **Proboscidea** have a single representative in the elephant, which is captured in pits, or driven into enclosures called keddahs, and tamed for use in dragging timber, for carrying baggage, and for ceremonial purposes at temples

Fig. 30. Wild Elephants captured in the enclosure or keddah.

or the palaces of Rājas. The term must (drunk) is applied to male elephants during their periods of excitement. The Government, it may be noted, pays rewards for the destruction of solitary rogue elephants, tigers, leopards, bears, and wolves.

Fig. 31. Gaur or "Bison."

The Ruminants include the sāmbar deer; spotted deer or chītal; muntjac, rib-faced, or barking deer (often called the jungle sheep); the little chevrotain or mouse-deer; the nīlgai, or blue-bull; gazelle or chinkāra; four-horned antelope; Indian antelope or black-buck; Nīlgiri wild goat (the "ibex" of sportsmen); the gaur or "bison"; wild buffalo; and the zebu or humped domestic ox.

Of the **Edentata**, or toothless mammals, there is only a single species, the scaly ant-eater or pangolin, wrongly called the armadillo, which burrows in the ground by means of its strong claws, and feeds mainly on ants, especially " white-ants," which it licks up with its extensile sticky tongue.

Among marine mammals, the **Cetacea** are represented by the whales and porpoises, and the **Sirenia** (sirens) by the dugong.

In 1864 a whale was cast on shore at Masulipatam, the old name of which place (Machlipatan, or fish town) is said to have been derived from a whale which was stranded there in the first half of the eighteenth century. The Madras Museum possesses the skeleton of a baleen or whalebone whale, about 48 feet in length, which was cast ashore near Mangalore in South Canara in 1874. The whalebone consists of a series of flattened horny plates on each side of the palate. The museum also possesses the skull of a toothed cachalot or sperm whale, which was washed ashore at Madras in 1890. This whale has a very wide range of distribution, being found in tropical seas, and as far as the polar regions. The oil contained in a cavity above the skull yields spermaceti, and the thick covering of blubber, which envelops the body, produces the sperm oil of commerce. Ambergris, which is used in perfumery, is a concretion found in the intestine.

The porpoises or dolphins usually travel about in herds or schools, and may often be seen out at sea along the coast, and in the tidal backwaters of the west coast, where they open into the sea.

The dugong, called in Tamil the sea-pig, is an inhabitant of the Gulf of Manaar, where it browses on sea-grasses. There is a tradition at Pāmban that a box of money was once found in the stomach of one of these animals, which was caught off that town.

Of the vast host of **Birds** which inhabit the plains, the hills, and the sea-shore, it is only possible to give a very brief summary. The birds are divided into twenty-one well-defined groups or orders, as follows :

1. Game-birds—peacock, jungle-fowl, spur-fowl, partridge, and quail.

2. Sand-grouse—painted and common sand-grouse.

3. Hemipodes—bustard-quail and button-quail.

4. Pigeon tribe—pigeons and doves.

5. Rail-like birds—banded rail, crake, water-hen, moor-hen, etc.

6. Grebe—the little grebe or dabchick, which inhabits lakes and tanks, on the hills and in the plains.

7. Gull tribe—sea-gulls and terns.

8. Plover tribe—curlew, plover, jacana, lapwing, bustard, oyster-catcher, sandpiper, stint, woodcock, snipe.

9. Crane-like birds—crane.

10. Heron tribe—ibis, spoonbill, stork, adjutant, heron, egret, bittern. The white herons which frequent rice-fields are commonly called paddy-birds.

11. Duck tribe—goose, duck, sheldrake, teal.

12. Flamingoes—flamingo.

13. Pelicans and their allies—pelican, cormorant, snake-bird.

14. Vultures, eagles, hawks—vulture, eagle, harrier, buzzard, sparrow-hawk, kestril kite. Of the kites, the best known are the pariah kite, which frequents kitchens, and the Brahminy kite, which is regarded with some veneration by Hindus.

15. Owls—horned owl, screech owl, spotted owlet (*Athene brama*), etc.

16. Parrot tribe—parroquet, loriquet.

17. Picarian birds—swift, edible-nest swiftlet, night-jar,

frog-mouth, roller or "blue jay" of Europeans, bee-eater, kingfisher, hornbill, hoopoe.

18. Trogon tribe—Malabar trogon.

19. Cuckoo tribe—cuckoo, coucal or crow-pheasant. The koel, whose plaintive cry, "ku-il, ku-il," is familiar to dwellers in the plains in the hot weather, lays its eggs in the nests of crows.

20. Woodpeckers and their allies—woodpecker, barbet. The crimson-breasted barbet is commonly called the coppersmith, from its cry "took, took," which resembles the sound produced by hammering copper.

21. Perching birds, which include all the song-birds, and are divided into singing and songless birds—crow, thrush, bulbul, babblers (seven brothers or sāt bhai, etc.), drongos (which include the king-crow), tailor-bird, weaver-bird, shrike, myna, magpie-robin, sparrow, flower-pecker, and very many others. A crow's nest in the Madras Museum is made of the wires from soda-water bottles interwoven, and lined inside with grass.

Some migratory birds only visit the south of the peninsula in the cool season. Of these the best known is the pin-tail snipe (*Gallinago stenura*), which is found, not only on the plains, but also at high elevations. Other temporary residents in the low-country include the ruddy sheldrake or Brahminy duck (*Casarca rutila*), common teal (*Nettium crecca*), blue-winged teal (*Querquedula circia*), and black-naped oriole (*Oriolus indicus*). Among the migratory birds of the Nīlgiris are the peregrine falcon (*Falco peregrinus*), marsh-harrier (*Circus æruginosus*), sparrow-hawk (*Accipiter nisus*), wood-snipe (*Gallinago nemoricola*), and woodcock (*Scolopax rusticola*). The course, which migratory birds follow, may sometimes be fixed by identifying those which are killed by striking against lighthouses. In this way, the large hawk-cuckoo (*Hierococcyx sparverioides*), an inhabitant of the Himalayas, which is a cold-weather visitor to the

Nīlgiris, was killed by striking against the Santapilly lighthouse on the Vizagapatam coast on October 28th, 1894.

Among the innocuous **Snakes**, are the burrowing or blind snake; freshwater and sand-snakes; the rat-snake (*Zamenis mucosus*); tree-snakes (*Dendrophis pictus* and *Passerita mycterizans*); and the python or rock-snake (*Python molurus*), often called the anaconda, which grows to a length of 20 feet or more. A python, apparently not exceeding 8 feet in length, has been said, on trustworthy evidence, to have swallowed a young antelope.

The venomous colubrine snakes include the hooded cobra (*Naia tripudians*) and snake-eating hamadryad (*Naia bungarus*), which grows to a length of 13 feet; the krait (*Bungarus cæruleus*); and the sea-snakes (*Hydrophidæ*), which have a flat paddle-shaped tail. The venom of sea-snakes has been said to be more virulent than that of any land snake, though deaths from their bite are infrequent.

The venomous viperine snakes include the Russell's or chain-viper (*Vipera russellii*); the small *Echis carinata*; several hill species of *Trimeresurus*; and *Ancistrodon hypnale*, called the karawala. The vipers have a pair of canaliculate or channelled fangs, which convey the venom from the poison-gland by means of an orifice near the sharp point of the fang to the puncture made in the skin of the human being or animal bitten.

The snakes, other than sea-snakes, which are known to inflict bites fatal to man, are the cobra, hamadryad, Russell's viper, krait, and *Echis carinata*.

Other reptiles are represented by the marine turtles, land and freshwater tortoises, crocodiles, and lizards. The **Turtles** include the edible green turtle (*Chelone mydas*) and the hawk-bill turtle (*Chelone imbricata*), whose imbricated dermal plates yield the tortoise-shell of commerce. **Crocodiles** (*Crocodilus porosus* and *palustris*), or muggurs, are frequently called alligators. The latter, however, are, with the exception of a Chinese species, found in the New, and not in the Old World. Of the **Lizards**, the largest is *Varanus bengalensis*, which is called the iguana or monitor, as it is supposed to give warning of the vicinity of crocodiles. It is also known as the bis-cobra (bish, poison), because it is believed, owing in all probability to its possessing a forked tongue, to be mortally venomous. The lizard (*Calotes versicolor*) with a spiny crest on its back, which is a common object of compounds in the plains, is generally called the blood-sucker, as the male, during the breeding season, assumes brilliant colours, including red, especially about the neck. It is also frequently called the chamæleon. The chamæleon is, however, quite different, and characterised by the mobility and independent action of its two eyes, a projectile tongue for catching insects, changeable hue of skin, and deliberate movements.

Of **Batrachians**, the most familiar are the big bull-frog (*Rana tigrina*) ; the green tank-frog (*Rana hexadactyla*) ; the burrowing *Cacopus systoma*, which makes the batrachian chorus during the rains; the common toad (*Bufo melanostictus*) often seen in houses ; and the chunam frog (*Rhacophorus maculatus*), which sticks on plastered walls by means of the discs on its fingers and toes. The tinkling frog of the Nīlgiris (*Ixalus variabilis*) has the reputation of being a ventriloquist. The limbless batrachians are represented by the burrowing Cœcilians (*Ichthyophis, Uræotyphlus*, and *Gegenophis*), often mistaken for earth-snakes, which live buried underground on the west coast.

The **Fishes** are represented by the Elasmobranchs (sharks and rays), and Teleostei (bony fishes). The largest shark recorded from South India is a specimen of *Rhinodon typicus*, the largest known fish, captured off Madras in 1880, which measures 22 feet in length. In this shark, each jaw is armed with a band of minute teeth, numbering several thousands. Among the rays may be noted the big saw-fish (*Pristis cuspidatus*), whose snout or saw is armed with a double row of sharp teeth; and the sting-ray (*Trygon uarnak*), whose tail is armed with a spine capable of inflicting very serious wounds. Among bony fishes, the most conspicuous is the large sea-perch (*Epinephelus lanceolatus*), which has been caught on several occasions by fishermen off Madras; and the sword or peacock-fish (*Histiophorus gladius*), which attacks whales, ships, canoes, and drift wood, and sometimes leaves its sword (snout) imbedded therein. Among curiously shaped bony fishes

Fig. 32.   *Rhinodon typicus.*

may be noted the sea-horse (*Hippocampus*, sp.); the remora (*Echeneis naucrates*), which has a sucking-disc on its head, by means of which it attaches itself to whales, turtles, sharks, and boats; the globe-fishes (*Tetrodon* and *Diodon*), which have great power of inflation; and the file or trigger-fishes (*Balistes*), which are accused of destroying the pearl-oysters by chiselling a hole through the shell with their sharp teeth, and extracting the soft parts of the animal.

The mahseer (*Barbus tor*), which sometimes weighs over 90 lbs., affords excellent sport in the Bhaváni, and other rivers.   The rainbow trout of New Zealand has been recently introduced with success on the Nīlgiri hills, and first provided sport for anglers in 1911.   The gourami (*Osphromenus olfax*), whose natural home is China and the Malay Archipelago, has been naturalised in the big pond at Government House, Madras.

According to one system of classification of zoo-geographical areas, more especially with regard to insect life, the following are recognised, in addition to the hill areas, in the south of the Peninsula:

1.   Deccan.   Well marked seasons, the dry hot weather following a marked cold weather, when hibernation sets in.

2.   West coast.   The fauna influenced by the neighbouring sub-tropical region of permanent forests and high humidity, which produce a very large fauna.   No hibernation in the places below the ghāts.   Many Ceylonese forms.

3.   Coromandel coast.   Less well marked seasons than the Deccan.   A large proportion of Ceylonese forms.

The most primitive existing forms of **Insects** are represented by the *Aptera* or wingless insects.   Included among these is the fish insect (*Lepisma*), which takes up its abode in almirahs or wardrobes, and book-cases, to the contents of which it does much damage.

Conspicuous among the **Orthoptera** are the leaf and stick insects, which bear a remarkable resemblance to leaves, sticks, and twigs, and afford examples of protective mimicry.   The praying mantis owes its name to its habit of standing on its four hind-legs, with the front legs held up close together.   The common *Gongylus gongyloides* is called the orchid mantis, because it simulates an orchid flower.   Cockroaches (*Periplaneta*) are common pests in houses and steamers.   Migratory locusts (*Acridium*), which sometimes travel in swarms so dense as to obscure the sun, do enormous damage to crops and vegetation.   A column of locusts, which invaded the Marātha country, was described as extending five hundred miles.

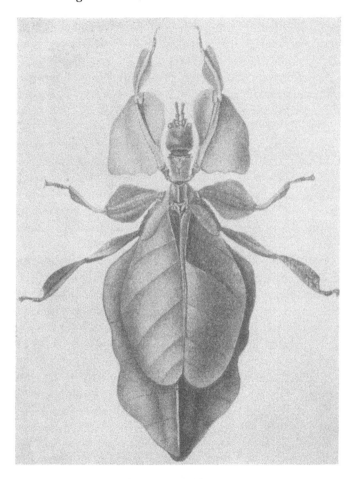

Fig. 33. Leaf insect.

Prominent among the **Neuroptera** are the "white-ants" (*Termes*), which are destructive to books, furniture, and wood-work. They live in large colonies, and build nests

consisting of cells connected by galleries, which form the
well-known ant-hills. The members of a colony consist of
wingless soldiers and workers, sexual winged forms, and
the Queen, who lives in a special cell, which she never
leaves. At certain seasons, hosts of sexual winged white-
ants come out from the ground, and fly about. Many of
them are eaten by birds, ants, and other enemies. Those
which escape shed their wings, which fall on the ground or

Fig. 34. Female white-ant, distended with eggs.

inside houses, and pair. In some places natives collect the
bodies, which they sun-dry, and store in large pots as an
article of food.

The **Lepidoptera** are divided into the Butterflies and
Moths. Some butterflies, *e.g.* various species of the yellow
Terias, illustrate season dimorphism, or variation of the
colouration and markings in the wet and dry season broods.

The upper surfaces of the wings of *Hebomoia glaucippe* and
Kallima horsfieldi are brightly coloured; but, when the
animals are at rest, with the wings folded and exposing the
dark under surface, they are protected by their resemblance
to dried leaves. In most cases of deceptive mimicry, the
mimicked form has an odour which is repulsive to birds
and lizards. Thus, the female of *Hypolimnas misippus*,
which is unlike the male (sexual dimorphism), mimics
Danais chrysippus, and the female of *Elymnias caudata*
mimics *Danais genutia*. The swallow-tail butterfly *Papilio
pammon* has two forms of female, which mimic respectively
the males of *Papilio aristolochiæ* and *Papilio hector*. Many
of the Nymphalidæ have what is called bird-misleading
colouration, the conspicuous colour-markings on the wings
diverting the bird's aim from the head and body, and
enabling the butterfly to escape with a piece bitten out of
its wings. The shawl butterfly, *Cethosia mahratta*, is said
to have suggested the pattern on the famous silk shawls.
The cocoons of the wild silk-moth *Antheræa paphia*, which
are the source of tasar silk, are collected in certain forest
areas, *e.g.* by the hill Pānos in the Ganjam Māliahs. The
rearing of the domesticated *Bombyx mori*, or mulberry silk-
worm, has for some time been a recognised industry in the
Mysore State. In recent years, silk-worm or sericulture
farms have been started under Japanese management, and
by the Salvation Army at Bangalore.

The **Hymenoptera** include the Wasps and Bees. Some
wasps, known as potters, make mud cells on walls, window-
panes, and other parts of houses, in which they deposit
paralysed caterpillars. The largest of the honey-bees is
Apis dorsata, which builds large nests in the forests. In
quest of honey some jungle folk, *e.g.* the Kādirs of the
Ānaimalai hills, climb lofty trees by means of bamboo
stems or pegs, or, torch in hand, descend steep precipices
on dark nights by means of a stout creeper or ladder made

of bamboo or rattan, and, having smoked out the bees, take away the honey.

To the **Diptera** belong the Flies and Fleas. The anopheline mosquitoes have earned a bad reputation, as the females have the proboscis modified for the purpose of sucking blood, and convey the germs of malarial fever to human beings. One of the mosquitoes (*Culex fatigans*) conveys the parasite which causes elephantiasis (filariasis).

Fig. 35. Jungle Irulas collecting honey.

Among the **Coleoptera** or Beetles are many weevils, which are destructive to crops or trees. For example, the palm weevil (*Rhynchophorus*) breeds in the coconut and date palms, and may reduce the tree to a shell. The mango weevil (*Cryptorhynchus*) breeds in the stone of the mango, the eggs being laid in the young fruit, through the pulp of which the mature larva (grub or caterpillar) eats its way. The nocturnal larvæ of Malacodermid Coleoptera

emit a bright greenish-white light from luminous organs
situated on the abdomen.   The dung-rollers roll the dung
of animals into pellets or balls, which they push along with
their hind-legs, and consume in some sheltered spot.   The
metallic green wings of a Buprestid beetle are used in
Madras for the ornamentation of articles of dress.

Included among the **Rhynchota** is the common house-
bug (*Cimex*), which lays its eggs in cracks in the floor,
cane-bottomed chairs, and other safe places.   The large
bug (*Belostoma*) commonly called the water-scorpion, which
has raptorial fore-legs, invades houses at certain seasons.
The green bug (*Lecanium viride*) is the green-scale of the
coffee plant, which proved disastrous to the coffee-planters.
The Cicadas or knife-grinders are responsible for the shrill
sound often heard in forests, which is produced by a
complicated structure on the abdomen.   The sound has
been likened to that of the wooden rattle used during the
boat-races at Cambridge.

CHAPTER XI

FLORA ; FORESTS

OWING to various causes, to its belonging to the oldest
geological region in India, to its great stretch of latitude
(from 8°—20° N.), to its many hill ranges culminating in
peaks over 8,000 feet above the sea, and to its varied rainfall from about 200 inches on the western ghāts to under
20 inches in some of the driest parts of the Deccan, the
Flora of the Madras Presidency is one of very varied
character and great number of species.   In all probability
the number of flowering plants and ferns reaches about
4,000.   Naturally, the greatest number of these are found

Fig. 36. Banyan avenue, Madras.

in the regions of heavy rainfall adjoining the west or Malabar coast, but other regions, such as the hills of the eastern side of the Presidency, give a considerable number.

The stranger who lands at the port of Madras is often disappointed in the vegetation. In and about the town he sees, it is true, many forms of more or less tropical appearance like the coconut (*Cocos nucifera*) and palmyra (*Borassus flabellifer*) palms, the banyan and pīpal figs (*Ficus bengalensis* and *religiosa*), the plantain (*Musa sapientum*) and papaya or papaw (*Carica Papaya*) fruit trees, the mango, tamarind, and jack fruit, and feathery bamboos. But the country around seems to be a somewhat uninteresting stretch of wet rice land with occasional rocky hills emerging from them here and there, and clothed with a shrubby and mostly thorny vegetation. And, travelling as he might about the cultivated low level areas of the Carnatic plain, he finds but little difference, little to tell him that the luxuriant tropical vegetation he may have expected to see exists at all in Southern India. Indeed, it is only when he has proceeded across the Peninsula, and finds himself at last on the Malabar coast in the narrow stretch of cultivated and forest land of steamy climate between the sea and the ghāt range, and in the valleys of that range, that he is rewarded by something like the vegetation he has looked for. On the coast itself, cultivated forests of the coconut palm, interspersed with occasional patches of mangrove swamp, are backed by green stretches of rice land and villages surrounded by trees. Here and there may be seen patches of the cultivated areca nut palm (*Areca Catechu*), and groves of bamboos, which are so valuable for the construction of houses and innumerable other domestic purposes. The forests begin chiefly on low hills, and contain principally a mixture of many species, often of an evergreen character. They clothe the slopes of the ghāt range, and among their chief trees are the teak (*Tectona grandis*), blackwood or rosewood (*Dalbergia latifolia*), and many *Dipterocarpeous*

Fig. 37. Tree Ferns.

giants. On the summit of the ghāt range there is a great change of character in the vegetation and scenery. Large

stretches of grass land dotted with flowers, among which
Senecio, Anaphalis, and *Strobilanthes,* are conspicuous, alter-
nate with patches of slow-growing shola (glade) forest
chiefly of evergreen type, and the hill cultivated lands, in
which the chief crops are kinds of millet, with maize,
tapioca, and leguminous vegetables. The highest peaks
are not usually precipitous, as is the western scarp of the
ghāt range, but are covered with grass and shola.

After the summit of the ghāt range comes a wonderful
transition of climate, and consequently also of vegetation.
By degrees, and rather speedy degrees, as the descent eastward is made, the rainfall gets less, the climate and soil
get dry, and both the cultivated crops and the general
flora change. Cotton cultivation is common, millets again
abound, sunn hemp and flax occur, trees are few and far
between, and the hedgerow vegetation presents such strange
plants as the various species of *Cactus,* the *Agave,* and the
curious tree *Euphorbias.* The palmyra palm may occasionally be seen, but more common is the wild date palm
(*Phœnix sylvestris*), cut and twisted into uncouth shapes
by the villagers for the sake of its sap, which gives a
fermented liquor. The forest in such regions is confined
chiefly to hilly places, and contains the same kinds of small
deciduous trees as may be found throughout the whole of
the centre of India. And so we come once more across
the Peninsula, and find ourselves again in the Carnatic rice
fields, which border the Coromandel coast. This coast
extends northwards up to about latitude 20°, where it runs
into Bengal, and everywhere presents the aspect of a dry
sandy shore, in places much disturbed by sand-dunes,
which have had to be tawed, and converted into protective
forests artificially. The chief agent in this protective work
has been the *Casuarina* tree, but there are others which are
noticeable, and among them the cashew nut (*Anacardium
occidentale*), the screw pine (*Pandanus odoratissimus*), and

a dwarf date (*Phœnix farinifera*). Northward along the coast, palmyra palms are common, with occasional coconuts and dates, and the forests produce such interesting

Fig. 38. Forest scenery.

plants as *Strychnos Nux-vomica*, the soapnut (*Sapindus emarginatus*), satinwood (*Chloroxylon Swietenia*), and ebony (*Diospyros Ebenum*). Inland from the coast rise the hills of the eastern ghāt range, reaching to 4,000 and occasionally

5,000 feet, and covered for the most part with deciduous forest, in which, in the southern parts, the most noticeable trees are the teak and ironwood (*Xylia dolabriformis*), and in the northern the sāl (*Shorea robusta*).

Behind the eastern ghāt scarp comes the Deccan plateau, partly covered with forest, partly cultivated. In the cultivated fields cotton is a common crop, especially on those areas of decomposed rock known as black cotton lands. Among the trees, red sanders (*Pterocarpus santalinus*) and sandal (*Santalum album*) are the most noticeable, and the small vegetation in the open country consists very largely of somewhat shrubby species of *Acanthaceæ*.

Sir Joseph Hooker, in his account of the Botany of India in the *Imperial Gazetteer*, divides the Peninsula into five regions, each of which contains a portion of the Madras Presidency. These regions are :—

(1) What may be called the **Northern Circars region**, the country north of the river Godāvari. It is all more or less hilly country, for, though here and there are some flat areas near the coast, especially the northern part of the Godāvari delta, the hills come more or less down to the sea, and in some places, *e.g.* near Vizagapatam, form quite bold headlands. The highest point is Mahendragiri (4,923 feet), the summit of which is scarcely more than 20 miles in a straight line from the coast ; but there are also other high peaks, especially in the densely wooded ranges of Golgonda and Rampa. The flora of the higher ranges shows a decided affinity to that of the hills of Assam and Burma, and possesses many plants of the temperate regions, and one especially noticeable plant on Mahendragiri is a date palm (*Phœnix robusta*?), while the bracken fern covers the grass lands as elsewhere in the world at suitable elevations. The main hill slopes are forest-clad, except for the patches of cultivation round the villages of the Kondhs and other primitive tribes. The

forests in the northern hills, in Ganjam and as far south as the Pālkonda hills of Vizagapatam, are noticeable for fine trees of sāl (*Shorea robusta*). Further south the chief noticeable tree is the ironwood (*Xylia dolabriformis*), and near the Godāvari the teak appears. The feathery kittul or bastard sago palm (*Caryota urens*) is often conspicuous, as also is *Cycas*. There are many *Acanthaceous* shrubs, and much bamboo, the common species being *Bambusa Tulda* and *arundinacea*, and *Dendrocalamus strictus*. Near the coast the hills are often composed of laterite, and here the bush vegetation is usually of a thorny character, and there is often much *Cactus*, while the screw pine and cashew nut abound near the sea-shore.

(2) The **Upper Deccan region** consists of the country between the rivers Godāvari and Kistna, and only a small part of it comes into the Madras Presidency, the rest being in the Hyderabad State. In the little Madras piece there is a strip of hilly country with forests of bamboo, teak and other trees, rising in the " Bison hills " to a considerable height, and the rest is the valuable and very fertile delta region of the two rivers. On the coast are some mangrove forests, the most common tree in which is probably *Avicennia*; but, in the Bay of Masulipatam, the sandy shore contains a number of sand-loving species such as the convolvulus (*Ipomœa Pes-capræ*) and the curious *Spinifex* grass.

(3) The **Mysore region** comprises the area between the Kistna river on the north and the Cauvery on the south, and includes the Mysore State, the Ceded Districts, the eastern ghāt scarp more or less parallel to the sea and chiefly covered with valuable forest, and the great cultivated plain of the northern Carnatic. In the interior, on the Bellary, Anantapur, and Kurnool plateau, the rainfall is very small, and the soil is sometimes black cotton, but more often red soil, covered largely with stones, and with

isolated and usually metamorphic hills rising from it here
and there, and often crowned by the interesting Poligar
forts, which testify to the disturbed times of previous
centuries. The forest vegetation is poor, but one valuable
tree is often noticeable, the *Hardwickia binata* sometimes
covering considerable areas of rocky country. The hedges
and roadsides have many thorny bushes, and the flora in
small plants such as grasses, *Acanthaceæ*, *Convolvulaceæ*,
Boraginaceæ, and *Compositæ*, is very interesting. On the
ghāt range in Cuddapah, North Arcot, and Salem, the
country is forest-clad, except for many villages with areas
of dry cultivation. Teak is fairly common, red sanders
(*Pterocarpus santalinus*) is the prevailing tree between
N. Lat. 13° and 15°, and a kind of sāl (*Shorea Tumbug-
gaia*) is very noticeable. In ravines, there is much bamboo
of the two ordinary kinds, but there are few or no palms.
In the coast belt, as already noted, the coconut and
palmyra palms are characteristic, the latter especially
among the villages. The hills are but lightly clothed with
thorny scrub, and the laterite lands bear forests of an
evergreen type, noticeable plants being the blue-flowered
Memecylon, two species of *Mimusops*, and many *Rubiaceæ*.
On the coast, the sandy dunes have been largely reclaimed
with *Casuarina*, and the river deltas show patches of mangrove.

(4) What may be called the **South Carnatic region**,
from the Cauvery river to Cape Comorin, is bounded on
the west by the bases of the Nīlgiri, Ānaimalai, Palni, and
Tinnevelly hills, in the Coimbatore, Madura, and Tinnevelly districts. The character of the flora of this region is
very similar to the last. The hill ranges are covered with
deciduous forest, in which the principal tree is teak, and in
places to the north, where the soil is poor, the half parasitic
sandalwood (*Santalum album*). The coast lands have their
sandy dunes, sometimes, as near Point Calimere, covering

considerable distances, which are being reclaimed to forest.
The cultivated lands have many groves of palmyra palm
and coconut, with mango and jack fruit; while, in the
Tinnevelly plains to the extreme south, a very characteristic plant is the umbrella-shaped *Acacia planifrons*.
The flora of small plants, *Compositæ*, *Acanthaceæ*, etc., is
very varied and interesting, and especially so are the many
and curious kinds of grasses.

(5) The **Malabar region** comprises the lands along the
western sea-coast and the ghāt range, including the hills of
Canara, Coorg, Wynaad, Nīlgiris, Ānaimalais, and Palnis.
The southern part of this region is chiefly in the Travancore
State. Being a region of great rainfall, as has been already
explained, the vegetation is characteristically tropical except on the higher hills, and the flora is a rich one. There
are many palms besides the coconut, areca, and occasional
palmyras, the most conspicuous being the tall *Coryphas*
which only flower once, produce enormous quantities of
seed, and then die, *Caryota*, *Arenga*, the endemic *Ben-
tinckia Coddapanna*, and the climbing rattan canes, species
of the genus *Calamus*. Noticeable among bamboos are
the thickets of the curious large-fruited *Ochlandra travan-
corica* in the south, besides species of *Oxytenanthera* and
Teinostachyum. Besides teak, of which the Government
plantation in the Benne forest extends over 244 acres, the
chief timber tree is the blackwood (*Dalbergia latifolia*),
and there are many species of *Guttiferæ*, *Dipterocarpaceæ*,
Myristicaceæ, *Anonaceæ*, and other Families with conspicuous large trees, the tree which probably reaches the
largest size of all being the soft-wooded *Tetrameles nudi-
flora*. The lower slopes and plateaux of the hills abound
in interesting plants of many families, *Leguminosæ* being
perhaps the most noticeable, while there are many *Orchideæ*,
both ground-species and epiphytes. The Todas of the
Nīlgiris may often be seen rooting up ground orchids with

a sharp-pointed digging-stick. The tubers are boiled in milk and taken "to make them strong." The shrubby

Fig. 39.   Bamboos on the Nīlgiri Ghāt Road.

vegetation largely consists of species of *Strobilanthes*, most of which, like some palms and most bamboos, flower only

once, and then die. On the higher hills, to which reference
has already been made, the grass lands have a characteristic vegetation, and the shola forests fill the hollows
with interesting trees, of which the most common are
myrtles (*Eugenia*), hollies (*Ilex*), *Rhododendron*, *Michelia*,
and *Meliosma*. Conspicuous plants also are the introduced gorse and arum lily. A beautiful white lily (*Lilium
neilgherrense*) is not uncommon, and in the peat bogs
occurs the curious *Hedyotis verticillata*. In these hills
many Australian plants have been introduced, chiefly
species of *Eucalyptus* and *Acacia*. Finally, it may be re-
marked that perhaps the most interesting point is the
almost complete absence of indigenous Conifers and
Oaks.

The forests of the Madras Presidency are found in all
districts, for nearly all the land in the Presidency, except
in the Native States and in a small number of granted
estates, is the property of the Government, who own the
forests. The area thus placed under management amounts
to about 20,000 square miles, and requires a considerable
staff of officers. The forests serve chiefly for the supply
of the requirements of the great agricultural population in
fuel and building material, the more valuable ones also
yielding a considerable amount of better class timber for
public works such as the railways, but scarcely any for
export. The most valuable forests are those of teak,
which are found principally in Malabar, the Nīlgiris, and
Coimbatore; but there are other teak forests in the Deccan
country, and up to and across the river Godāvari. Sāl
forests occur chiefly in the most northernly district, Ganjam; red sanders wood in Cuddapah and North Arcot;
sandal in Coimbatore and Coorg; and *Hardwickia* in
Anantapur and Bellary. In most other regions the forests
are of mixed species, the chief timber-givers being trees
of the genera *Dalbergia*, *Xylia*, *Pterocarpus*, *Terminalia*,

Lagerströmia, *Adina*, *Vitex*, *Acacia*, *Albizzia*, and *Arto-carpus*. In the hilly regions, introduced Australian trees of quick growth are very conspicuous, and some Coniferous woods have been recently brought in. Nearly all the forests are managed under simple plans of working, designed to produce as much material as possible without endangering the capital stock, though this is by no means an easy matter in a country where every village possesses huge herds of often very poor cattle requiring forest grazing for their support.

CHAPTER XII

ECONOMIC USES OF PALMS

OF the palms which are useful for economic purposes, the most important are the coconut (*Cocos nucifera*), palmyra or tar (*Borassus flabellifer*), betel-nut palm (*Areca Catechu*), wild date or date-sugar palm (*Phœnix sylvestris*), the Indian sago palm or salop (*Caryota urens*), which yields the kittul fibre used in brush-making, and the several species of *Calamus*, of which the rope-like stems yield the canes and rattans of commerce. According to a Tamil proverb, 801 uses are ascribed to the palmyra palm.

The **coconut palm** grows luxuriantly along the littoral of both the west and east coasts, and is also cultivated far inland, *e.g.* in Coimbatore and Mysore. It is further an important source of livelihood to the Laccadive islanders, who bring their produce to Malabar. A very important industry in Malabar is the extraction of the fibre known as coir (kāyar) from the outer walls of the fruits or husks of the coconut. These are retted (or rotted) by burying them in pits on the margin of rivers, streams, or back-waters, in which they are left to soak for six months, a

Fig. 40. Coconut Plantation.

8—2

year, or even longer. When the husks are removed from
the pits, the fibre is beaten out with sticks by women of
the Tiyan and other castes, dried in the sun, and twisted
into yarn for export to Europe, where it is manufactured
into matting, rope, etc. The fibre was introduced into
England about 1836, and it is on record that, at the baptism of the late King Edward VII in 1842, the floor of
St George's Hall at Windsor Castle was covered first with

Fig. 41.   Coir-picking, Malabar.

matting made of the husk of the coconut. The white
kernel of the coconut fruit, when sliced and dried, is called
kopra, and is the source of coconut oil, which is largely
used as an illuminant, in cooking, and in soap manufacture.
For the illuminations on the occasion of the marriage of
Queen Victoria, Price's Candle Company introduced a
cheap candle composed of stearic acid and coconut stea-
rine, which did not require snuffing. The oil-cake, which

remains after the oil has been expressed from the kernel, is used as food for cattle. The "milk" of young or green coconuts affords a refreshing drink. The wood, commercially known as porcupine wood, is used for a variety of purposes, *e.g.* for rafters of buildings, the manufacture of walking-sticks, etc.

The extraction of the juice of the coconut, palmyra, and wild date palms, gives employment to the various **toddy-drawing castes**, of which the most important are the Tamil Shānars, Telugu Idigas, Malayālam Tiyans, Canarese Halēpaiks, and Tulu Billavas. The Shānars, when employed in the palmyra forests of Tinnevelly, are said to climb from forty to fifty trees, each forty or fifty feet high, three times a day. The story is told by Bishop Caldwell of a Shānar who was sitting upon a leaf-stalk at the top of a palmyra palm in a high wind, when the stalk gave way, and he came to the ground safely and quietly, sitting on the leaf, which served the purpose of a parachute. Woodpeckers are called Shānar kurivi by bird-catchers, because they climb trees like Shānars. There is a legend that the Shānars are descended from Adi, the daughter of a Pariah woman, who taught them to climb the palm tree, and prepared a medicine which would protect them from falling from the high trees. The squirrels also ate some of it, and enjoy a similar immunity. In Malabar, the toddy-drawer's outfit consists of a knife, a bone (the leg bone of a sāmbhar deer from choice) loaded with lead for bruising the flower-stalk, a few earthen pots, and two rings of rope with which to climb the tree. The Telugu toddy-drawers use a ladder about eight or nine feet in length, which is placed against the tree. The Shānars climb up and down with their hands and arms, using a soft grummel of coir to keep the feet near together. The juice or sap, which exudes when the flower-stalks are cut, is collected in the pots. If the juice is to be drunk fresh, in which state it is known as sweet

Fig. 42. Toddy-drawer climbing palm-tree.

toddy (a corruption of tari), the pots are coated inside with lime, to prevent fermentation from setting in, and yielding the intoxicating beverage. If the toddy is subjected to distillation, a form of spirituous liquor or palm wine, called **arrack**, is obtained. Arak means perspiration, and hence exudation of sap. A corruption of the word is rack, which occurs in rack punch. The excise or abkāri revenue is largely derived from the sale of arrack carried on in licensed shops, the right of sale in which is put up to auction annually. A further source of revenue is the tax levied on each tree which is tapped for toddy. In the hill-tracts of Ganjam and Vizagapatam, spirit is distilled from the flowers of the mahua tree (*Bassia*). The hill tribes of these districts also obtain alcoholic liquor from the fermented juice of the salop palm.

The juice of the various palms, when boiled down, yields a coarse, dark-coloured sugar called **jaggery** (a corruption of the Sanskrit sarkarā, sugar), which is very largely used by the poorer classes. Small round cakes of jaggery are said to have formerly passed as a kind of currency in Tinnevelly, and do even now to a small extent.

The seeds of the areca palm, which are in appearance like small nutmegs, are commonly called **betel-nuts**. The name betel, however, strictly applies to the leaves of the *Piper Betle* or pān, which is chewed by Indians with the areca seeds (supāri). The presentation and distribution of pān-supāri are an important feature of many ceremonial occasions.

CHAPTER XIII

LANGUAGE

SOUTH INDIA is essentially the home of the Dravidian languages, which are spoken by over 90 per cent. of the population. The word Dravidian has been simply defined as the name given to a collection of Indian people, and their form of language comprising all the principal forms of speech in Southern India. In the *Linguistic Survey of India*, Mr G. A. Grierson writes that the name Dravidian "is derived from an older Dramila, Damila, and is identical with the name of Tamil. The name Dravidian is, accordingly, identical with Tamulian, which name has formerly been used by European writers as a common designation of the languages in question. The word Dravida forms part of the denomination Andhra-Drāvida-bhāshā, the language of the Andhras (*i.e.* Telugu), and Dravidas (*i.e.* Tamilians), which Kumārila Bhatta (probably 7th century A.D.) employed to denote the Dravidian family."

The five principal **Dravidian languages**, spoken in South India, are Tamil, Telugu, Malayālam, Canarese, and Tulu. The population speaking each of these languages, as recorded at the Census, 1901, was as follows (see Table on p. 122).

Tamil is the language of the southern districts of the Madras Presidency from a few miles north of Madras as far west as the Nīlgiri hills and western ghāts, and southward to Cape Comorin. **Telugu** is mainly spoken in the districts north of Madras, except the west of Bellary and Anantapur, the Agencies, and the northern part of Ganjam, where it gives place to the Indo-Aryan Oriya language,

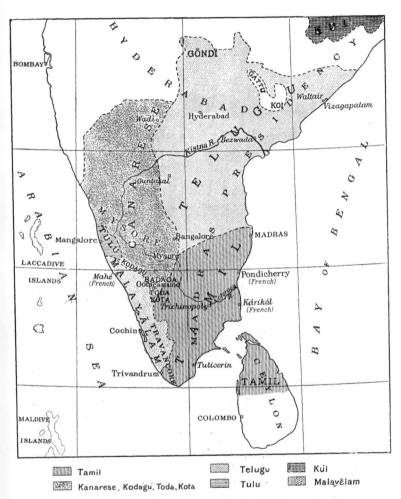

Fig. 43. Map showing distribution of the Dravidian languages.

Classification of the Population according to the principal Languages.

	Tamil	Telugu	Malayālam	Canarese	Tulu
Madras Presidency	15,543,383	14,315,304	2,854,145	1,530,688	495,717
Mysore	187,427	820,691	2,365	4,039,575	20,644
Coorg	5,189	2,974	14,039	76,608	12,994
Travancore	492,273	7,460	2,420,049	1,454	1,321
Cochin	54,171	12,676	715,847	4,180	657
Total.........	16,282,443	15,159,105	6,006,445	5,652,505	531,333

which is spoken by various Oriya castes in Ganjam and Vizagapatam, who belong ethnically to Bengal rather than to Madras. It has been said that, of all Dravidian languages, Telugu, which has been called the Italian of the East, is the most musical, and sounds harmonious even in the mouth of the most vulgar and illiterate. **Canarese** is essentially the language of the western portions of Bellary and Anantapur, and the Mysore State. The **Kodagu** or Coorg language is said to be a dialect of Hala Kannada, or old Canarese. **Malayālam** is practically confined to Travancore, Cochin, Malabar, and South Canara. A dialect thereof is said to be spoken by the Yeravas of Coorg. **Tulu** is the prevalent language in South Canara (the ancient Tuluva).

Of the tribes inhabiting the Nīlgiri hills, the Badagas are said to speak an ancient form of Canarese, the Kotas a mixture of Canarese and Tamil, and the jungle Irulas and Kurumbas dialects of Tamil and Canarese. As regards the language of the Todas, Bernhard Schmid, who wrote in 1837, ascribed two-thirds of the vocabulary to Tamil. Bishop Caldwell was also of opinion that it is most closely allied to Tamil, whereas, according to Dr Pope, it was originally old Canarese, to which a few Tamil forms were added. It is noted by Dr Rivers, in his book entitled *The Todas* (1906), that they have undoubtedly borrowed many words from the Badagas.

A Dravidian language, called **Gōndi**, and a dialect thereof named Gattu, are spoken by the Gōnds, who have migrated from the Central Provinces to Ganjam and Vizagapatam; and a dialect thereof occurs among the hill Koyis. The Kondhs of the Ganjam and Vizagapatam hills also speak a Dravidian language, called **Kui**.

The hill Savaras and Gadabas of Ganjam and Vizagapatam speak languages, which are placed by Mr Grierson in the Mundā linguistic family, called **Kolarian** by Sir George Campbell, of which the principal home is the Chota Nagpur plateau.

Of Indo-Aryan languages other than Oriya, **Marāthi** is spoken by the descendants of the former Marāthas of Tanjore, and by various castes in the Bellary district and Sandur State, which were formerly under Marātha dominion, in South Canara, Mysore, etc. In South Canara, and southward into the Cochin and Travancore States, a dialect of Marāthi, called **Konkani**, is the language of Sārasvat and Konkani Brahmans, Roman Catholics, and others. The Konkanis are said to have migrated southward to escape from the religious persecution of the Portuguese, and found a safe haven in Travancore and Cochin, where they developed their commerce, and built temples, which were richly endowed. A dialect of Gujarāti, named **Patnūli** or Khatri, is spoken by the Patnūlkāran immigrants from Saurāshtra in Gujarāt, who settled as weavers in the town of Madura, at the invitation, it is said, of one of the Nāyak kings.

Hindustani (including the Deccani or Dakhini dialect) is the language of the Muhammadan population. For the purpose of the education of the children of Labbai and Marakkāyar Muhammadans, the Koran, and other books, have been published in the Tamil language, with Arabic characters. It is said that a book of a religious character, written or printed in Tamil, may be left on the ground, but a kitāb (book) in Arabic, of even secular character, will always be placed on a seat, and, if it falls to the ground, is kissed and raised to the forehead.

The nomad Lambādis, Brinjāris, or Sugālis, have a language, which has been said to be usually based on one of the local vernaculars, embroidered and diversified with thieves' slang and expressions borrowed from the various localities, in which the tribe has sojourned. Like the Lambādis, the wandering Koravas or Yerukalas, who call their language Oodra (possibly a corruption of Oriya), have a thieves' slang, and call a head-constable the man who rides on an ass, a constable a red-headed man, rupees milk eyes, and so on.

CHAPTER XIV

PEOPLE——RACE, RELIGION

ACCORDING to many writers on Indian ethnology, the oldest existing race in the Indian peninsula is represented by the **Dravidians,** who make up the bulk of the population in South India. Tradition has it that the warlike Asuras and Daithias (Danavas), who opposed the proto-Aryan invaders of the Punjab, sent expeditions to the Deccan, where they found the semi-civilised States of South India, and imposed their speech and culture on the aborigines. It is the Pre-Dravidian aborigines, and not the later and more cultured

Dravidians, who must be regarded as the primitive existing race. According to modern nomenclature, these **Pre-Dravidians** belong to the group of melanous, dolichocephalic cymotrichi, or dark-skinned, narrow-headed people, with wavy or curly (not woolly) hair, who are differentiated from the Dravidian classes by their short stature and broad (platyrhine) noses. There is strong ground for the belief that the Pre-Dravidians are ethnically related to the Veddas of Ceylon, the Toalas of the Celebes, the Batin of Sumatra, and possibly the Australians. The theory of the connexion between the Pre-Dravidians and Australians is based partly on the strength of certain characters which the Dravidian and Australian languages are said to have in common, and partly on the supposed resemblance of the curved throwing-sticks (valai tadi) of the Tamil Kallans and Maravans to the Australian boomerang. The throwing-stick is used for knocking over hares and other small game, and, at some Kallan weddings, the bride and bridegroom exchange sticks.

Of the Pre-Dravidian tribes, the most typical examples are afforded by the **Paniyans** of Malabar, who carry out most of the rice cultivation ; the **Kurumbas** of the Nīlgiri and Mysore jungles ; the **Yeravas** of Coorg ; the **Paliyans** of Tinnevelly ; and the **Kādirs** of the Ānaimalai hills. The Kurumbas are dreaded by the other tribes of the Nīlgiris, owing to their supposed magical powers ; and, if sickness or misfortune of any kind visits them, some Kurumba is held - responsible. Some years ago, a whole family of Kurumbas was murdered, because the head thereof, who had a reputation as a "medicine-man," was believed to have brought disease and death into a Badaga village. The Kādir women wear in their hair bamboo combs, the designs on which bear a remarkable resemblance to those on the combs worn by some tribes in the Malay peninsula. Like the Mala Vēdars of Travancore, and some Malay

tribes, the Kādirs have the incisor teeth chipped to a
point. The description of tree-climbing with the assistance of pegs by the Dayaks of Borneo, as given by Wallace
in his *Malay Archipelago*, might have been written on the

Fig. 44. Jungle Paliyan.

Ānaimalai hills. A Kādir will build a house or raft out of
bamboo, bridge a stream with canes and branches, make
a fishing-line out of fibre, set effective traps for catching
beasts and birds, and find food among the forest trees and
roots. Some jungle tribes, *e.g.* the Kādirs, Kurumbas, and

Yānādis, work for the Forest Department, and collect minor forest produce, such as deer horns, elephant tusks, rattans, cardamoms, myrabolams, soap-nuts, nux-vomica etc.

In their **religion**, the primitive tribes are animists, " seeking to influence the shifting and shadowy company of unknown powers or influences for evil rather than for good, which reside in the primeval forest, in the hills, in the rushing river, in the spreading tree; which give its spring to the tiger, its venom to the snake, which generate jungle fever, and walk abroad in the terrible guise of cholera, smallpox, or murrain." Some jungle folk, how-ever, now worship Hindu deities, visit the plains at times of Hindu festivals, make offerings at Hindu shrines, daub their forehead and bodies with sandal paste, and give their children Hindu names.

As in other countries, civilisation is fast bringing about a radical change in so-called manners and customs. The Paniyans of the Wynaad, and Irulas of the Nīlgiris, now work regularly for wages on European planters' estates. The primitive method of making fire by friction with two pieces of wood or bamboo is fast disappearing before the use of lucifer-matches. The practice of **human or meriah sacrifice** by the hill Kondhs, to propitiate the earth goddess, has been abolished within the memory of men still living, and the sacrifice of a buffalo or sheep substituted for it. The Kondhs of Bara Moota promised to relinquish the meriah rite on condition that they should be at liberty to sacrifice buffaloes, monkeys, goats, etc., to their deities, and that they should be at liberty to denounce to their gods the Government as being the cause of their having abandoned the great rite. Twenty-five descendants of persons who were reserved for sacrifice, but were rescued by Government officers, returned themselves as Meriah at the census, 1901. The practice of **female infanticide** was formerly very prevalent among the Kondhs, and, in the middle of the last century, many villages were found without a single female child in them. The custom of killing the female infants also prevailed among the Todas of the Nīlgiris, among whom there is, even at the present day, a very marked preponderance of males over females. The

Fig. 45. Yānādis making fire by friction.

institution of **polyandry**, in accordance with which, when a girl marries a man, she becomes also the wife of his brothers, is still in force among the Todas. It is, however, noted by Dr Rivers that "there is a tendency for the polyandry of the Todas to become combined with polygyny. Two brothers, who in former times would have had one wife between them, may now take two wives, but, as a general rule, the two men have the two wives in common. In addition, polygyny of the more ordinary kind exists, and is probably now increasing in frequency, as one of the results of the diminished female infanticide." The picturesque, but barbarous custom of **hook-swinging** is now regarded with disfavour by the Government; and, in the Mysore State, instead of a human being with strong iron hooks driven through the small of the back, a little wooden figure, named Sidi Vīranna, dressed up in gaudy attire, and carrying a shield and sabre, is hoisted on high, and swung round.

Abundant evidence exists in support of the belief that some of the primitive tribes, as well as the slave (*adscripti glebæ*) and other depressed classes, once held a high position, and were indeed masters of the land. In a note on the **privileges of the servile classes**, Mr M. J. Walhouse writes that "many curious vestiges of their ancient power still survive in the shape of certain privileges, which are jealously cherished, and, their origin being forgotten, are much misunderstood. These privileges are a remarkable instance of survivals from an extinct state of society." At one of the agricultural ceremonies of the Badagas of the Nīlgiris, a Kurumba heads the procession, scattering fragments of the sacred tūd tree (*Meliosma pungens*), brings a few sheaves of millet (*Setaria italica* : tenai) to the temple, and ties them to a stone set up at the main entrance. At the festival of Siva at Tiruvalur in the Tanjore district, the headman of the Paraiyans (Pariahs) is mounted on the elephant with the god, and carries the chauri (flyflapper). In Madras, at the annual festival of the goddess of the Black Town, when the tāli (marriage badge) is tied round the neck of the idol, a Paraiyan is chosen to represent the bridegroom. At the festival of some village goddesses, a Paraiyan is honoured by being invested with the sacred thread, and permitted to head the procession. At Mēlkote in Mysore, the Holeyas (agrestic serfs) have the right of entering the temple as far as the dhvaja-stambham or consecrated monolithic column on certain days. It is said that the temple is afterwards ceremonially purified. The privilege is reputed to have been conferred on the Holeyas, in return for their helping Rāmānuja to recover the image of Krishna, which was carried off to Delhi by the Muhammadans.

Conversion to the **Muhammadan faith** has had a marked effect in liberating the depressed classes in Malabar from their former burthen, and the same follows on their embracing Christianity. A melancholy picture has been drawn of a Cheruman in Malabar tramping along the marshes in mud, often wet up to the waist, to avoid polluting his superiors. In the scale of pollution, the jungle Nayādis of Malabar occupy the lowest place, and are said to pollute a Brahman at a hundred yards. By conversion to Christianity or Islām, both Cherumans and Nayādis escape from many of the disabilities resulting from their degraded position in the social scale.

I pass on to the consideration of the more highly civilised classes, which, at times of census, have come under the general head of **Hindus**, or those who worship any of the recognised gods of the Hindu Pantheon. Hinduism has been summed up as a term which is used, for the sake of convenience, to designate the religious creeds and practices, differing from one another in their principles and in the social principles with which they are organically connected, of more than two hundred millions of Hindus. Included in the definition are the four traditional castes, viz. Brahman (priestly), Kshatriya (ruling or military), Vaisya (trading), and Sūdra, which are said to have arisen respectively from the head, arms, thighs, and feet of Brahma. These four castes have been said to be distinguished by their colour, viz. Brahman, white; Kshatriya, red; Vaisya, yellow or turmeric colour; Sūdra, black. Sūdra is a very indefinite term, and has been summed up as including a congeries of castes, in which we find all the varying grades of social respectability, from industrious artisans and cultivators to vagrants and scavengers. The word caste (casta), meaning race or kind, was introduced by the Portuguese, and has been universally adopted. The terms high caste and low caste are familiar to all who have lived in India.

The **Brahmans** occupy the highest position socially and intellectually, and are divided into a series of linguistic groups (Tamil, Telugu, etc.), which are split up into territorial, sectarian, or occupational divisions. From a religious point of view, the Brahmans are either Saivites or Vaishnavites. Among the latter, two important divisions are the Vadagalais (northerners) and Tengalais (southerners). The Vaishnavites are followers of the Tamil Brahman Rāmānuja, Madhva Āchārya, or Chaitanya. The Oriya Brahmans, who follow the creed of Chaitanya, are called Paramarthos. Many of those who claim Sankara Āchārya as their founder are Saivites. The birthplace of Sankara has been located at a village in Travancore, and a garden on the bank of the Periyar river is pointed out as the spot at which he consigned his mother's body to the earth. The priest of the temple at Gurhwāl in North India, which is said to have been established by Sankara Āchārya, must be a Nambutiri Brahman. The Nambutiris form the socio-spiritual aristocracy of the west coast, where many are large landowners. Every Brahman wears the sacred thread, with which he is invested during boyhood at the upanāyanam ceremony. At the present day, many Hindus disregard certain ceremonies, in the performance of which their forefathers were most scrupulous. But no Brahman, orthodox or unorthodox, would dare to omit the celebration of the annual srādh (oblation made in faith) in memory

of his deceased father.   Popular traditions allude to whole-
sale conversions of non-Brahmans into Brahmans.   Accord-

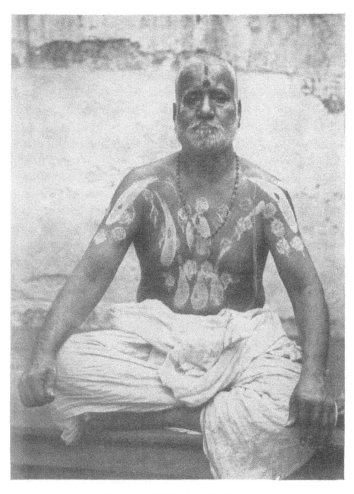

Fig. 46. A Madhva Brahman.

ing to such traditions, Rājas used to feed very large numbers
of Brahmans (a lakh of Brahmans), in expiation of some

sin, or to gain religious merit. To make up this large number, non-Brahmans are said to have been made Brahmans at the bidding of the Rājas. Here and there are found a few sections of Brahmans, whom the more orthodox Brahmans do not recognise as such, though the ordinary members of the community regard them as an inferior class of Brahmans. As an instance, the Mārakas of the Mysore State may be cited. Though it is difficult to disprove the claim put forward by these people, many demur to their being regarded as Brahmans.

The **Lingāyats**, or Vīra Saivas, who are most numerous in the Mysore State, have been described as a Puritan order, who revolted from the Brahman supremacy and caste rule under a certain Basava in the twelfth century. The outward and visible sign of their religion is a red silk scarf or metal casket containing the linga (phallic emblem), which they wear on some part of the body.

The **Jains**, named after the twenty-four Jinas or Tīrthankaras (conquerors or teachers of schools of thought), whose origin goes back to the sixth century B.C., are another sect of nonconformists to Brahmanism. They are chiefly found in Mysore, with headquarters at Srāvana Belgola, in the North and South Arcot districts, and South Canara. The two main divisions are Digambara (sky-clad, *i.e.* nude) and Swetambara (white-robed). A series of paintings in the Mīnakshi temple at Madura illustrate the persecution and impaling of the Jains on stakes by the Saivites.

It has been said that there are, in South India, possibly a few representatives (Rājputs) of the old **Kshatriya** caste, but the bulk of those who claim to belong thereto are pure Dravidians. The Rājas of Jeypore (named after the celebrated town in North India) trace their pedigree back through more than thirty generations to one Kanakasēna of the solar race of Kshatriyas. The Mahārāja of Mysore belongs to the Arasu caste of " Kshatriyas." And there is said to be an old Sanskrit verse, which describes eight classes of Kshatriyas as occupying Kērala from very early times, namely Bhupala or Mahārāja, such as those of Travancore and Cochin, etc. The indigenous "Kshatriyas" of Kērala are now divided into four classes, viz. Koil Pandala, Rāja, Tampan, and Tirumulpād.

The Telugu Komatis, and some other trading classes, claim to belong to the **Vaisya** caste, and the Komatis have established a Vysia Association for the advancement of the community.

The **non-Brahman Hindu** community is split up into a very large number of castes, which include cultivators, artisans, fishermen, traders, shepherds, and a host of others. The two great Tamil and Telugu cultivating castes, Vellāla and Kāpu, alone account for about five millions of the population. In illustration of the manner in which castes increase and multiply, two examples must suffice. Among the divisions of the Kēvuto fishing caste of Ganjam are three, called Thossa, Liyāri, and Chuditiya. Of these, the Thossas are cultivators, the Liyāris make a preparation of fried rice (liya), and the Chuditiyas are engaged in parching grain (chuda, parched rice). By reason of this change of occupation, the Liyāris and Chuditiyas have practically become distinct castes, and some deny that there is any connection between them and the Kēvutos. The Jātāpus are a civilised section of the hill Kondhs, who have given up eating beef, taken to infant marriage, adopted the Telugu type of marriage ceremonies, worship Hindu gods, and have practically developed into a new caste. It has been well said that "a man's **caste** affects his life from its beginning to its end. It frequently determines his occupation, and it often fixes his residence for him, most villages being divided into caste quarters. The social position and the limits within which he may marry are decided by his caste, and so is his name, and even sometimes the clothes

which he and his womenkind may wear." Many castes
are divided into endogamous divisions, which form the
limit within which a man is obliged to marry, and exogamous septs, which, on the other hand, form the limit
within which he may not marry, *i.e.* he must marry a girl
of a sept other than that to which he belongs. In many
cases, especially among the Telugu, Canarese, and Oriya
castes, the exogamous septs are totemistic, and bear the
name of some animal, tree, plant, or object, natural or
inanimate, which a member of the sept is prohibited from
killing, eating, cutting, burning, carrying, or using. In one
of the Telugu castes, members of the frog sept will not
injure frogs, and those of the thanda sept abstain from
using the fruit or leaves of the thanda plant (*Cephalandra
indica*), which is a very common Indian vegetable. In
another caste, women of the magili (*Pandanus fascicularis*)
sept do not use the flower-buds for the purpose of adorning
themselves, and a man has been known to refuse to pur-
chase bamboo mats, because they were tied up with the
fibre of this tree. In yet another caste, if the totem is
a plant, it is said that a person who breaks the taboo will
be punished by being born as an insect for several generations. A person who wishes to eat the forbidden fruit may
do so by performing the funeral ceremonies of the totemic
ancestor at Gaya in Bengal, where obsequial ceremonies
for ancestors are celebrated. Many of the lower classes,
though nominally worshippers of Vishnu or Siva, worship
more especially the **village deities** or Grāma Dēvatas, concerning which Bishop Whitehead writes as follows: " In
almost every village of South India may be seen a shrine
or symbol of the Grāma Dēvata, and the Grāma Dēvata is
periodically worshipped and propitiated. Very often the
shrine is nothing more than a small enclosure with a few
rough stones in the centre, and often there is no shrine
at all ; but still, when calamity overtakes the village,
when pestilence or famine, or cattle disease, make their

appearance, it is to the village deity that the whole body
of villagers turn for protection. Siva and Vishnu may be
more dignified beings, but the village deity is regarded as
a more present help in trouble, and is more intimately con-
cerned with the happiness and prosperity of the villagers."

The **Muhammadan community** has been divided into :
(*a*) those who are immigrants from other provinces and
countries, and pure-blooded descendants of such immigrants ; (*b*) those who are the offspring of immigrant men
by Hindu women of the south ; (*c*) those who are full-
blooded natives of the south, who have been converted to
Islām. Included among the Muhammadans are the Labbais
and Marakkāyars of the east coast, and Māppillas (Moplahs)
of the west coast, many of whom are prosperous traders and
boat-owners ; the Dūdēkula cotton-cleaners of the Telugu
country; and the Dāyarē Muhammadans of Mysore, who
differ from orthodox Muhammadans on a point of belief
concerning the advent of Imām Mahadi. The Dūdēkulas
are said to have adopted or retained many of the customs
of the Hindus, tying a tāli on the bride's neck at weddings,
dressing like Hindus, and giving their children names with
Hindu terminations, *e.g.* Hussainappa or Roshamma.

The White and Black **Jews**, as they are commonly
called, are settled in Jew's Town at Mattāncheri, adjoining
the British quarter of Cochin. It has been said that, passing through a native bazar crowded with dark-skinned
Malayālis, one turns off abruptly into a long, narrow street,
where faces as white as those of any northern European
race, but Semitic in every feature, transport one suddenly
in mind to the Jewish quarters at Jerusalem, or rather
perhaps to some ghetto in a Polish city. The circum-
stances under which, and the time when the Jews migrated
to the west coast, are wrapped in obscurity. The Black
Jews believe themselves to be descendants of the first
captivity, who were brought to India, and did not return
with the Israelites who built the second temple. It seems

probable that the White Jews are late arrivals, who came
to Cochin as traders, and built their synagogue and quarters
after the Black Jews were established there. Each section
has its own synagogue. The floor of the synagogue of the
White Jews is paved with blue and white Canton china
tiles.

The **Syrian Christians**, who form an important community in Travancore and Cochin, trace their origin back
to a very remote period. On one occasion, the wife of a
European official asked one of the pupils at a school how
long they had been Christians. " We," came the crushing
reply, " were Christians when you English were worship-
ping Druids, and stained with woad." According to tradition, the apostle St Thomas landed near Cranganore on
the west coast about 52 A.D., and founded seven churches
in Cochin and Travancore. The Syrian Christians are
divided into several groups, *e.g.* Romo-Syrians, Jacobite
Syrians, and Reformed or St Thomas' Christians. In an
address presented to Sir M. E. Grant-Duff, when Governor
of Madras, it was stated that this was the first occasion
which, after ages of separation, witnessed the spectacle of
all the different sects of their community, following di-
vergent articles of faith, sinking for once their differences,
to do honour to their friend.

Principal Religions, according to the Census, 1901.

	Hindu	Animist	Muhammadan	Jain	Jew	Christian
Madras Presidency	34,436,586	641,825	2,477,610	27,431	45	1,038,854
Mysore	5,048,449	86,627	268,131	13,578	21	32,933
Coorg..................	159,817	3,305	13,654	107		3,683
Travancore	2,035,615	28,183	190,566			697,387
Cochin	554,255	3,897	54,492		1,137	198,239
Total......	42,234,722	763,837	3,004,453	41,116	1,203	1,971,096

CHAPTER XV

OF the widespread distribution of prehistoric man in Southern India in the palæolithic and neolithic ages, and in the era of rude stone monuments, ample proof is afforded by the dolmens, cromlechs, and kistvaens of the Deccan, Nīlgiri and Palni hills, and many other localities; the hat stones (topi kallu) and umbrella stones (kuta kallu) of Malabar, etc.

Of the ages referred to, the palæolithic or old stone age is represented by implements manufactured by chipping and flaking stones of suitable hardness to an edge or point. In the later neolithic or new stone age, in which the art of making pottery came into existence, the implements were made by chipping, and subsequently rubbing down and polishing the stones. The neolithic age passed into the iron age, in which the art of smelting iron, and making pottery on the wheel, had been discovered, and stone implements were almost entirely displaced by iron ones.

Extensive finds of **palæolithic implements** have been made, among other places, in the country round Madras, *e.g.* at Pallāvaram, Arkonam, and Pundi near Tiruvallur, and along the valley of the Penner river in the Cuddapah district. The implements found at Pundi, and other places in the neighbourhood, were situated in the laterite beds. These beds contain boulders of quartzite, from which the implements were made.

Neolithic implements, believed to be the thunderbolts of Vishnu, are preserved in little shrines or cells cut in the rocks, and set up on end round the foot of sacred trees on the Shevaroy hills. In the country round Bellary, *e.g.* near the summit of Peacock hill, Mr R. Bruce Foote found many evidences of the former settlements of neolithic man, in the shape of terraces revetted with rough stone walls, near which were great accumulations of pottery, bones of bovine animals, tanks made by damming streams, and shallow troughs hollowed out in the rocks, which were

Fig. 47. Palæolithic and neolithic implements.

apparently used for crushing corn. Mr Foote further discovered stone celts in all stages of manufacture, chipped, ground, and polished, and flakes struck off them during the process of fabrication.

The **kistvaens** (underground stone chambers or vaults) are called by natives Pāndu kulis, or pits of the Pāndava heroes of the Mahābhārata. According to tradition, they were constructed for the purpose of concealing treasure, and this may possibly account for so many of them having been ransacked. It is further believed that spells were placed over them as a guard, the strongest of which was to bury a man alive in the vault, and order his ghost to protect the treasure against robbers.

The **dolmens**, or stone tables of upright stones with a cap-stone resting on them, are believed to have been built by a race of Pāndava dwarfs a cubit high, who were never-

Fig. 48.   Dolmens on the Nīlgiris.

theless able to lift the huge stones with ease. The dolmens on the Nīlgiri hills are supposed to have been made by a race of pygmies, assisted by hares and porcupines. The Badagas of the Nīlgiris have turned the dolmens into sacred places, not looking on them as temples, but as actual gods. When it was proposed to remove some of the stones to a museum, the Badagas remonstrated, saying, "They are our gods." Close to the village of Bethalhada is a row of dolmens, carved with figures of human beings,

animals, the sun and moon, etc., and enclosed within a
stone circle, which the Badagas claim to have been the
work of their ancestors, to whom periodical offerings are
made. At the time of my visit, there were within one
of the dolmens a conch shell, lingam, bell, and flowers.
The jungle Kurumbas of the Nīlgiris are said to come up
annually to worship at a dolmen on the higher hills, in
which one of their gods is believed to reside. It is on
record that some Kurumbas, who burn their dead, deposit
a bone and a small round stone in the sāvu mane (death
house), which is an old dolmen. Writing concerning the
Kurumbas and Irulas of the Nīlgiris, Mr. M. J. Walhouse
says that " after every death among them, they bring a long
water-worn stone, and put it into one of the old cromlechs
(dolmens), which are sprinkled over the Nīlgiri plateau.
Some of the larger of these have been found piled up to
the cap-stone with such pebbles, which must have been the
work of generations. Occasionally, too, the tribes mentioned make small **cromlechs**, for burial purposes, and
place the long water-worn pebbles in them. On the
higher ranges in Travancore, there are three of the so-
called cairns of Parasurāma where the Mala (hill) Arraiyans
still keep lamps burning. They make miniature cromlechs
of small slabs of stone, and place within them a long pebble
to represent the dead." The conjecture has been made
that the construction of these miniature dolmens is an echo
from remote times, which keeps up the tradition of a
primeval usage, when the hill tribes were a great race.

The possible connection of the jungle **Kurumbas** with
the more civilised **Kuruba** shepherd caste of the plains,
between whom there is a marked difference in physical
characters, has long been a disputed question. It is
interesting, therefore, to note that, in the North Arcot
district, the temples of the Kurubas are sometimes "rude,
low structures supported upon rough stone pillars, with a

small inner shrine, where the idols are placed during
festival time. A stone wall encloses a considerable space
round the temple, and this is covered with small structures
(miniature dolmens) formed of four flat stones, three being
walls, and the fourth the roof. For each person of rank,
one of these monuments is constructed, and here periodically,
and always during the annual feasts, pūja (worship) is
made, not only to the spirits of the deceased chiefs, but

Fig. 49. Kuruba dolmen-like graves.

also to those of all who have died in the clan." In the
Kuruba quarter of the town of Kadur in Mysore, the
shrine of Anthargattamma is a regular dolmen beneath a
margosa (*Melia Azadirachta*) tree, in which the goddess is
represented by round stones imbedded in a mound of
earth. Just outside the same town, close to a sacred fig
tree (pīpal, *Ficus religiosa*), are two small dolmen-like
structures, in which two Kuruba Dāsaris, one a centenarian,
are buried.

Dolmens of the type called **holed dolmens** are found in large numbers in the Deccan, and elsewhere. Concerning these, Mr W. Crooke writes that "many explanations of the meaning of these holes in the door-stone have been given—that they are intended as a means of exit for the ghost, when it feels disposed to leave its home; that they are a means of passing in offerings of food or other articles for the comfort of the ghost; that they illustrate the habit of creeping through an orifice or narrow entrance to a cave or structure of the kind, which is supposed to be efficacious for the cure of disease."

The excavations carried out in the "cairns, cromlechs, and barrows" of the Nīlgiris by Mr J. W. Breeks, when Commissioner of the district, brought to light a splendid series of unique **pottery jars, iron implements, agate and carnelian beads, bronze vases and bowls**, etc. The bulk of the collection is now exhibited in the Madras Museum. The pottery jars are surmounted by lids, on which are modelled grotesque representations of human beings and animals. Concerning these figurines, Mr Foote writes that "those representing men and women are extremely interesting from the light they throw upon the stage of civilization their makers had attained to, for they illustrate the fashion of the garments as also of the ornaments they wore, and of the arms and implements carried by them. The animals they had domesticated, those they chased, and others that they probably worshipped, are all indicated." Among the most interesting figures are those of bearded men riding on horses, and large-horned buffaloes, which might have been modelled from the Toda buffaloes of the present day, and like these, at funerals, and the migrations of the sacred herd from place to place, bear a bell round the neck.

It was noted by Mr Breeks that the characteristic feature of the Nīlgiri cairns and barrows is the circle of

Fig. 50. Pottery from excavations on the Nilgiris.

stones. At the funeral of a Toda, at which I was present,
the corpse was placed in front of the entrance to a circle
of loose stones, about a yard and a half in diameter, which
had been specially constructed for the occasion. According
to Mr Walhouse, at some Toda funerals, the ashes of the
deceased are collected, and buried under a large stone
at the entrance of an ancient circle (azaram). And Dr
W. H. R. Rivers, during his recent study of the Todas,
was informed that all the hills inhabited by their gods
have on their summits ancient stone circles, which the
Todas call pun. Among the dairies of the Todas are
several of circular form, one of which is well known to
Europeans under the name of the " Toda Cathedral." It is
recorded by Dr Rivers that the circular wall which once
surrounded one of these dairies has been converted into a
buffalo pen.

A few years ago, extensive excavations were carried
out by Mr A. Rea, of the Archæological Survey Department, at the vast prehistoric or **protohistoric cemetery** at
Āditanallur in the Tinnevelly district. From this early
burial-ground, a large number of elongated, globular urns,
made of red earthenware, and averaging less than three
feet in diameter, with a slightly greater height, were dug
out. Some of the urns contained human skulls and other
bones, with no signs of cremation. In those urns which
contained complete skeletons, the position of the bones led
to the conclusion that they had been placed inside in a
squatting or sitting attitude. Of the skulls examined by
me, several were conspicuously prognathous (with projecting lower jaw)—a character, which is occasionally found
in South India at the present day. The general type of
the skulls was, like that of the existing inhabitants of the
Tamil country, dolichocephalic (narrow-headed), and some
were conspicuously hyperdolichocephalic. The excavations
at Āditanallur further brought to light large numbers of

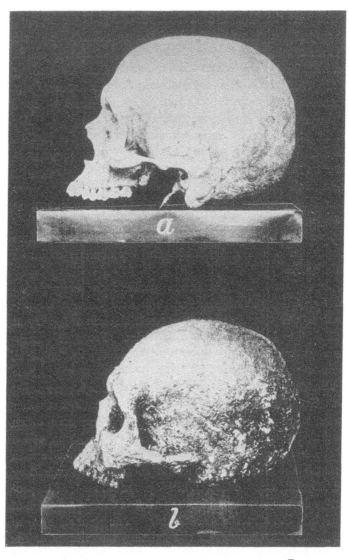

Fig. 51. Prognathous skulls (a) of Tamil man ; (b) from Āditanallur.

pottery vessels of various shapes and sizes, with ring-stands; iron swords, daggers, arrows, trisulas or tridents, mamutis (spades), saucer-lamps, tripods, etc., bronze jars, cups and sieves, and figures of large-horned buffaloes, and grotesque birds; carnelian beads; stone curry-grinding rollers; and many other objects. The discoveries further included a few diadems, of the same shape as those found at Mycenæ, consisting of thin oval gold plates, which were bound round the foreheads of the corpses, probably of persons of rank. Even at the present day, among some Tamil castes, a plain strip of gold is placed on the forehead of the dead.

At Jaugada in the Ganjam district, is one of the various **rock-cut edicts** of the Buddhist Emperor Asoka or Piyadasi (264—227 B.C.), grandson of Chandragupta, who founded the Maurya dynasty. The edict, which has been translated by Dr G. Bühler, records that it was incised by order of King Piyadasi, beloved of the gods, and refers to the stopping of the slaughter of animals as burnt sacrifices, and festive assemblies; the foundation of hospitals, and cultivation of herbs, for men and animals; decorous behaviour towards Brahmans and ascetics; the prevention of unjust imprisonment, and corporal punishment; religious tours made by the King, and so forth. Other examples of Asoka's edicts, at Siddāpura, Jatinga-Rāmēsvara, and Brahmagiri, in the Chitaldroog district of Mysore, have been described by Mr L. Rice.

Near the village of Bhattiprolu in the Guntur district, a mound, known as Lanja Dibha, and composed of a solid mass of brickwork, covers the remains of a **Buddhist stupa**. Excavations led to the discovery of three large stone receptacles, each containing a crystal casket. Of the caskets, two have the lids shaped like a Buddhist dagoba, and the remaining one is a cylindrical phial $2\frac{1}{2}$ inches in diameter $\times 1\frac{1}{4}$ inch in height. Within the stone receptacles were found gold flowers, trisulas, trinacrias, and beads;

pearls; amethyst beads, etc. One of the caskets encloses a small relic casket made of beryl (aquamarine), within which are three small fragments of bone. The greatest interest attaches to the cylindrical phial, which was enclosed not only by the outer stone receptacle, but further by a small globular black stone casket, and contains a flat piece of bone about $\frac{1}{2}$ inch broad. Cut on the outer casket is an inscription, identified by Dr Bühler as being in a Prakrit dialect closely allied to the literary Pali, which records that by the father of Kura, by the mother of Kura,

Fig. 52. Caskets and their contents, Bhattiprolu.

by Kura, and by Siva (has been defrayed the expense of) the preparation of a casket and a box of crystal, in order to deposit some relics of Buddha. The sacred relic is now preserved in safe custody at the Madras Museum.

Near the town of Dharanikota in the Guntur district, which is situated in the old Andra-dēsa or country of the Andhras, the remains of an ancient Buddhist stupa, known as the Amarāvati stupa, were discovered, towards the end of the eighteenth century, on the south bank of the Krishna or Kistna river. The discovery is said to have been made by the servants of a local Rāja, who, during a search for building materials, sunk a shaft, and came across a soapstone casket containing a pearl and some relics. Excavations have been carried out on the site by Colonel Mackenzie, Sir Walter Elliott, Mr R. Sewell, and the Archæological

Fig. 53. Slab from inner rail, Amarāvati.

Survey Department. The large series of sculptured slabs or marbles, and other objects, are now exhibited at the British Museum, London, and in the Madraṣ Museum. The transition from the Sānchi and Gandharam types to the ideal Hindu-Buddhist type is said by Mr E. B. Havell to be very evident in the sculptures. These consist mainly of the fragmentary remains of the carved outer and inner railings, which enclosed the central stupa. Many of the carved slabs represent dagobas, various scenes in the life of Buddha, and the Jatakas (legends of his previous incarnations), Ganas or dwarfs, and abound in illustrations of tree and serpent worship. Some of the slabs forming a plinth bear representations of two-winged lions, which recall to mind the sculptures at Nineveh. On isolated slabs, the feet of Buddha (sripāda), with the chakra, svastika, and other symbols, are carved. The large stone lions doubtless stood at the gateways. Many crystal relic caskets enclosed within stone caskets were discovered during the excavations, and a single gold casket, shaped like a dagoba, and containing a small fragment of bone and six gold flowers, was brought to light in recent years.

In the Andhra-dēsa, large finds of **lead coins** of the Andhras have been made. The coins belong mainly to the horse, lion, and elephant types, and bear the chaitya or shrine, tree with a railing, the Ujjain symbol, or cross with each of its arms terminating in a ball or circle, and other emblems.

Thirty-five miles south of Madras, are situated the antiquarian remains at Mahābalipuram or Māmallapuram, commonly known as the **Seven Pagodas**. Of these pagodas two are situated on the sea-shore, and, according to tradition, five are buried beneath the sea. The submerged pagodas are thus referred to by Southey in 'The Curse of Kehama':—

"When now the ancient towers appear'd at last;
    Their golden summits in the noon-day light;
    Shone o'er the dark green deep that roll'd between;
    For domes, and pinnacles, and spires were seen;
    Peering above the sea—a mournful sight!"

The monuments are said to have been constructed by Pallava kings, whose capital was at Conjeeveram, from about the beginning of the seventh century A.D. onward. They have been said to contain some of the finest examples of Indian sculpture, and consist of bas-reliefs, raths or monolithic temples, and cave temples. The last are believed by Natives to have been constructed by Rishis (sages), or by a sovereign named Mahābali, to accommodate the gods who visited him. The caves at the present day afford shelter to Hindu pilgrims, who flock to the spot, to bathe in the sea, at the Mahodayam, or special new moon day, which occurs once in thirty years, and is considered extremely sacred. The great bas-reliefs, carved on the face of two huge granite boulders, about thirty feet high, with a combined length of about ninety feet, are traditionally supposed to depict Arjuna practising austerities, to gain the arms of Indra. In the illustration, according to the graphic description given by Mr Havell in his 'Ideals of Indian Art' (1911), "the emaciated figure, supposed to be Arjuna, is seen practising his austerities, standing on one leg with his arms raised over his head. The figure of a four-armed deity standing by him, armed with a huge mace, and attended by dwarfs, seems to be that of Siva. Immediately below the supposed figure of Arjuna there is a small temple of Vishnu, at the base of which a number of devotees are grouped. The upper part of both rocks is covered with a great crowd of celestials, gods, and sages; and Gandharvas, the heavenly musicians with bird-like legs, and various four-footed denizens of the Hindu Olympus are hastening to watch the wonderful penance. The right-hand rock is distinguished by the magnificent group of elephants, Indra's noble beasts, which are very realistically treated. The foremost tusker, which gives shelter to a delightful group of baby elephants, stands gravely watching Arjuna, while the female impatiently waits her turn behind

Fig. 54. Bas-relief, Mahābalipuram.

him.   The cleft between the rocks is skilfully used to show
a Nāga and Nāgini, and other snake-deities, as coming up
from the depths of the ocean, drawn by the ascetic's magnetic power, to pay him homage."

At Srāvana Belgola in Mysore, which is the chief seat
of the Jains in South India, are two hills, called Indra-
betta and Chandra-betta.   On the summit of the former
stands a **colossal stone figure** of Gomatēsvara, Gummata,
or Gomata Rāya, which, according to the inscriptions, was
erected about 983 A.D. by Chāmunda Rāya, the minister
of the Ganga king Rāchamalla.   The figure is nude, and
surrounded up to the thighs by "white-ant" hills, from
which snakes emerge, with the tendrils of a climbing plant
entwined round the legs and arms.   The hair is curled in
spiral ringlets, and the lobes of the ears are represented as
having been artificially dilated.   The height of the figure
is given as 57 feet.   Other colossal statues, resembling the
figure at Srāvana Belgola, are situated on the summits of
hills outside the towns of Karkal and Vēnur or Yēnur in
South Canara.   In connection with the statues of Bāhu-
balin or Gummata Jinapati at Karkal, there is a legend
that Bāhabalin was so absorbed in meditation in the forest,
that climbing plants grew over him.   A character, which
all the colossal figures possess in common, is that the
arms are so long that the tips of the fingers reach nearly
to the knees.   One of the good qualities of Sir Thomas
Munro, the celebrated Governor of Madras, was that he
resembled Rāma in that his hands reached to his knees;
or, in other words, he possessed the good qualities of an
Ājanubāhu, which is the heritage of kings, or those who
have blue blood in them.   Rob Roy, it may be remem-
bered, was able to tie his garters without stooping, as his
hands reached below his knees.

CHAPTER XVI

ARCHITECTURE

ARCHITECTURE in India, as in medieval Europe, has nearly always found its highest expression in the service of religion, and to this general rule Southern India forms no exception. In pre-Muhammadan times the orthodox Hindu kings and nobles rarely presumed to make their palaces vie in splendour with the temples of the gods, or with the great religious foundations attached thereto, and sumptuary laws were sometimes enforced, forbidding the use of stone and precious materials for domestic buildings. Even at the present day, the same feeling prevails among strict Hindus.

In ancient India, owing to the vast extent of primeval forest, wood was always the most convenient building material, and was probably mostly used for the super-structure of all buildings, great and small. Their character, therefore, can only be judged by the representations of them carved in stone in the early Buddhist and Jain sculptures, and from the modern wooden architecture of the sub-Himalayan districts, and that of Western India, which has some affinity with them.

Of **Buddhist religious buildings**, the earliest extant belong to the time of the great Emperor Asoka (B.C. 264—227), and many remains of his time are scattered over the districts adjoining the deltas of the Kistna and Godāvari rivers in the Madras Presidency. They consist of stupas or topes, chaityas, and vihāras. The **stupas** were either relic shrines or memorials of a sacred place, surrounded by a procession path or ambulatory for pilgrims, which was generally enclosed by a stone railing, plain or carved, exactly reproducing a wooden prototype. A **chaitya** was the Buddhist church, in which the members of the Sangha assembled for worship ; sometimes a simple group of cells surrounding an enclosed quadrangle with an adjoining shrine and an assembly hall in the centre; sometimes a many storied pyramidal structure, each one of the lower stories containing cells and a pillared assembly hall allocated to different grades of the monastic order, and the topmost one a shrine or chapel surmounted by a domed or barrel-vaulted roof. The monasteries of the different sects of Hinduism (in which Buddhists, Jains, and orthodox Brahmans are included) grew, like the abbeys of medieval Europe, into great educational centres devoted to the study of philosophy, science and art, as well as religious dogma.

The stupa or tope at Amarāvati (p. 148), which was probably commenced about the time of Asoka and elaborated by successive Buddhist dynasties down to the 3rd century A.D., is famous for its fine sculptures, the best of which are now divided between the Madras and British Museums.

As Buddhism gradually merged into the two principal sects of modern Hinduism, the Saiva and Vaishnava, its architectural forms were modified to suit their ritual, and in Southern India developed into the styles named by Fergusson **Dravidian and Chalukyan**. The process of transformation can be seen in the group of monolithic temples carved in granite at Māmallapuram near Madras, known as the Seven Pagodas (p. 150). The unfinished Dharmarāja rath is a sculptured model of a Saiva shrine, the design of which is directly derived from a four-storied pyramidal Buddhist vihāra or monastery. This rath, together with the noble sculptured reliefs found at the same place, was

executed under the Hindu kings of the Pallava dynasty of
Kānchi (Conjeeveram) about the 7th and 8th centuries
A.D. Another very beautiful, though unfinished example

Fig. 55. Dharmarāja Rath, Mahābalipuram.

of this class of monolithic sculptured temples is at Kalu-
gumalai in the Tinnevelly district. It is probably of the
10th or 11th century, and is said to have been originally

Fig. 56. Tanjore Temple.

intended for Jaina worship, but is now dedicated to the Hindu war god Subramanya.

One of the finest examples of Dravidian temple architecture is the great Saiva temple of Tanjore, the principal shrine of which belongs to the beginning of the 11th century, when South Indian art may be said to have reached its zenith, though the remains of that period now existing are very scanty. Here the vimāna, or shrine, standing in a cloistered courtyard 500 feet in length, rises in a pyramid of thirteen stories to a height of 190 feet. A pillared porch leads up to the vimāna, in front of which is a smaller shrine containing a remarkable colossal sculpture of the bull Nandi, sacred to Siva. Within the quadrangle there are several smaller temples of later date, including a very fine one dedicated to Subramanya. The approach to the temple quadrangle is through two lofty gopurams, or gate towers of many stories, which are distinctive features of the Dravidian style, also adapted from Buddhist prototypes. A temple at Darāsaram in the Tanjore district, and others at Gangaikonda Cholapuram in the Trichinopoly district, belong to the same period, and contain some of the most beautiful sculptures to be found in Southern India.

The majority of the South Indian temples were not built at one time, but consist of successive enclosures, sometimes of vast extent, containing an aggregation of temples, pillared halls, and bazars for pilgrims, which were built in successive centuries round some village shrine of special sanctity. Fergusson first called attention to the striking similarity in general arrangement and conception between the great South Indian temples and those of ancient Egypt. In spite of the capriciousness, their planning, in which the holy of holies is made the smallest and least ornamental feature, conforms to the philosophical tenets of Hinduism regarding the evolution of the universe,

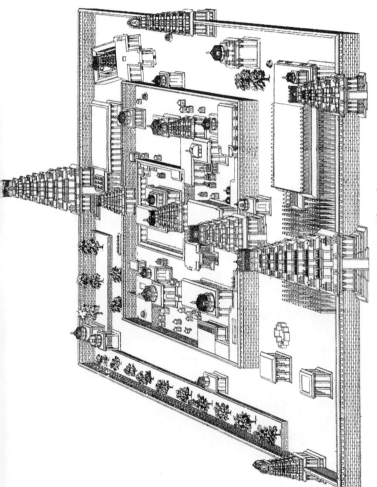

Fig. 57. Pagoda, Tiruvalur.

Fig. 58. Srivilliputtur Pagoda.

and to the rules of design based upon Hindu philosophy laid down in the Silpa Sastras, the canonical books of Indian builders and craftsmen.

The gopurams or gate-towers, which in the later more ornate examples are decorated from the base to the summit with sculptures of the Hindu Pantheon, increase in size with the size of the walled quadrangles, the outer ones becoming imposing landmarks, which are visible for miles around, and are strikingly similar to the pylons of Egyptian temples. Among the most splendid of these temples is that at Chidambaram with its beautiful porch and hall of a thousand columns; Srīrangam with its fourteen lofty gate-towers; Madura with its pillared hall and characteristic Dravidian sculptures, known as Tirumala Nayak's choultry from the king of that name who built it; Rāmēsvaram with magnificent corridors 4000 feet in length. Excepting small portions, all of these, as they now exist, are of comparatively modern date, *i.e.* from about the sixteenth century downwards, as a great deal of the older work was destroyed in the Muhammadan invasions of Southern India, and subsequently restored.

At Vijayanagar in the Bellary district there are very extensive remains of a great city, still containing many remarkable buildings of the later Dravidian style, founded by a Hindu dynasty which, from the 14th to the 16th century, successfully resisted the Moghul sovereigns of the north.

At Srāvana Belgola in Mysore, besides the remarkable colossal figure (p. 153), there is an interesting group of temples of the Jain sect, dating from about the 12th century, which also belong to the Dravidian style. These, and other temples in the Canarese districts of the west coast, are distinguished by their lofty and very beautiful stambhas or carved obelisks resembling those found near Buddhist stupas, which are placed outside the entrances. In Hindu temples such pillars are called dīpdāns, and are surmounted by a sacrificial lamp, but the Jains place images, or sometimes a miniature shrine, at the top of them.

The districts of the west coast have a style of temple architecture distinct from any other part of Southern India, but very similar to that of Nepal and other sub-Himalayan districts. The roofs so far resemble the Buddhist and Dravidian type that they are built in stories gradually diminishing towards the top; but, being entirely of wood or thatched, they are sloping instead of being terraced, and have deep projecting eaves supported by brackets. The substructure is of stone, with richly carved columns supporting the roof. The Jain temples at Mudabidri in South Canara, built in the 15th century, are typical examples.

The Hindu style of architecture which is intermediate between the Northern and Southern styles, and called **Chalukyan** by Fergusson, belongs properly to the Deccan, though some fine examples of it are found in Mysore, and in the Canarese districts of the Madras Presidency. In this style the vimāna, or shrine, remains the dominant architectural feature, but, instead of being square at the base, as in the Dravidian type, it becomes more and more polygonal and circular, until the plan at last is like the opened petals of a lotus. The roof also, instead of being in distinct stories and pyramidal, is stepped, and tends to resemble the curved spire, or sikhara, of the Northern Hindu style. The exquisitely carved doorways of the Chalukyan temples are particularly noticeable. The purest examples of the style date from the 10th to the 12th century A.D. The temple of Kuruvatti on the Tungabhadra river, not far from Harpanahalli, is one of the best. The famous temples at Halebid and Somnathpur in Mysore, though designed on a much larger and more imposing plan, belong to the later decadent style.

Fig. 59.   Temple Stambha, South Canara.

There are no important monuments of **Moghul or Indo-Saracenic** architecture in Southern India, though in Kurnool, on the borders of the Nizam's territory, a few Muhammadan mosques show the fine style which originated in the Deccan under the Bijapur dynasties of the 16th and 17th centuries. The Darya Daulat, Tīpu Sultan's palace, and the tombs of the short-lived Muhammadan dynasty of Mysore at Seringapatam, are fairly good specimens of 18th century architecture, but cannot compare with similar buildings of the same period in Northern India.

The traditions of the Hindu temple builders are still alive in the south, as well as in other parts of India, the best **Indian craftsmen** being always the master masons, wood and metal-workers, attached to the temple service. In recent years, a considerable impetus has been given to the building craft of Southern India by the Nāttukottai Chettis (bankers) towards the restoration and extension of South Indian temples. The building of a new palace for the Mahārāja of Mysore, and of important public offices in Madras from designs by European architects, and consequently purely eclectic in their Indian style, give promise of a coming revival of indigenous architecture in the south.

None of the **royal palaces** of Southern India are older than the sixteenth century, when wooden construction was almost entirely superseded by brick and stone, and the Saracenic arch began to be used by the Hindu builders. The most interesting of these palaces are at Vijayanagar, Chandragiri in the North Arcot district, and at Madura, where the splendid hall of Tirumala Nayak's palace is now used as a Court of Justice. The palace of Tanjore, built in the 18th and 19th centuries, is a very degenerate mixture of Italian and Indian styles.

Many good examples of **domestic architecture**, distinguished by fine doorways, verandahs, and cloistered inner courtyards, with elegantly carved pillars and brackets,

Fig. 60. Indian architect, with elevation of a new temple
drawn on a wall.

are to be found in every considerable town in Southern India, but the wealthy English-educated Indian of the present day, despising his own art, affects a style of house devoid of any kind of architectural distinction, which is a more or less bad copy of Anglo-Indian buildings. There is, however, a reaction of feeling among the more enlightened Indians against a slavish imitation of European fashions, which may eventually lead to a new style of Indian domestic architecture being founded on the basis of the old by an intelligent adaptation of the living Indian craft traditions to the needs and habits of modern life.

The **hill fortresses** scattered over many South Indian districts are interesting memorials of medieval and later times, when rival Hindu dynasties were fighting against each other, or resisting the Musalman invaders from the north, or when British, French, Dutch, and Portuguese, were struggling for supremacy in India. But, though some are considerable in size, none of them are to be compared as architecture with similar military works in Northern India. Several of the Hindu temples, like those at Tanjore and Vellore, both of which are distinguished by very fine architectural sculpture, are enclosed by fortifications, which have been the scene of eventful struggles in the history of British India, but these too are insignificant as architecture.

CHAPTER XVII

HISTORY

THE sequence of events, commencing with the first arrival of the Portuguese, which led up to the supremacy of the British, and the constitution of the Madras Presidency and Mysore in their present form, is briefly set out in the following chronological summary of the principal incidents.

1498. The Portuguese navigator, **Vasco da Gama**, arrived off the coast of Malabar, and anchored near Calicut. The quinquecentenary of the event was celebrated at Calicut in 1898. The first land sighted by Vasco da Gama is said to have been Mount Delly, a conspicuous hill near the coast, which was called by the Portuguese Monte d'Eli. The name is said to be derived from the Malayālam eli mala (high hill), or from the ancient Eli State in Malabar.

1502. Second voyage of **Vasco da Gama** to Malabar, and establishment of a factory at Cochin.

1503. **Pedro Alvares Cabral** was placed in charge of an expedition, and came to Calicut and Cochin.

1503. **Albuquerque** assisted the Cochin Rāja by defeating the Zamorin of Calicut, and received sanction for the construction of a fort, which was called Manoel after the reigning King of Portugal. The names Da Gama, Cabral, Albuquerque, and many others, whose exploits are handed down to posterity in the Indo-Portuguese archives, survive among Eurasians of the west coast to the present day.

1565. Battle of **Tālikota**, at which the great Hindu kingdom of Vijayanagar, which extended from the Kistna to Cape Comorin, was overthrown by the Muhammadans. The reigning sovereign, Rāma Rāya, was taken prisoner, and decapitated.

1600. The first Royal Charter was issued for establishing an **East India Company**, in consequence of the commercial rivalry between London and Amsterdam, the Dutch having in the previous year raised the price of pepper against the English from 3*s.* to 6*s.* and 8*s.* per pound. The Company was incorporated under the title of the Governor and Company of Merchants of London trading into the East Indies, and five ships were chartered for the first voyage. Special silver coins, bearing the arms of Queen Elizabeth and the Tudor portcullis, were struck for the use of the Company.

1602. A priest of the **Syrian Christians** of St Thomas was sent by the Portuguese Bishop of Malabar to Todamala (the Nīlgiri hills), to investigate a race—the Todas—who were supposed to be descendants of the Christians of St Thomas. In the following year, Father Yacome Finicio was deputed thither on a similar mission.

1602—9. Certain private Dutch Companies were amalgamated into the Vereenigde Oost-Indische Com-

Fig. 61. Portcullis money of Queen Elizabeth.

pagnie, or **United Dutch East India Company.** Pulicat on the east coast was the site of the earliest settlement of the Dutch, who built there a fort, which they called Castel Geldria. Just as the Portuguese struck coins with the initial G for Goa and D for Diu, so the Dutch struck copper coins bearing the initial letter P for Pulicat, and N for Negapatam. Dutch coins, called duits and half-duits or challis, bearing on one side the monogram V.O.C., and on the other the arms of Zeeland, Friseland (Frisia), Holland, Utrecht, and Gelderland, are met with in large quantities in the bazars, and are still to some extent current on the west coast.

1611. **Captain Hippon**, of the ship "Globe," founded English settlements or agencies at Nizāmpatam and Masulipatam.

1620. A treaty was concluded between Denmark, which had despatched ships to the east, and the Nāyak of Tanjavur (Tanjore), by which **Tranquebar** was ceded to the Danes. A fort called Dansborg was built, and a factory established. Coins struck by the Danes in India bear the initials DB, or TB, standing for Dansborg and Tranquebar.

1625. The English under **Francis Day** founded a trading establishment at Dugarāzupatnam, and called it Armagon or Armeghon after a friendly local chief named Arumuga Mudaliyar.

1628—32. On account of the oppression which was experienced at the hands of the Native Governor, it was resolved in 1628 to abandon the factory at Masulipatam. The representation of the Agent at Bantam to the President and Council at Surat (in Bombay) of the necessity of being supplied with Coromandel cloth, to furnish that station and the southern markets with the means of increasing their investments in pepper and spices, gave rise to a decision, in 1632, to re-establish the factory at Masulipatam, and to strengthen Armagon. This was effected by a firman from the King of Golconda, called the **Golden Firman**.

1639. Francis Day, struck with the quality and prices of the cloths at Madraspatam, as compared with those of Armagon, obtained through a subordinate of the Rāja of Chandragiri, a representative of the old Vijayanagar dynasty, a lease of the revenues of the locality, and permission to build a fort, which was named **Fort St George**. The necessity for this fort was impressed on the East India Company in a letter stating that "it hath been a continued tenet among as many of your servants as have been employed in these parts that goods, especially paintings

Fig. 62. Fort St George, Madras, at the present day.

(*i.e.* prints, chintzes) cannot be procured, nor secured when acquired, unless you have some place of your own to protect the workmen from the frequent enforcements of these tyrannous governors, and to lodge your goods free of the mischievous attempts which these treacherous Gentues are too often ready to adfer against them." The name Gentou is said to be a corruption of Gentio, a gentile or heathen, which the Portuguese applied to the Hindus in contradistinction to the Moros or Moors, *i.e.* Muhammadans. It has been suggested that the reason why the term Gentoo became specifically applied to the Telugu people is because, when the Portuguese arrived in Southern India, the Telugu kingdom of Vijayanagar was dominant. In the records of the seventeenth century, the Black Town of Madras is referred to as Gentue Town.

1642. Cardinal Richelieu founded a **French Company**, on the lines of the Dutch Company, which did not have a prosperous career.

1653. Fort St George was raised to the rank of a separate **Presidency**, independent of Bantam in Java.

1658. **Negapatam**, which was one of the earliest settlements of the Portuguese on the Coromandel coast, was taken by the Dutch.

1663. The town and fort of Cochin were captured from the Portuguese by the Dutch, assisted by the Rāja of Cochin. Between 1661 and 1664, the Dutch also drove the Portuguese from Quilon, Cannanore, and other places on the west coast.

1664. The French statesman Colbert reconstituted the French Company, under the name of the **Compagnie des Indes Orientales**. This Company lasted till 1719, and was then united to the Compagnie d'Occident for trade with Louisiana, under the title of the Compagnie perpétuelle des Indes.

1669. The Moghul Emperor Aurangzīb issued a firman,

permitting the French to have a factory at **Masulipatam**. Coins were struck here by the French later on, bearing the name Machlipatan, and the regnal year of the Moghul Emperors Ahmad Shāh and Ālamgir II.

1672. The Frenchman Caron seized **Saint Thomé** (now a suburb of Madras) from the Dutch, to whom it was restored two years later.

1683. Francois Martin took up his abode at **Pondicherry**, which was purchased from the Rāja of Gingee, and fortified it.

1686–90. The Dutch took possession of **Masulipatam**, putting restrictions on the English trade "on purpose to lay the English low in the eyes of the natives, according to their usual treatment." Three years later, Zu-l-Fikar Khān, the Moghul Commander-in-Chief in the Carnatic, seized the factory, and, in 1690, the full right of trade at Masulipatam was secured by the English from the Emperor Aurangzīb.

1690. The fort at Dēvanapatam, Thevnapatam, or Tegnapatam, close to Cuddalore, which was re-named **Fort St David**, was purchased by the English from the Marāthas with the surrounding country "within the randome shott of a great gun." The name Fort St David was probably given by Elihu Yale, Governor of Madras (1687—92), who was a Welshman, in honour of the patron saint of Wales.

1692. Zu-l-Fikar Khān was created first **Nawāb of the Carnatic** by Aurangzīb. Elihu Yale helped him with war materials, and, in return, he procured a firman from the Moghul Emperor, by which the villages of Egmore, Pursewaukum, and Royapuram (now districts in the city of Madras) were secured to the East India Company.

1693—99. **Pondicherry** was taken from the French by the Dutch, and restored to them by the Treaty of Ryswick in 1699, when Francois Martin was appointed Governor.

1701. The English East India Company and London

East India Company, between which there had been great rivalry during the last few years, came to terms, and assumed the title of the United Company of Merchants of England trading to the East Indies, commonly known as the **Honourable East India Company**. The title Honourable English Company in Persian characters occurs on some of the gold coins. The bale-mark of the United Company, with the initials V.E.I.C., is reproduced on many of the copper coins. Other coins, which were struck long after the establishment of the new Company, bear the initials G.C.E. which are presumably those of the original Governor and Company of Merchants trading to the East Indies.

1725. The French settled at Mayazhi in Malabar, which was re-named **Mahē** after Mahé de la Bourdonnais.

1741. Husain Dost Khān, better known as Chanda Sahib, a son-in-law of Dost Ali Khān, Nawāb of the Carnatic, was defeated by the Marāthas at Trichinopoly, and taken prisoner to Satara. In this year, **Dupleix** became Governor of Pondicherry, and subsequently proclaimed himself Nawāb of the Moghul Empire. It has been suggested that a series of copper coins, bearing the French Fleur-de-lis and Gallic cock, and the word Vijaya (victory) and other legends, may have been struck in honour of the French by some Native Prince impressed by the power of the French arms during the government of Dupleix, or were possibly struck by the French themselves.

1742. Sanction to coin Arcot (Arkāt) rupees was given to the East India Company by Nawāb Saadatullah Khān, Subah of Arcot. The **Arcot rupees**, and their fractions, struck in the name of the Moghul Emperor Ālamgir, "in the sixth year of his propitious reign," were long current in the Madras Presidency. It was not till 1835, in the reign of William IV, that the British struck coins in India, bearing the effigy of the reigning monarch.

1746. Mahé de la Bourdonnais, who had equipped a fleet at his own expense, besieged Madras, which surrendered. The Governor, Nicholas Morse, a descendant of Cromwell, and the chief merchants, were carried off as prisoners to Pondicherry. **Robert Clive**, at that time a young civilian, escaped to Fort St David, and obtained an Ensign's commission.

1749. Fort St George was restored to the English under the Treaty of Aix-la-Chapelle, and taken possession of by **Admiral Boscawen** ("old Dreadnought"). In this year, Chanda Sahib, whose release from prison had been obtained by Dupleix, was, with the support of the French, proclaimed Nawāb of the Carnatic. Three years later, he was put to death by the Rāja of Tanjore, and his head was sent to Muhammad Āli, the British candidate for the office of Nawāb.

1750. **Masulipatam**, with the surrounding country, was given to the French by the Nizam, and, from 1753 to 1759, the English were excluded.

1751. **Clive** was besieged by an army under Chanda Sahib's son in the fort of Arcot, and, after a siege of fifty days, the enemy was compelled to retire. For his brilliant services during the siege, Clive was pronounced by Pitt "a heaven-born genius."

1752. **Captain John Dalton**, the commandant at Trichinopoly, defended the town on behalf of Muhammad Āli against the Regent of Mysore and the Marātha Morari Rao, till he was relieved by Stringer Lawrence.

1753. The whole of the **Northern Circars** were handed over to the French by the Subadar, or Moghul Viceroy of the Deccan. In this year, the French were defeated by Stringer Lawrence on the plain near Trichinopoly close to the spot now known as Fakir's Rock, at the battle of the Golden Rock. Iron cannons and shot found at Trichinopoly, and preserved in the Madras Museum, are probably

Fig. 63. Stringer Lawrence and Nawāb Walajah.

relics of the fighting round Fakir's Rock. A painting in
the Banqueting Hall, Madras, represents Lawrence walking
with Nawāb Walajah of the Carnatic on the island of
Srīrangam near Trichinopoly. Copper coins struck by the
Nawābs bear the name Walajah or Wala in Persian or Tamil.

1756. **Clive appointed Governor of Fort St David.**

1757. **Vizagapatam**, where an English factory was
founded in the seventeenth century, surrendered to the
French General Bussy. At a nautch in the fort of the
Mandasa zamindar in honour of Sir Mountstuart Grant Duff
when Governor of Madras (1881—6), the dancing-girls
danced to the French air of Malbrook se va t'en guerre,
which must have been originally learnt from the French
troops under Bussy.

1758. Colonel Forde defeated the French under the
Marquis de Conflans at the decisive battle of **Condore** near
Pithapuram in Vizagapatam. The French General **Thomas
Arthur Lally**, son of an Irish officer who emigrated to
France, besieged Madras. An old house, recently dis-
mantled in the course of additions to the Madras Christian
College, which contained an extensive series of elaborately
carved wooden beams, lintels, etc., was, according to tradition,
occupied by Lally during the siege.

1759. **Comte d'Ache**, who commanded the French
Navy in India, was defeated off Fort St David, and is said
to have lost in a few months the French cause in Southern
India.

1760. Colonel (afterwards Sir) Eyre Coote defeated
Lally at the battle of **Wandiwash** in North Arcot. Colonel
Forde captured Masulipatam, and the Subadar of the
Deccan made a treaty, agreeing to drive out the French.
The treaty was ratified by a firman from the Moghul
Emperor in 1765, and a further treaty with the Subadar
in the following year, by which the English acquired the
whole of the Northern Circars.

1761. **Pondicherry** surrendered to the English, who destroyed the town and fortifications. Lally was sent to England as a prisoner of war. The Frenchman **Claude Martin** deserted to the English. He subsequently amassed a large fortune, built a palatial residence at Lucknow called Constantia (now La Martinière), and became a Major-General.

1763. **Pondicherry** restored to the French by the Peace of Paris.

1766. **Haidar Ali**, who had deposed the reigning Rāja of Mysore, conquered Malabar.

1769. **Warren Hastings** appointed second in Council at Madras.

1778. **Pondicherry** once more fell into the hands of the English under Hector Munro.

1780. Commencement of the **first Mysore war**, which lasted till 1784. When attempting to join Munro's army, Colonel Baillie was taken prisoner by Haidar. He was sent to Seringapatam, where he died in captivity two years later.

1781—2. Haidar Ali was defeated by Eyre Coote at Porto Novo, and also lost heavily at the battle of Sholingur. He died in 1782, and was succeeded by his son **Tīpu Sultan**. A gold pagoda struck by the Danes bears on the obverse the crowned monogram of King Christian VII, and on the reverse the Persian letter ‎چ (Haidar's initial). This coin, it has been suggested, tends to show that the Danish power in the East did homage to the Mysore usurper, consistently with the unambitious policy of peace adopted by them in dealing with the dominant Indian powers. Tīpu retained his father's initial on his gold and silver coins, devised new names for the mint towns, introduced on the coins a special era commencing from the birth instead of the hijra of Mohammed, and employed a new method of expressing the date by a system of

alphabetical numeration. Seeing the bale-mark of the East
India Company on the arms captured from the English, he
imitated it on his own muskets and cannon, but replaced
the initials V.E.I.C. by his father's name.

1783. **Pondicherry**, and the other French factories,
were restored to the French by the Treaty of Versailles.

1790—92. **Second Mysore war**. Seringapatam was
besieged by the English, led by the Governor-General, the
Marquis Cornwallis, and Tīpu ceded the country round
Dindigul, and the districts of Salem and Malabar.

1793. On the breaking out of war in Europe between
France and England, the French Possessions in India were
once more taken by the English.

1794. The Rāja of Vizianagram was defeated by the
English at the battle of Padmanabham. The country
ceded to the Company was governed by a Chief and
Council at **Vizagapatam**, which was divided into three
Collectorates.

1795. On the conquest of Holland by the French, the
Dutch factories and possessions were handed over to the
East India Company. They comprised three groups,
those on the Coromandel coast, with head-quarters at
Pulicat; those on the Madura coast, as it was called, with
head-quarters at Tuticorin; and those on the Malabar
coast, with head-quarters at Cochin.

1799. **Third Mysore war**. Tīpu Sultan was slain at
the storming of Seringapatam. The storming party was
led by General David Baird, who some years previously
had been imprisoned by Haidar Ali at Seringapatam. On
the day of the battle, which, being the last day of a lunar
month, was inauspicious, an astrologer repeated the un-
favourable omen to Tīpu. It is recorded that "to different
Bramins he gave a black buffalo, a milch buffalo, a male
buffalo, a black she-goat, a jacket of coarse black cloth, a
cap of the same material, ninety rupees, and an iron pot

Fig. 64. Fort Wall, Seringapatam.

filled with oil; and, previous to the delivery of this last
article, he held his head over the pot for the purpose of
seeing the image of his face; a ceremony used in Hindo-
stan to avert misfortune."

An officer took from off the right arm of the dead body
of Tīpu a talisman, consisting of a charm made of metal,
and some manuscripts in magic Arabic and Persian characters, sewed up in pieces of flowered silk. The standards,
which were taken at Seringapatam, were brought home
for the King of England by General Harris, who subsequently became the first Lord Harris. After its capture, at
which he was in command of the reserve, **Arthur Wellesley**
(the first Duke of Wellington) was placed in charge of
Seringapatam, and appointed to the military and political
command in Mysore. The British Government restored
the Hindu Rāj of Mysore, and placed on the throne
Krishna Rāja Wodeyar, with Purnaiya as Regent during
his minority. The British share of Tīpu's territories included Canara, Coimbatore, and the Wynaad.

1800. The Cuddapah, Bellary, Anantapur, and Kurnool
districts, which had fallen to the share of the Nizam in the
re-distribution of territory after the death of Tīpu, were
ceded to the British by Azīm-ud-daula, Nawāb of the
Carnatic.

1801. The French possessions were restored to the
French, but again taken away in the following year by the
Treaty of Amiens, which was signed on behalf of England
by the Marquis Cornwallis.

1808. **Tranquebar**, with the other Danish settlements,
was taken by the British, but restored in 1814.

1814—15. By the treaties of these years, **Pondicherry**,
and the other factories, were restored to the French.

1831. The **Mysore Rāja** deposed, and his territories
administered by a British Commission.

1839. The territories of the Nawāb of **Kurnool**, who

had been guilty of treasonable intrigues, annexed by the British.

1845. **Tranquebar**, and the other Danish settlements, were purchased by the East India Company. In the collection of arms transferred from Tranquebar to the arsenal of Fort St George, and now in the Madras Museum, are several large guns bearing the monogram C 7 of the Danish King, Christian the Seventh.

1855. On the death of the last Nawāb of the Carnatic, Ghulam Muhammad Ghaus Khān, Azīm Jah, and other members of the Carnatic family, became pensioners of the Government. Some years later, the title of **Prince of Arcot** was conferred on Azim Jah and his descendants.

1881. **Rendition of Mysore** (p. 6).

CHAPTER XVIII

ADMINISTRATION

THE administration of the Madras Presidency is at the present time vested in the **Governor and three members of the Executive Council**, all of whom are appointed by the Crown for a period of five years. Of the members of Council, two belong to the Indian Civil or Covenanted Service, and the third is an Indian of distinction. The term Covenanted Civilian is a survival from the days of the East India Company, whose servants entered into a covenant therewith, as the Civil Servants, and many other Government officials, do at the present day with the Secretary of State for India. The name Competition Wallah has been applied to those who entered the Civil Service by the system of competitive examination, which was introduced in 1856. The East India College at

Haileybury was closed in the following year.   Prior to the abolition of the appointment, the Commander-in-Chief of Madras was a member of the Executive Council.   The addition of an Indian member thereto was brought about by the India Councils Act of 1909, when Lord Minto was Viceroy and Lord Morley Secretary of State, by which it was enacted that the Council shall not exceed four, of whom two at least shall be persons who have been in the service of the Crown in India for at least twelve years. The first Indian to hold office was the Mahārāja of Bobbili. All Orders of Government are issued in the name of His Excellency the Governor in Council.   The work of the Council is distributed among the members, who are assisted by Secretaries.   The Departments of the Secretariat are divided into :—(*a*) political, financial, ecclesiastical, marine, and pensions ; (*b*) revenue ; (*c*) local, municipal, educational, and legislative·; (*d*) public works, including roads and buildings, irrigation, and railways.   For the purpose of making laws, subject to confirmation by the Governor-General and the Secretary of State, the Governor presides over a **Legislative Council**, composed of the members of the Executive Council, and a number of members, official and non-official.   Of the non-official members, some are nominated, and others elected.   The revenue administration is carried out by the **Board of Revenue**, which has control over matters connected with the land revenue, revenue settlement, land records and agriculture, forests, salt, abkāri (excise), customs, stamps, income-tax, etc.

For the purpose of general administration, the Presidency is divided into **twenty-four districts**.   The principal district officers are the Collector (*i.e.* of revenue) and District Magistrate, and the District and Sessions Judge. The Collector is assisted in his manifold duties by the Divisional Officers and Assistants, Executive Engineer, District Forest Officer, District Medical Officer, and

Superintendent of Police. The subdivisions of the district
are divided into **tāluks** in charge of native Tahsildars
or revenue officers (tahsil, collection). " The ultimate
unit," it has been said, " for all fiscal and administrative
purposes is the **village**. Each of these has a headman,
who is responsible for the due collection of the revenue,
and possesses small judicial powers ; an accountant
(Karnam, or Shānbōg), who maintains all its records, and
a varying number of menial servants under the orders of
these two officers. Succession to these village offices is
usually hereditary, and the powers and duties of their
incumbents have undergone but little change since the
earliest days of which history gives us any account."
Among the powers of the village headman is still that of
confining persons belonging to the lower classes in the
stocks for trivial offences, such as using abusive language,
or inconsiderable assaults or affrays.

The time-honoured **panchāyat** (pānch, five), or council
of five members of the community to arbitrate on caste
disputes and questions affecting the interests of the village,
has in some measure degenerated in recent times. Liti-
gants now resort freely to the British Courts, and employ
vakils to plead their cause, with a resultant expenditure of
much money.

The larger towns in the Presidency are governed by
Municipal Councils, composed of *ex officio* members, and
members nominated by Government and elected by the
rate-payers.

The Government of Madras is represented in the **Native
States** of Travancore and Cochin by a British Resident,
who has official Residencies in both States. He is also
Collector of the isolated British settlements of Anjengo
and Tangassēri. The British Resident of Mysore, who has
official relations with the Government of India, is also
Chief Commissioner of Coorg. The administration of

Mysore, Travancore, and Cochin is conducted by a Dīwān or Prime Minister, who is, in Mysore, Travancore, and Pudukkottai, assisted in ascertaining the views of the people by a Popular or Representative Assembly, composed of members representing various classes of the community and interests. In Mysore, the Dīwān has the assistance of Councillors, and Pudukkottai is administered by a Council, composed of the Rāja, the Dīwān, and a Councillor. The divisions of Travancore, Cochin, and Pudukkottai are administered by Dīwān Peshkars, who correspond to the Collectors of the British districts, and the Deputy Commissioners of Mysore. The States of Pudukkottai, Banganapalle, and Sandur have respectively as Political Agents the Collectors of the adjacent British districts of Trichinopoly, Kurnool, and Bellary. The Banganapalle State has, in recent times, been managed by a member of the Indian Civil Service, entitled the Assistant Political Agent.

The administration of **Pondicherry** is vested in the Governor, and a Council composed of official and non-official members. A General Council, composed of representatives elected by universal suffrage in the five French settlements of Pondicherry, Kārikāl, Yanam, Mahē, and Chandernagore (in Bengal), meets annually at Pondicherry. The settlements other than Pondicherry, to which they are subordinate, are administered by local Governors or Chefs de Service. A Senator and Deputy are elected by universal suffrage by the five settlements, to represent them in the Chambers at Paris.

CHAPTER XIX

THE chief lines of communication in the Madras Presidency by means of **roads**, which were originally made to satisfy military requirements, are the northern road from Madras to Calcutta, the southern to the Travancore frontier, and the western to Calicut in Malabar. Tīpu Sultan is said to have been the pioneer of the roads in Malabar, making, in the course of his campaigns, an extensive chain of roads, which connected all the principal places of Malabar, and pervaded the wildest parts of the country. Traffic along the roads is mainly carried on by means of springless bullock-carts, and two-wheeled covered boxes with venetian windows called jutkas (jhatkā, swift), drawn by country-bred ponies or tattoos (tats). The palanquin of former days is now only found in out-of-the-way places ; but I have travelled along the high road in South Canara in a muncheel or hammock-litter with a cover to keep off the sun and rain, carried on the shoulders of coolies. The name Boy, applied by Anglo-Indians to their domestic servants, is derived from the Bestha or Boyi caste, which was, in former times, employed in carrying palanquins. Thus it is recorded by Carraccioli, in his 'Life of Lord Clive,' that the Boys with Colonel Lawrence's palankeen, having straggled a little out of the line of march, were picked up by the Marathas. Writing in 1563, Barros states that " there are men who carry the umbrella so dexterously to ward off the sun that, although their master trots on his horse, the sun does not touch any part of his body, and such men are called Boi."

The Indian **trunk railways** were sketched out by Lord Dalhousie when Governor-General (1848–56), and his schemes included the linking up of Madras with Bombay and Calicut. The east coast railway, to connect Madras with Calcutta, found a place among the recommendations of the Royal Famine Commission (1878–80). Among the manifold purposes subserved by railways, are the development of commercial requirements, the lowering of the cost of articles imported to the sea-ports, and the transport of food-grains, when famine or local distress, from failure of the crops, prevails. In times of famine, railway relief works give employment to many of those who are affected thereby.

The railways of South India belong to two main systems, viz., the Madras and South Mahratta Railway, and the South Indian Railway.

The **Madras and South Mahratta Railway** forms a complex network of main and branch or feeder lines, of which it is only possible to refer to the more important ones. The north-west line, which connects Madras with Bombay, passes through Cuddapah, Tadpatri, Gooty, Guntakal, and Adoni, and joins the Great Indian Peninsula Railway at Raichur. From Guntakal, a branch line runs through Bellary to Hubli. Another line, by which Bombay is eventually reached from Madras, passes through Bangalore, Tumkur, Arsikere, and Harihar in the Mysore State, and Hubli, and meets the Great Indian Peninsula Railway at Poona. Between Jalarpet and Bangalore, the line ascends to the Mysore plateau, and a branch line from Bowringpet to Marikuppam taps the Mysore gold-fields. From Bangalore, a line runs through Seringapatam to Mysore, and thence to Nanjangōd, the temple at which place attracts large numbers of devotees. The north-east line, which connects Madras with Calcutta, passes through Nellore, Bezwāda, Rājahmundry, and Sāmalkot, and joins the Bengal-Nagpur Railway at Waltair near Vizagapatam. From Bezwāda, a line runs through Nandyāl and Kurnool Road to Guntakal, where it joins the north-west line. Short lines run from Bezwāda and Sāmalkot respectively to Masulipatam and Cocanāda on the coast. The Bengal-Nagpur Railway passes through Vizianagram, Chicacole Road, and Naupada; and, skirting the Chilka lake, runs into Bengal. A line, built by the Rāja of Parlākimedi, connects the town of Parlākimedi with Naupada.

The **South Indian Railway** has two main lines, with various branches, which run respectively to the west coast, and southward to Tuticorin. The former, with running powers from Madras to Jalarpet, passes through Salem, Erode, Podanur, and the natural break in the western ghāts called the Pālghāt Gap, to Malabar. Striking the coast, it runs northward through Calicut, Tellicherry, and Cannanore, to Mangalore in South Canara. For those proceeding to Yercaud on the Shevaroy hills, Salem is the most convenient station. From Podanur, a line runs through Coimbatore to Mettupalaiyam, and there joins the rack-rail Nīlgiri Mountain Railway, which, winding up the ghāt through many tunnels, touches at Coonoor and Wellington, and has its terminus at Ootacamund. The railway has displaced the service of vehicles called tongas, drawn by horses, by which travellers formerly ascended the ghāt road. At Shoranur, the main line joins the Shoranur-Cochin State Railway from Shoranur to Ernākulam, whence the backwater can be crossed to Cochin. The southern line, starting from Madras, runs, now near the coast and now far inland, to Tuticorin, whence a steamer service conveys passengers to Colombo. It is a very important pilgrim route, passing as it does, directly or by means of its branches, through many towns celebrated for

Fig. 65. Nilgiri Railway.

their Hindu temples—Conjeeveram, Chidambaram, Kumbakonam, Tanjore, Trichinopoly, Madura, and Rāmēsvaram.
It is estimated that, on the occasion of the Mahāmakham
festival at Kumbakonam, nearly half a million Hindus are
present.   At Kodaikānal Road, passengers for Kodaikānal
on the Palni hills alight.   The most important branch
lines are those between Villupuram and Katpādi, and

Fig. 66.   Up-country Railway Station.

Trichinopoly and Erode in the interior; and those which
run to Pondicherry, Kārikāl, and Negapatam on the east
coast, and to the island of Pāmban, on which the Rāmēsvaram temple is situated.   From Maniyāchi a line goes
through Tinnevelly and Ambasamudram, from which the
temple at Papanāsam is not far distant, to Quilon on the
Travancore coast.   The western ghāts are pierced by

several tunnels, one of which, at Ariyankavu, is 2,294 feet in length.

The west coast, from the extreme north of Malabar, through the Cochin State, to Trivandrum in Travancore, the country of "land-locked water and water-locked land," is traversed, with slight intervals, by a chain of **navigable backwaters** or lagoons. These backwaters are connected together by a series of artificial canals. Between Trivandrum and Quilon, the Varkala cliffs are pierced by two tunnels, respectively 2,364 and 924 feet in length, through which the canal passes. The backwaters open into the sea at various points, and are either expansions of rivers at their mouths, or broad, irregular sheets of water, into which the rivers flowing from the western ghāts discharge their water. Some of the backwaters are of very considerable size, the Vembanād backwater in Travancore, for example, being 32 miles long and 9 miles broad. The shores of the backwaters, and banks of the canals, are often lined with extensive coconut plantations, and studded with villages and hamlets. The traffic along the water-system is carried on by means of cabin-boats rowed by many oars, native boats called vallams, which are propelled by poles or tattered and torn mat sails, dug-outs or canoes, and other small craft.

The **Buckingham Canal** is a salt-water navigation canal, named after the Duke of Buckingham, a former Governor of Madras, in whose term of office its completion was undertaken, during the great famine of 1876–8. It extends along the east coast 66 miles southward from Madras, through which it passes, to Merkanam, and northwards 195 miles from Madras to Pedda Ganjam, where it communicates with the freshwater canal system of the delta of the Kistna river, which again communicates with the canal system of the delta of the Godāvari. The Buckingham Canal is tidal to a great extent when the river bars are

Fig. 67. Backwater and Canal, Malabar.

Fig. 68. Lake opening into the sea.

open. It runs within three miles of the coast throughout its entire length, and, in many parts, separated from the sea only by a line of sand-dunes. The traffic along the canal consists chiefly of salt from the salt factories, and firewood for use in Madras.

During its course, the Buckingham Canal enters and emerges from the Pulicat lake, which is a shallow salt-water lagoon, about 37 miles in length. The lake is separated from the sea, into which it opens at several places, by the island of Srīharikota, and the spit of land on which the town of Pulicat stands.

In the extreme north of the Madras Presidency, the **Chilka lake**, studded in places with green islands, which has been described as a gulf of the original Bay of Bengal, extends southwards from Bengal into Ganjam. This lake is the largest of the sheets of fresh or brackish water called tamparas. It consists of an open sheet of water, 44 miles long, fed by the Bhargavi and Dayā rivers, and separated by a ridge of sand from the Bay of Bengal, into which it opens by a narrow mouth. At the latter end of the eighteenth century, the mouth was so wide that it had to be crossed in "large boats." The lake is connected with the Rushikulya river by a tidal navigable canal, along which grain from Orissa, and salt, are carried in flat-bottomed boats, propelled by poles or "crazy mat sails."

CHAPTER XX

AGRICULTURE AND CROPS

Of the total population, of the Madras Presidency, roughly 70 per cent. are engaged in agriculture. The name **ryat** (ra'ā, to pasture) is generally applied to a tenant of the soil, or individual occupying land as a farmer or cultivator.

In the Madras Presidency there are two main divisions of
the land revenue system, called respectively zamindāri and
ryotwāri.   The former has been defined as a system of
intermediaries and transferees of interest between the State
and the cultivator, and is a survival from the days prior to
the British occupation, when the land was chiefly held by
zamindars (landholders) and feudal chieftains.   Under the
ryotwāri system, which prevails, the settlement for land
revenue is made directly by the Government agency with
each individual cultivator holding land, not with the village
community, nor with the middleman or landlord, payment
being also received directly from every such individual.
It is said that a large number of ryats are continuously in
debt, unable to subsist during the growth of the crop
except by petty borrowing, and returning at harvest time
all but a moderate surplus to the creditor.   Much has been
heard, in recent years, of the adaptation of the Raffeisen
system to Indian requirements, and, during the vice-
royalty of Lord Curzon, an Act was passed, giving legal
sanction to the operations of a system of co-operative banks
and credit societies for the benefit of the humbler classes.

The **agricultural year** nearly coincides with the Fasli
(fasl, season or crop), which commences on 1st July.   Fasli
has been defined as the name applied to certain solar eras
established for use in revenue and other civil transactions,
under the Muhammadan rulers (including Akbar), to meet
the inconvenience of the lunar calendar of the Hijra, in its
want of correspondence with the natural seasons.   The
present year is Fasli 1322.

The **soils** of South India are classified as dry, or not
irrigated ; wet, or irrigated otherwise than from private
wells ; and garden, or dry land watered from private wells,
on which dry and wet assessment is charged.   Of the
occupied ryotwāri area, 81 per cent. is dry, including
gardens, and 19 per cent. wet.

Many cultivated economic plants have been introduced from other parts of Asia, from Africa, or from Europe. Such, for example, are the cabbage, cauliflower, pomelo, peach, betel pepper, niger seed, and Italian millet. Others have been supplied from America, and include the pineapple, custard-apple, guava, papaw, chilli, ground-nut, potato, sweet potato, and Indian corn.

Of the gross area of **crops** cultivated on ryotwāri and inām lands (rent free, or on a quit rent) a few years ago, 80 per cent. was devoted to food-grains, which consist of cereals, or grains of grasses, and pulses, or seeds of leguminous plants. Of the cereals, the most important are rice (24.7 p.c.), cholam (15.6 p.c.), kambu (10 p.c.), and rāgi (5.8 p.c.). Rice (*Oryza sativa*: Tamil, arisi) in the husk is called paddy, and the name paddy-field is commonly applied to the plot of ground on which rice is growing. Cholam (*Sorghum vulgare*: the great millet) is not only valuable as food for man, but is said to be one of the best fodders in the world for milch cattle. Kambu (*Pennisetum typhoideum*) is, in many parts of India, the staple food of the lower classes. So, too, is rāgi (*Eleusine Coracana*), which receives its name (rāga, red) from the colour of the grain. *Zea Mays* (Indian corn or maize), of which the edible heads are called cobs, yields pop-corn, when parched in hot sand or over a fire. Dhāl (*Cajanus indicus*: pigeon-pea) is a highly esteemed pulse, which is sold in the form of split peas. It has been suggested that the name is derived from the Sanskrit root dal, to divide. Another highly valued pulse is *Phaseolus Mungo*, of which the grains are sometimes split, like dhāl. Among the pulses known as gram (Portuguese, grão, grain), are *Dolichos biflorus* (horse-gram), *Dolichos Lablab*, and *Cicer arietinum* (chick-pea or Bengal gram). The term gram-fed mutton is familiar to Anglo-Indians. The pulse *Lens esculenta* forms the basis of the food for invalids, called Revalenta.

The Badagas and Kotas of the Nīlgiris cultivate, among other crops, bearded wheat, barley, sāmai (*Panicum miliare*), tenai (*Setaria italica*: the Italian millet), and kīrai (*Amarantus paniculatus*: red amaranth), which is, in its season, a striking feature of the cultivated patches on the hills. Among some hill tribes, e.g. the Kondhs of Ganjam, the chief feature of the dry cultivation is the destructive practice of shifting cultivation called kumari (kumbari, a hill slope of poor soil), or jhūm. A strip of forest, primeval if possible, as being most fertile, is burnt, cultivated, and then deserted for a term of years, during which other sites are similarly treated.

Among the many **vegetables** which are cultivated is the brinjal or egg-plant (*Solanum Melongena*), the egg-shaped fruit of which is eaten by Indians and Europeans. The edible sweet potato (*Ipomœa Batatas*), called in North India shakar kand (sugar-candy), is, in some parts of the world, cultivated as a source of sugar.

The bendikai, vendikai, or lady's fingers (*Hibiscus esculentus*) is very mucilaginous. A former Collector of a district was known as Vendikai Dorai, with reference to the sticky nature of the mucilage, as he had the reputation of smoothing matters over between conflicting parties. The nickname Velakkennai (castor-oil) is given for a similar reason. The pods of the sword-bean (*Canavalia ensiformis*), and cow-pea (*Vigna Catjang*), constitute the French beans of Europeans in India. Onions, and garlic (*Allium Cepa* and *A. sativum*), are extensively cultivated.

The several species and varieties of *Capsicum* (chilli) are cultivated for consumption and export. The fruit, when dried and powdered, yields the red pepper of commerce, and is the basis of various pungent sauces, such as Tabasco. The cultivation of the climbing pepper plant (*Piper nigrum*), which grows wild in the forests of the west coast, has long been an important industry in Malabar.

In recent years, a Government farm has been established near Tellicherry for the scientific cultivation thereof. The betel plant (*Piper Betle* : vettilai) is largely cultivated for the sake of its leaves, which are chewed with areca nuts and chunam (lime). There is a 'very general belief in the existence of an imaginary poisonous animal called vettila poochi (insect), vettila pāmpu (snake), or vettila thēl (scorpion), which may cause illness, or even death, if chewed with the leaf. For this reason, the leaf is often carefully examined, and dusted with a cloth, before it is introduced into the mouth.

The rhizomes or underground root-like stems of *Zingiber officinale* are the source of **ginger**, which is sold fresh or dried, and exported in large quantities. The powdered rhizomes of *Curcuma longa* yield **turmeric**, which is not only used as a food-adjunct, but enters largely into Hindu ceremonial observances. In South India, turmeric is commonly called saffron. This is, however, obtained from the flowers of *Crocus sativus*.

Several important **oil-seeds**, including castor-oil (*Ricinus communis*) and niger (*Guizotia Abyssinica*), are cultivated. The ground-nut, earth-nut, or pea-nut (*Arachis hypogæa*), derives its name from the fact that the young pod forces its way beneath the surface of the earth, where it ripens. It is extensively cultivated in South Arcot, and exported thence to Europe. It is noted by Sir George Watt that there is little doubt that large quantities of ground-nut oil are passed off as olive-oil, the chief centre of which industry is at Marseilles. Gingelly oil, obtained from the seeds of *Sesamum indicum*, is largely used for culinary purposes, as an illuminant, and in Hindu ceremonial.

Various species of *Citrus* yield the **lime**, which is presented to Europeans by Indian retainers and others on New Year's day, the orange, and the pomelo, shaddock, or grape-fruit, which is more appreciated in the West Indies

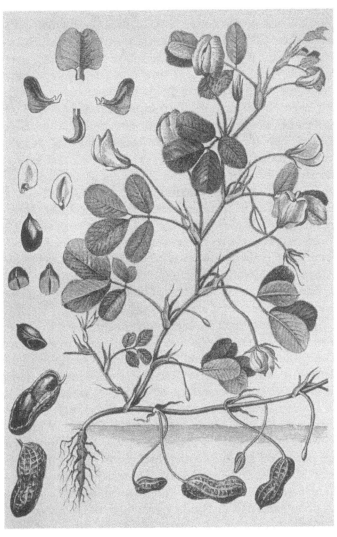

Fig. 69. Ground-nut.

than in India. The **plantain** (*Musa sapientum*), or banana of the West Indies and the English market, of which each plant bears a large bunch of fruits, is sometimes cultivated in large gardens extending over many acres. In connection with the specific name, it is interesting to note that the plantain was formerly confused with the jack fruit, which was described by Pliny as the fruit "quo sapientiores Indorum vivunt," i.e., the fruit on which the more learned of the Indians (Brahmans) live. The **jack tree** (*Artocarpus integrifolia*), which grows wild in the hills, and is extensively cultivated, receives its name from the Malayālam chakka. In young trees the fruits, which are sometimes 18 inches or more in length, grow on the branches, and in older trees on the trunk. The **cashew-nut** tree (*Anacardium occidentale*) yields the kidney-shaped nuts, which grow on a pear-shaped fleshy receptacle, and are usually eaten roasted. The fruit of the **mango** tree (*Mangifera indica* : mān-kai or mān-gai), when of good quality, and free from the odour of turpentine, is undoubtedly the best fruit in India. The Naulākh Bāgh, or nine lakh garden of mango and other trees, near Rānipet in the North Arcot district, was planted by one of the Nawābs of the Carnatic. The **custard-apple** (*Anona squamosa*), known as sharīfa (noble) and Sītaphal or fruit of Sīta, is cultivated for its luscious fruit. It is very common in a wild state near old forts in the Deccan, e.g. at Gooty, Gurramkonda, and Penukonda. The **papaya** or papaw tree (*Carica Papaya*), which derives its name from the Carib ababai, is extensively grown in gardens. The fruit is eaten, and the digestive properties of its milky juice are utilised for the purpose of rendering meat tender by rubbing it therewith. It has even been said that tough meat is rendered tender by merely hanging it, when freshly killed, amongst the foliage of the tree. The best melons (*Cucumis Melo*) are grown in the Cuddapah district, chiefly at Sidhout and Cuddapah. Vine (*Vitis vinifera*) or grape cultivation, from cuttings imported from Australia, has been carried out in recent years in the Mysore State.

CHAPTER XXI

IRRIGATION

IRRIGATION has been defined as an artificial application of water to the land in order to promote cultivation. Where, as on the west coast, there is an abundant rainfall, there is no need for irrigation except of a simple kind. East of the western ghāts, however, irrigation is extensively carried out by means of dams thrown across rivers, tanks, wells, etc. Of 671 square miles of land, which were irrigated in the Coimbatore district in 1903–4, 502 square miles were watered by wells, 119 square miles by Government canals, and 35 square miles by tanks. In that district, there are said to be 100,000 wells, sunk, in many cases, through hard rock, to a depth of 80 to 90 feet. The name "tank" is applied to artificial ponds or lakes, made either by excavating or banking, which sometimes breach during the wet season, and dry up altogether in the hot weather. The number of tanks in the Madras Presidency and Mysore is said to be about 75,000. Some tanks are of immense size, and resemble great natural lakes. For example, the Vīrānam tank, which is a very ancient work, has an area of 35 square miles, and an embankment 12 miles long. The great tank at Cumbum in the Kurnool district, which is by tradition attributed to the sage Jamadagni, was formed by damming a gorge through which the Gundla-kamma river flows. It has a capacity of 3,696 million cubic feet, and a drainage area of 430 square miles. The Chembrambākam tank in the Chingleput district, which

is fed by the Cooum river, has an embankment more than
3 miles long, and irrigates more than 12,000 acres of wet-
weather crops. Madras receives its supply of water from
the Red Hills tank, situated about eight miles distant from
the city. The Telugu Oddēs, or Wudders, who are the
navvies of the country, have practically a monopoly of the
work of sinking wells, digging tanks, and constructing
tank bunds (embankments), and other kinds of earthwork.
The caste insignia of the Oddēs, as given in the Kanchi
(Conjeeveram) records, 1807, is a spade. Among other
insignia recorded there, are a Cupid for the Dēva-dāsis
(dancing-girls), and a curry-comb for Christians.

The methods resorted to by cultivators for lifting water
are primitive and simple. One of the best known methods
is by means of a **picota** or picottah, which consists of a
long lever or yard, pivoted on an upright post, weighted
on the short arm, and bearing a bucket suspended by a
bamboo from the long arm. The picota has also been
described as the trunk of a tree, resting near the middle
of the fork of another tree, like a see-saw, on which men
run up and down to raise a large bucket of water. Picota
is a Portuguese word, and is also applied to the lever of a
ship's pump, and post in which it works. The ship's picota
was also used as a pillory. Thus it is recorded by Gaspar
Correa that Vasco da Gama gave orders that no seaman
should wear a cloak, except on Sunday ; and if he did so,
he was to be put in the picota for a day.

The **Persian wheel** for lifting water consists of a large
wheel, which is turned by bullocks walking round in a
circle, and revolves in water by means of cogged gearing.
The wheel carries a number of buckets or pots, and, as it
revolves, the water contained therein is lifted, discharged
into a trough, and conveyed thence by channels. In the
Deccan, and elsewhere, water is often lifted by means of a
mot or large leather bag, which is hauled up with a rope

and pulley by a pair of bullocks walking down an earthen ramp or slope. In some places, water is baled out by means of hand scoops, or by a basket swung on ropes by two men.

Fig. 70. Lifting water by means of a picota.

The Madras Government has quite recently started a **Pumping** and **Boring** Department in connection with the Department of Industries. In the annual report thereof,

1909–10, it is recorded that "the utilisation for cultivation of such underground supplies of water as may be revealed by boring depends to a large extent on the cost of raising the water to the surface. The oil-engines and pumps now being installed in the Pumping Department at present represent the most economical form of water-lift; but, even so, they involve considerable initial and recurring expenditure, and are frequently beyond the means of ryots (cultivators). If a cheaper source of power than that represented by the oil-engine could be introduced, the practice of lift irrigation could be enormously stimulated. The water of the Periyar, if harnessed for power, represents such a source." There are said to be fully 60,000 acres dependent on pumps, the popularity of which is steadily increasing.

Of the **major irrigation works** undertaken by the Madras Government, priority of place must be given to what is known as the **Periyar Project**. Briefly, the object of this great undertaking was to divert the waters of the Periyar river, which flowed through Travancore, where the rainfall is heavy, into the Arabian Sea, across the western ghāts, to the more arid eastern side of the peninsula, and so into the Bay of Bengal. The work, which was carried out in a malarious jungle, included the construction of a solid masonry dam 176 feet high, to close the valley of the Periyar, and form a vast lake or reservoir, which has an area of 8,000 acres, for the storage of water. A tunnel, 5,704 feet long, drilled and blasted through hard rock, with sluices and subsidiary works, conducts the water from the reservoir down the valley of the Suruli, by which it reaches the Vaigai river, which runs past the town of Madura. The bed of this river is utilised to carry water to places where it is wanted, and canals have been constructed for the distribution of water for the irrigation of over 100,000 acres of land in the Vaigai valley. It has been picturesquely said that "we are adding an Egypt a year to the (Indian) Empire by our canals, but England takes no notice."

Fig. 71. Periyar dam during construction.

Another good example of **combined storage and canal systems** is afforded by the works in connection with the Palar river. By means of an **anicut** (Tamil, anai-kattu) or dam, four miles below the town of Arcot, the water is diverted, through a series of main and branch canals, to a number of tanks, in which it is stored for the purpose of irrigation. The anicut was originally designed to improve the supply of water to old channels fed by a series of old native tanks.

The Rushikulya river in Ganjam has been utilised for irrigation by means of a series of works, known as the **Rushikulya Project.** They consist of two canals from the Rushikulya and its tributary the Mahānadi, supplemented by two reservoirs named after the towns of Russellkonda and Surada. Of these, the former was formed by damming a valley in the basin of the Mahānadi, while the latter was constructed across the Pathama river, which is an affluent of the Rushikulya. The cultivable area thus placed under irrigation has been estimated at 142,000 acres. The project has been classed among the protective works, i.e. protective against famine, in contradistinction to productive works, the revenue derived from which not only pays the cost of maintenance, but also a percentage on the capital expended on them.

The best examples of **deltaic canals** are those at the deltas near the mouths of the Godāvari, Kistna, and Cauvery rivers, where the soil is a rich alluvium produced by silt washed down thereby. The head-works of the **Godāvari system** are situated at Dowlaishwaram, where the river bifurcates into two main streams, the Gautami and Vasishta, which are named after two Rishis. The works consist mainly of a masonry dam across the river, above the bifurcations, in four sections connected by islands, which are altogether about $2\frac{1}{2}$ miles in length. From the dam nearly 500 miles of navigable main canals, and 2,000 miles of smaller distributary canals, commanding over 1,250,000 acres of irrigable land, take off. The Gunnavaram aqueduct extends the irrigation system of the river called the Vainateyam Godāvari to the

Nagaram island, which is said to be one of the most fertile parts of the Godāvari district.

The **Kistna irrigation system** has been carried out by damming the river at Bezwāda, and constructing canals, which communicate on the north with the Godāvari canals, and on the south with the Buckingham canal.

In connection with the **Cauvery river**, the grand anicut was constructed by one of the Chola kings below the island of Srīrangam, to separate the Cauvery from the

Fig. 72. Dowlaishwaram Anicut.

Coleroon, and direct it towards the Tanjore district. During the last century, as the Cauvery was silting up, and the irrigation channels were becoming dry, the upper anicut, 2,250 feet long, was constructed across the Coleroon at the upper end of Srīrangam island, and a regulation dam, 1,950 feet long, was built across the Cauvery near the grand anicut. Subsequently, a similar regulator was constructed across the Vennar, a main branch of the Cauvery. It has been estimated that, in the Tanjore,

IRRIGATION

207

Trichinopoly, and South Arcot districts, the Cauvery and Coleroon water 1,107,000 acres of land.

In deltaic country, the river branches run on the watersheds, and so command the adjacent country. Hence

Fig. 73. Kistna Anicut, with river in moderate flood.

irrigation is easy. In non-deltaic country, the river runs in a valley, so, to irrigate a given area, the stream must be dammed far above that area.

CHAPTER XXII

INDUSTRIES

THE cotton plant (*Gossypium*) is most extensively cultivated in the Ceded Districts, especially the Bellary district,
in Coimbatore and Tinnevelly. Its cultivation is largely
carried out on the black loamy soil, called in the vernacular
rēgur or rēgada, and by Europeans black cotton soil, which
is very soft and adhesive during the monsoon rains, and
fissured by huge cracks in the dry season. The cotton of
commerce consists of the unicellular hairs, which are attached to the seeds of the plant, and, in South India,
produce the commercial forms known as Tinnevellys,
Westerns, Cocanādas, and Salems. The separation of the
fibre or lint from the seed is effected by ginning (gin, a
contraction of engine). The cotton is brought for sale to
the factories by the bigger ryots (farmers or cultivators),
the smaller ones disposing of it, ginned or unginned, to
native brokers, who have advanced money on the crop.
It is noted, in the 'Imperial Gazetteer of India,' that
"originally all the cotton-presses were in Black Town,
Madras, and the raw cotton was brought to them in carts,
taking months upon the road. The cotton famine in
Lancashire, which was caused by the American War
(1861–5), gave a great impetus to the trade, and it was
shortly afterwards further encouraged by the construction
of the Madras Railway towards the cotton-growing areas
in the Deccan. As the line advanced, the cotton was
carted to the nearest station, and, when it reached the
Deccan, the presses were transferred thither from Madras.

Ginning and cleaning mills followed, but most of the
Deccan cotton is still hand-ginned. Much the same course
was followed in Tinnevelly and Coimbatore." Many ginning and cleaning mills, and steam-presses are now at
work in the most important centres of the cotton industry;
and spinning or weaving mills have been established,
especially in Madras, Bellary, Madura, Tuticorin, Coimbatore, and Bangalore. During a visit to Tuticorin in

Fig. 74. Weaving on hand-loom.

1887, I used to watch massive blocks of stony corals
(*Porites, Astræa*, etc.) being brought in canoes from the
reef, and thrown into the ground to form the foundation
of the new cotton mills, which have in consequence been
named the Coral Mills. At a cotton-press at Adoni, in
the Bellary district, I have seen many Basavis (women
dedicated to the deity) working for a daily wage of three
annas. The Madras Government has, in recent years,
established a weaving factory at Salem, with the object

of affording training in improved methods of weaving on hand-looms, and advancing the welfare of the weaving classes. Fly-shuttle looms are reported to be coming steadily into use; and successful experiments have been carried out in adapting the Jacquard harness to country looms making bordered cloths. Weaving is taught in various mission schools, and the woven fabrics manufactured by the Basel Mission on the west coast have earned a widespread reputation.

The **sugar-cane** plant (*Saccharum officinarum*) is widely cultivated in South India, and there is a large native industry in the manufacture of jaggery (raw sugar), country sugar, molasses, and other products of the juice. The sugar factory and distillery at Aska in Ganjam was long associated with the name of Mr F. J. V. Minchin. At Nellikuppam, in the South Arcot district, there is a sugar factory belonging to the East India Distilleries and Sugar Factories Company, in which large quantities of spirit are distilled, and sugar is made from the juice of the canes cultivated in the neighbourhood, and palmyra jaggery imported from Tinnevelly. The ryats, who bring the canes to the factory, are paid according to the weight of the jaggery obtained from a sample thereof, which is crushed, and the juice boiled down to jaggery in their presence. The ryat is said to be sometimes caught, adding sand, concealed within his clothes, to the juice as it boils, to increase the weight. During the last few years, an experimental sugar-cane station, from which canes are distributed among the ryats, has been established at Sāmalkot in the Godāvari district, under the direction of the Government Botanist. From the latest reports, it is gathered that, in the Godāvari and South Arcot districts, the new Mauritius canes which have been introduced are rapidly ousting the inferior local canes grown before. The new canes are said to give about twice the produce of the old, and their harder rind makes them almost proof against jackals—a source of great loss before.

Tobacco (*Nicotiana Tabacum*) is cultivated, on a large or small scale, in every district of the Madras Presidency. The leaf is manufactured in European factories, employing large numbers of Indians, at Dindigul in the Madura district, into the well-known Dindigul, or, as they are often called, Trichinopoly or Trichy cheroots. The word cheroot, it may be noted, is derived from the Tamil shuruttu, a roll (of tobacco). The cheroot manufacture in the Trichinopoly district is said to have declined, owing to the competition of the milder and better rolled cheroots, which are made at Dindigul and Madras. It is pointed out by Sir George Watt that the discovery, made about 1881, that, by importing wrappers from Java and Sumatra, cheroots could be turned out, which were better than those made throughout of Indian leaf, gave the impetus that was needed to bring them to the favourable notice of the world at large. Tobacco, called lunka tobacco, grown on the banks of the Godāvari river, and the lunkas or islands, which are very fertile owing to the silt deposited on them, is exported in large quantities in the form of leaf to Burma from the port of Coconāda. According to the Review of Trade in the Madras Presidency, 1910–11, the importation of cigarettes decreased to the extent of 77 per cent. in quantity, owing to the enhanced duty on tobacco (Act VIII, 1910). Cheap American cigarettes suffered most severely, their place being taken by cigarettes of Indian manufacture. Enormous numbers of cheap cigarettes are now turned out in India, especially in Bengal.

One result of the discovery and introduction of aniline and alizarine dyes has been that the cultivation of some of the plants used by native dyers in the manufacture of **vegetable dyes**, has been abandoned. The imports of aniline and alizarine dyes into India during 1910–11 were

valued at £685,000. The effect of the discovery of syn-
thetic indigo on the indigo industry has been very marked.
The indigo trade of the Madras Presidency decreased, in
1910–11, from Rs. 5·45 lakhs to Rs. 3·92 lakhs, or 28 per
cent. in value, and the area under cultivation was 25 per
cent. less than in the previous year. The leguminous
plant (*Indigofera tinctoria*), which yields the natural blue
dye, is most widely cultivated in the Cuddapah and South

Fig. 75. Tobacco crop.

Arcot districts. The dye, when it has been extracted from
the plant by either a wet- or dry-leaf process, is finally
pressed into hard cakes.

A few years ago, the manufacture from the imported
metal **aluminium**, of cooking-pots, water-bottles, and other
articles for domestic, military, and medical purposes, was
introduced at the Madras Government School of Arts,
and successfully launched as a new industry, which has

since been taken up by the Aluminium Company and others.

More recently, the Madras Government established a **Chrome Tanning** Department, with the primary object of replacing the country leather by a better leather for kavalais or water-bags used for raising water from wells. The industry was extended to the manufacture of boots, shoes, and sandals. Among the various articles tanned for private individuals were crocodile, tiger, leopard, sāmbar deer, and snake skins. The departmental report, 1908–9, records the manufacture of a false ear for a policeman's charger, and a leopard skin waistcoat. In 1908–9, a Company, called the Mysore Tannery Limited, erected a large chrome tannery near Bangalore in the Mysore State. The Madras Government Chrome Tanning Factory was sold in 1910 to the Rewah Durbar (Government), and the machinery and plant set up at Umaria. According to the census returns, 1901, the number of people (Chakkiliyans or chucklers, Mādigas, Muhammadans, etc.) engaged in the tanning and leather-working trade in the Madras Presidency, was 190,011. Of this number, 111,865 were returned as boot, shoe, and sandal makers ; 50,796 as makers of water-bags, well-bags, buckets, and ghī (clarified butter) pots ; and 9,294 as engaged in the manufacture of leather from hides (cow, buffalo, and calf) and skins (sheep and goats). It is said that ghī, if carefully enclosed in skins while still hot, may be preserved for many years, without the addition of salt or other preservative.

Beer has been brewed on the Nīlgiri hills since 1826, and various breweries have since been established there from time to time. In the breweries at the present day, beer is brewed for the taverns, and for the troops at Wellington and other military stations. For the beer supplied to the taverns, the barley of the Nīlgiris (called beer ganji), which is cultivated by the Badagas and Kotas, is used; but for " English beer " the grain is imported from the Punjāb.

A Government **Cordite** Factory is established on the Nīlgiris, in the Aravanghāt valley above Coonoor. The machinery is driven by electricity generated at the Kartēri falls. The factory gives employment to many Badagas. Cordite is a smokeless explosive, used by the Army and Navy. Its name is derived from the fact that it is produced in the form of cylindrical strings or cords, looking like macaroni, by pressing it, while in a pasty condition, through dies or perforations in a steel plate.

CHAPTER XXIII

PLANTING INDUSTRIES

THE prosperity of the **coffee** (*Coffea arabica*) industry in South India was at its height in the decade 1870–80. The profits were so good that the cultivation of the plant spread all over the suitable areas of the western ghāts. Before the appearance of leaf disease or blight caused by the fungus *Hemileia vastatrix*, the heavy rainfall during the south-west monsoon did not affect the growth or yield, and, in consequence, Travancore, Wynaad, Coorg, and Mysore, gave up large tracts of forest land to the enterprise of the planter. But the appearance of leaf disease worked a complete and rapid change. The disease first appeared in Ceylon, and gradually crept along the line of the ghāts until it invaded every planting district in South India. Now it has completely killed coffee out of Travancore, and almost entirely out of Wynaad. Districts with heavy rainfall have succumbed, and it survives only in comparatively dry climates, where the fungus can be successfully combated by high cultivation. A heavy fall in the price of coffee owing to the extension of cultivation in Brazil has also

Fig. 76. Coffee bushes.

lowered the price of coffee to a point at which planters in India find it hard to make a profit. Consequently, except in favoured localities, such as parts of Coorg and Mysore, and a few other remnants, the cultivation of coffee has given place to tea.

The coffee fruit, when ripe, is popularly called the cherry, owing to its red colour, and the twin seeds or beans are known as the berries. In the preparation of the seeds for the market, the succulent pulp, parchment, and silver skin which surround it, are removed by machinery. Coffee-curing works, in which the berries are prepared for export and consumption in India, are established at Calicut, Telli-cherry, Mangalore, Coimbatore, and other places.

The **tea plant** (*Camellia Thea*) has been grown, especially on the Nīlgiri hills, for a great number of years, but its cultivation on a large scale is of quite recent growth. When *Hemileia* destroyed the coffee industry of Ceylon, planters turned their attention to other products, especially to cinchona and tea. The planters of South India were not slow to follow the example. The coffee districts of South Travancore and Pīrmed were the first to be planted up on a large scale. It was soon found that these areas could produce a tea which, though not of first class quality, could command a ready sale at profitable prices. Tea will grow at any elevation, but, in general terms, it may be said that, the higher the elevation, the better is the quality of the tea produced, but the smaller is the yield. Tea grown near sea-level gives an abundant yield of very low quality. The leaves, which are hand-plucked by coolies, are manufactured into various classes of tea, e.g. black and green tea, which receive market names, such as Orange Pekoe, Pekoe, etc.

The days of profitable cultivation of **cinchona** were short, owing to the rapid and scientific development of the industry by the Dutch Government in Java. Cinchona plantations are now maintained by the Madras Govern-ment on the Nīlgiri hills, at Naduvatam, on the slopes of Dodabetta, and the Hooker estate (named after the dis-tinguished botanist), to meet the demand for sulphate of

Fig. 77. Tea Estate.

quinine and cinchona febrifuge in the Madras Presidency, and other Provinces and States. The factory at Naduvatam is on the site of the old Nīlgiri jail, in which Chinese convicts from the Straits Settlements were formerly confined. On the expiration of the sentence, they settled between Naduvatam and Gudalur, and, contracting alliances with Indian women, now form, with their Indo-Chinese offspring, a small colony of market-gardeners, gaining a modest livelihood by cultivating vegetables and coffee. Of the various species of cinchona, *C. officinalis* (loxa or crown bark) is said to have proved the most useful, and hybrids between this species and *C. succirubra* (red bark), and *C. Calisaya*, var. *Ledgeriana* ("Ledger"), are also cultivated. Quinine powders are sold, in cheap packets, by postmasters throughout South India.

Experimental cultivation of **rubber-producing trees** (*Hevea, Manihot, Castilloa, Landolphia*, etc.) has long been carried out on the Nīlgiris, in Malabar, and Mysore. The systematic cultivation thereof in the planting districts has extended rapidly during the last few years, owing to the increasing demand for rubber in the English market, and is now carried out in Travancore, Cochin, Malabar, Mysore and Coorg, and on the Nīlgiri and Shevaroy hills. It has been said that the varying elevations of the land in South India are adapted for the growth both of para (*Hevea braziliensis*) and ceara (*Manihot Glaziovii*), the former loving the hot moist climate of the lowlands, and the latter thriving best at high elevations where the rainfall is slight. The rubber is obtained by cutting or scoring the bark, so as to produce a flow of the inspissated milky fluid called the latex, which coagulates on exposure to the air.

CHAPTER XXIV

SEA-FISHERIES

In the British trade, fish are classified as prime and offal, the former being consumed by the richer, and the latter by the poorer classes. In India the fish supply is essentially a poor man's question, and the prosperity of the industry depends largely on the offal, and not on the prime. At Cochin, out of forty different kinds of fish classed as edible by the natives, only four—seir, whiting, mullet, and "sardines"—were regarded as of the prime quality. The economic fishes comprise: (*a*) round fishes, e.g. seir, pomfret, mackerel, and herring; (*b*) flat fishes (the so-called soles); (*c*) cartilaginous fishes (sharks and rays or skates). Sharks and skates are known as pāl sora or milk producers, and, when salted, are considered very good for women nursing infants. **Sharks' fins** are sold in the local markets for food, or exported to China. At Cannanore, one fish daily from each boat, and half the sharks' fins, used to be claimed as a perquisite for the Rāja's cat, or poocha mīn (cat-fish) collection. In his speech on the budget some years ago, the Finance Minister stated that he had to come down from the regions of high finance to grovel among sharks' fins and fish maws, but these articles would bring in sufficient income to pay the salary of a High Court Judge for half a year. **Fish-maws** are the sounds or air-bladders of fishes, such as the cat-fish (*Arius*), which are shipped to China and Europe for the manufacture of isinglass. In former times, hundreds of tons of **fish oil**, obtained by boiling "sardines" (*Clupea longiceps*), which in some years arrive in huge shoals off the west coast, are said to have been exported from Cochin. The oil trade is, however, reported to have decreased in recent years. The Natives believe that the oil which is exported to Europe returns in the guise of cod-liver oil. The "sardines," which are called nalla mathi (good fish), are highly appreciated as an article of food, and are of importance to planters, whose agents have them sun-dried for the purpose of manure.

The importance of the fisheries of the west as compared with those of the east coast is brought out by the following statistics of a single year, which show that, with half the number of yards, the outturn of fish on the west coast exceeded that of the east coast by 533,533 maunds.

	Eight east coast sub-divisions	Calicut (west coast) sub-divisions
Number of yards	85	43
Weight of fish brought in for operation, maunds	322,702	856,235
Value of salt sold, Rs	21,023	108,465
Weight of salt sold, maunds	39,139	118,583

The **fish-curing operations**, which are carried on in yards near the sea-shore, are controlled by the Salt Department, which supplies salt to the fish-curers. The sea fisheries of the west coast are conducted mainly by Mukkuvans, Mogērs, and Māppillas (Muhammadans) from small rowing and sailing boats, within a few miles of the shore But fishermen come, during the fishing season, to Malpe in South Canara, from Ratnagiri in the Bombay Presidency, with a flotilla of larger keeled and outrigged sailing boats. The Pattanavan fishermen of Madras go out fishing on catamarans (kattu, binding; maram, tree), which have been described by Lady Dufferin as "two logs of wood lashed together (with ropes). The rower wears a fool's cap, in which he carries betel and tobacco, and, when he encounters

Fig. 78. Small Catamaran, Madras beach.

a big wave, he leaves his boat, slips through the wave himself, and picks up his catamaran on the other side of it. Some large deep barges (masūla boats) came out for us, with a guard of honour of the mosquito fleet, as the catamarans are called." Catamarans have further been described as getting through the fiercest surf, sometimes dancing at their ease on the top of the waters ; sometimes the man completely washed off, and man floating one way and catamaran another, till they seem to catch each other again by magic. In one of the early Indian voyagers' log-books there is an entry concerning a catamaran to the effect that "this morning, 6 a.m. we saw distinctly two black devils playing at single-stick. We watched these infernal imps about an hour, when they were lost in the distance. Surely this doth portend some great tempest."

The **pearl fisheries**, which are conducted from Tuticorin in the Gulf of Manaar at irregular intervals, have been celebrated from a remote period, and, in comparatively recent times, have been carried out successively by the Portuguese, Dutch, and English. The mollusc (*Avicula fucata*), popularly known as the pearl oyster, which is the source of the pearls, grows in dense masses on the sea-bottom, some miles from the coast, and anchors itself by means of its silky byssus filaments to another shell, coral-rock, or other object. The pearls of commerce are for the most part those which are formed within the soft tissues of the animal, and not the irregular pearly excrescences (odumuttu), which are found as outgrowths of the nacreous or mother-of-pearl layer of the shell. The pearls are formed by the deposition of carbonate of lime in concentric layers like the successive scales of an onion, round some irritating foreign body, such as a parasitic worm, grain of sand, or the frustule of a diatom. The shells are collected by Tamil and Arab divers, who wear no diving dress, but are let down from boats on a stone to which a rope is attached.

On arrival at the bottom, they collect as many shells as they can in a basket or net, and come to the surface to regain their breath. At the fishery in 1890, a scare was produced by a diver being bitten by a shark, and a "wise woman" was engaged to officiate as shark-charmer. The shells, with the exception of the divers' share, are sold at the end of each day by a government auctioneer, and piled up in a shed (kottu), where they are left for some days, so that the animal matter undergoes decomposition. The pearls are finally extracted by means of sieves of graduated sizes from the putrid residue, which is submitted to repeated washings, to free it from the prevailing maggots, sand, etc. The Jāti Talaivan, or head of the Parava fishing caste, which originally held the fishing rights, is entitled to a fixed share of the shells as his perquisite.

The **chank** (sankha) or **conch fishery** is also conducted from Tuticorin, and is a more regular source of income than the pearl fisheries. The shells are found in the neighbourhood of the pearl banks, buried in the sand, lying on the sea-bottom, or in sandy crevices between blocks of coral-rock. They lie scattered about, and not aggregated together like the pearl oysters, so that the divers have to move about from place to place on the bottom in search of them. The shells are stored in a godown or store-room, where the animal matter is got rid of by the process of putrefaction, and periodically sold by auction to the highest bidder. The chank is a sacred shell, and is used as a musical instrument in Hindu temples. It is also cut into armlets, bracelets, and other ornaments. It appears on the coins of the Chālukyan and Pāndyan kingdoms, and on the modern coinage of Travancore. The rare right-handed chank (i.e., one which has its spiral opening to the right) is said to have been sometimes priced at a lakh of rupees (Rs 100,000), and to have sold for its weight in gold.

One of the edible holothurians (sea-cucumbers), known as the **trepang** or bêche-de-mer, is very abundant in the mud on the south shore at Pāmban, and in the vicinity of Rāmēsvaram, and is prepared for exportation to Penang and Singapore. The process of preparation is as follows. The animals are collected as they lie on the mud at low water, and placed in a cauldron, which is heated by a

Fig. 79. Chank shell.

charcoal fire. As the temperature rises in the cauldron, the living animals commit suicide by ejecting their digestive apparatus and other organs, and become reduced to leathery sacs. At the end of twenty minutes or half-an-hour, the boiling process is stopped, and the shrivelled animals are buried in the sand until the following morning, when the boiling is repeated. Bêches-de-mer are

highly esteemed as an article of food by Chinese and
Japanese epicures, being made into a thick gelatinous
soup.

During the last few years, a **Fishery Department** has
been organised, under the direction of Sir F. A. Nicholson,
K.C.I.E.   The work in connection therewith includes
improved methods of curing fish, the manufacture of fish-
oil and guano, freshwater pisciculture and conservancy, the
stocking of big tanks with fish, the culture of edible oysters,
the care of pearl and chank fisheries, and cooperation.

CHAPTER XXV

INDUSTRIAL ARTS

OF the indigenous arts of South India, the only one
which now employs any considerable number of persons is
the **weaving** on hand-looms of silk and cotton fabrics, and
even this is in a declining state.   Little more than a
century ago (1796–7), the value of the cotton fabrics exported from India to England was £2,777,000, or one-third
of the total of all Indian exports.   When, as at the present
day, the bazars of South India are flooded with imported
piece-goods of British manufacture, it is curious to look back
and reflect that the term piece-goods was originally applied
in trade to the cotton fabrics exported from India.   In
1700, a law was passed, mainly with a view to the protection
of the Spitalfields weavers, by which all wrought silks,
mixed stuffs, and figured calicoes, the manufacture of
Persia, China, or the East Indies, were forbidden to be
worn or otherwise used in Great Britain.   The exports at
the present day include bright coloured Madras and
Ventupallam "handkerchiefs" for Indian emigrants to

Fig. 80. Painted cloth, made at Kālahasti.

distant countries. Madras handkerchiefs are repeatedly referred to in *Uncle Tom's Cabin*; and, in *Tom Cringle's Log*, President Petion, the black Washington, is described as wearing the everlasting Madras handkerchief round his brows. It is said that the Indian purchasers of the printed and dyed fabrics which find a market in Africa set as much store by the odour of the cloth, which Manchester cannot imitate, as by the pattern and colour.

An industry for which South India was till quite recently celebrated was the manufacture of block-printed and hand-painted **palempores**, and other cotton fabrics. Nowadays, at former centres of this industry, e.g., Masulipatam and Walajapet, old wood-blocks, many with beautiful patterns of Persian origin, may be seen piled up in corners or in the roof, and covered with the dust and cobwebs of years. The printed cottons of Masulipatam consisted of canopies, screen-cloths, prayer-cloths, etc. At Kālahasti, painted cloths are made, on which are depicted crude illustrations of scenes from the Hindu epics, the Mahābhārata and Rāmayana, with the story in Telugu characters; and at Cocanāda fabrics with the tree of life pattern are also made.

European manufacturers have not yet produced anything which can compete with the **fine cotton** and **silk** cloths for female attire made at Madura, Tanjore, Kuttālam, Kornād, Kampli, Adoni, and other places; and the satins made at Ayyampet, Ariyalur, Arcot, and Walajapet, are of considerable beauty. The fine lace-like patterns on the fabrics of Karuppur, Paramagudi, Mānamadurai, etc., which are drawn by skilled hands with an iron pen fed with melted wax, are exceedingly beautiful. The muslins manufactured at Chicacole and Arni, the delicacy of which has been compared with a spider's web, have been justly celebrated. Rugs made of silk floss are manufactured at Ayyampet, and good carpets are made at Ellore, and the Vellore and Bangalore jails.

The manufacture of fine **ornamental brass** and **bronze** work, in the shape of many-branched lamps, images of

Fig. 81.   Metal Image of Siva as Natarāja.

gods, etc., for which South India was once famous, has become almost a lost art.   The Madras Museum possesses a magnificent collection of **arms** from the Tanjore palace armoury, which show to what a high state of perfection the ironsmiths had brought their art in the days when skilled artisans were specially employed by Indian Princes at their

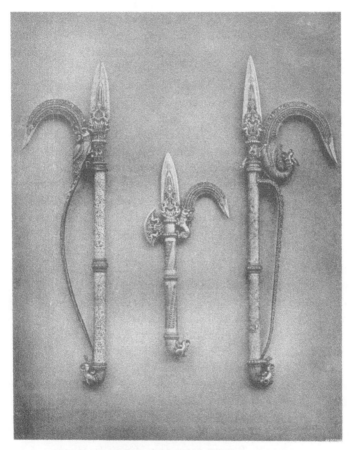

Fig. 82. Elephant goads from the Tanjore palace.

palaces. The collection includes three magnificent damascened elephant goads (ancus) of chiselled steel, and several Genoa blades attached to hilts of Indian workmanship. It

is a matter of history that the Marātha Rāja Sivaji's favourite
sword Bhāvani was a Genoa blade. Tanjore is now the
chief centre for metal-work, consisting of combinations of
copper and silver, brass and copper, and graven brass.
The crusting of copper with silver figures is a modern
adaptation of an older art, and the demand for these wares
is almost entirely European. Madras has a reputation
for its silver-ware, adapted to European requirements,
with figures of Hindu deities (swāmis) crowded together.
Brass trays and plates, into which thin plates of copper are
let in or damascened, with crude representations of gods,
are made at Tirupati. There is also a considerable trade
in small brass and copper deities of local manufacture,
which are sold to pilgrims to the sacred shrine. At Vellore
exists an industry in pierced brass trays with mythological
figures. An interesting type of brass-work is carried on at
Belugunta and other places in Ganjam, in the form of
grotesque animals and human figurines, cast by the *cire
perdue* process, which are said to be used as wedding
presents by the Kutiya Kondh hill tribe. Pliable brass
fishes are made at Russellkonda. At Sivaganga and
Madura, brass models of lizards, cobras, frogs, and other
animals are made. At Kurumbalur, in the Trichinopoly
district, there is a small industry in the manufacture of
brass trays and vessels inlaid with zinc.

The Gudigars of Mysore are highly skilled **carvers in
sandalwood**, and were employed during the building of
the Mahārāja's new palace at Mysore. The designs of the
cabinets, caskets, etc., which they turn out, are very elaborate
and intricate, and frequently consist of delicate scroll-work
interspersed with figures from the Hindu Pantheon. The
finer portions of the work are sometimes done with tools
made from European umbrella-spokes. At the Cannanore
jail, double coconuts (coco-de-mer) are richly carved, for
use as liquor-cases, with Burmese figures. Coconuts, for

use as sugar-basins, teapots, etc. are also carved with representations of peacocks, Burmese figures, and Hindu deities. The industry was originally started by Burmese convicts confined in the jail after the Burmese war of 1885, but has since been taken up by Māppillas, Tiyans, and others in forced retirement. In Travancore very spirited and well executed designs are carved on coconut shells, and at Karkal in South Canara young coconuts are, in like manner, neatly carved with floral, conventional, and mythological designs.

In Travancore, **ivory-carvers** used to be regularly employed by the Mahārājas, and some fine specimens of their work, in the shape of tankards with representations of the tulabhāram (weighing against gold), and other ceremonies, are preserved in the palace at Trivandrum. The throne sent to the London Exhibition of 1851 as a gift to Queen Victoria is a notable production from this locality. In recent times, ivory-carving has been developed at the Trivandrum School of Arts. Western influence has greatly affected the design and character of the articles turned out, which include hand-mirrors, combs, paper-knives, deer, hunting scenes, and the lion of Lucerne. At Vizagapatam several firms make fancy boxes, card-cases, picture-frames, etc. of sandalwood, rosewood or ebony, inlaid or overlaid with ivory fretwork. Representations of Hindu deities, and floral designs, are incised in the ivory, and filled in with black lacquer (sgraffito). At Vizagapatam are also made various articles, e.g. animals, boxes and book-slides, in "bison" horn obtained from the hill-tracts, tortoise-shell, and porcupine quills.

The "**lacquer**" **ware** of Kurnool has been said to be perhaps the finest gesso work, or ornament modelled in plaster and glue in low relief, which is produced in India. It consists mainly of boxes, trays and tables. The work turned out at Mandasa in Ganjam is much bolder, and is suitable for decoration on a large scale. A similar method of decoration was formerly much used in Saracenic architectural decoration of interiors in many countries. At Nosam, leather dish-mats are painted with pictures of deities and floral designs. Native playing-cards and fans made of palm leaves, lacquered and painted, are also made there.

Fig. 83. Portion of a lacquered table, Nandyal, Kurnool.

At Trichinopoly, models of the great temples, artificial flowers, and bullock coaches, are made of the pith of the sola plant (*Æschynomene aspera*). The pith is further employed in the manufacture of sola (not solar) topis or sun-hats, and in the construction of the decorated tazias or tābuts, representing the tombs of the martyrs Hasan and Husain, at the Muhammadan Mohurrum festival.

Of the mats of South India, those made at Tinnevelly

Fig. 84. Pith model of the Tanjore temple.

and Pālghāt in Malabar are the best known. They are
woven with the split stalks of a sedge. It is said that a
good mat will hold water for twenty-four hours, and that
a Tinnevelly mat long enough for a man to lie upon can
be rolled up and packed into the interior of a moderate-
sized walking-stick. The reed mats of Parlākimedi,
Shiyāli, and Wandiwash may also be noted.

The Victoria Memorial Hall, Madras, has, under the
auspices of the Victoria Technical Institute, been set apart
as a permanent place of exhibition and sale for selected
samples of the artistic handicrafts of the Presidency, with
a view to fostering the art industries and improving the
prospects of the artisans.

CHAPTER XXVI

THE ROLL OF HONOUR

MANY of the early travellers and pioneers, from the
thirteenth century onwards, have left in their published
writings relating to Malabar and other parts of South India
material of very great value. The book of **Ser Marco
Polo** the Venetian, written in the thirteenth century, is
said to have been one of the influences which inspired the
navigator Columbus. **Ibn Batuta**, the Arab traveller, who
visited South India in the fourteenth century, wrote an
account of his wanderings in Arabic. To the sixteenth
century belong **Ludovico di Varthema** ; **Gaspar Correa** ;
Duarte Barbosa, a relation of Magellan, whom he accom-
panied on his voyage for the circumnavigation of the globe ;
Fernao Lopez de Castanheda ; **Ralph Fitch** ; **Cæsar de
Federici**, merchant of Venice ; **van Linschoten**, who came
to the east in the train of the Archbishop of Goa ; and the

Portuguese poet **Luiz de Camoens**, who was the author
of *Os Lusiadas* (the Lusiad). To the seventeenth century
belong **Philippus Baldæus**, a Dutch chaplain; **John Fryer**,
F.R.S.; and **Jean Baptiste Tavernier**, who travelled as
a jeweller. The eighteenth century produced **Francois
Valentijn**, an army chaplain in the Dutch service; **Alex-
ander Hamilton**; **J. Canter Visscher**, chaplain at Cochin;
Edward Ives, a surgeon in the navy; **Mr Grose**, a writer in
the East India Company's service; **J. Splinter Stavorinus**,
Rear-Admiral in the service of the States General; **P.
Sonnerat**, the French naturalist, after whom the grey
jungle-fowl is named *Gallus sonnerati*; **Frao Paolino di
San Bartholomeo**, who published a Sanskrit grammar in
Tamil characters; **Joao de Barros**; and **Robert Orme**.
Orme, who was at one time a Member of Council in
Madras, and afterwards Historiographer to the East India
Company, was born at Anjengo. So, too, was **Elizabeth
Draper** (" Sterne's Eliza"), the wife of Daniel Draper of the
East India Company's service, who came to England, and
became acquainted with Laurence Sterne. The cyclone at
Masulipatam in 1864 washed away a tree which was known
as Eliza's tree. To the nineteenth century belong **Francis
Buchanan** (afterwards Buchanan-Hamilton), author of *A
Journey through the Countries of Mysore, Canara, and
Malabar*; **Mark Wilks**, the historian of Mysore, who was
Resident in Mysore (1803–8); and **George Bruce Malleson**,
the author of various books relating to Indian history, who
was guardian of the young Mahārāja of Mysore (1869–77).

In the chapter devoted to History, reference has been
made to many of those who made history during the troublous
times commencing with the arrival of the Portuguese off
the Malabar coast, and lasting till the end of the eighteenth
century. Conspicuous among these are **Vasco da Gama,
Albuquerque, Zu-l-Fikar Khān, Chanda Sahib, Mahé
de la Bourdonnais, Robert Clive, Dupleix, Stringer**

Lawrence, Nawāb Waḷajah, Bussy, Lally, Warren
Hastings, Eyre Coote, Haidar Ali, Tīpu Sultan, Arthur
Wellesley (the first Duke of Wellington), the Marquis

Fig. 85. Lord Clive.

Cornwallis, and General Harris, afterwards Lord Harris
of Seringapatam and Mysore. Sir Frederick (afterwards
Earl) Roberts was Commander-in-Chief of Madras, 1881–85.

General (afterwards Sir) **Harry Prendergast** was in command of the Burma expedition, 1885–6, which resulted in the deposition of King Theebaw, and the annexation of the country.

Mohammed Yusuf, Governor of the Madura country, who eventually rebelled against the Nawāb of Arcot, and was captured by the Nawāb and the English, and hanged as a rebel in 1764, is referred to in Malcolm's *Life of Robert Lord Clive*, as the bravest of all the native soldiers that ever served the English in India.

Umdat-ul-Umara, Nawāb of the Carnatic (1795—1801), who built the "Thousand Lights" in Mount Road, Madras, was initiated as a Freemason in the Trichinopoly Lodge about 1775.

The long line of Agents, Presidents, and Governors of Madras commencing with **Francis Day**, in whose time the building of Fort St George was begun (1640), contains many names distinguished in Indian history. In some cases, the appointment of Governor was combined with that of Commander-in-Chief. Thus, **Sir Archibald Campbell**, who was wounded at the taking of Quebec by Wolfe in 1758, fulfilled the dual *rôle*. So, too, did Major-General **William Medows**, who took the field against Tīpu Sultan in 1790. In the following year, the Governor-General, the **Marquis Cornwallis**, who capitulated at York town in America in 1781, took the command against Tīpu. **George Foxcroft**, Agent and Governor, was arrested and imprisoned by Sir Edward Winter in 1665, but reinstated three years later. The Yale University in America was named after **Elihu Yale** (1687–92), in gratitude for a present of books, pictures, and other effects, the sale of which realised £560, to the struggling school at Connecticut. **Lord Pigot** was kidnapped by his Councillors in 1776, and kept in confinement at St Thomas' Mount, whence he was removed to the Governor's Garden House, where he died. **Sir Thomas**

Rumbold (1778–80), after his retirement, was held responsible for Haidar Ali's invasion of the Carnatic, and dis-
missed from the service by the Court of Directors, but
subsequently acquitted. Hobart Town in Tasmania derives
its name from **Lord Hobart**, who became Secretary of
State for the Colonial and War Departments subsequent
to his Governorship of Madras (1794–8). **Sir Thomas
Munro**, who, during his administration of the Ceded
Districts, did much to develop the ryotwāri system of land
tenure, died of cholera at Pattikonda in Kurnool when
Governor of Madras (1827).

Tiruvallavar (the divine soothsayer), who was the
author of the poetical work entitled the Kurāl, is said to
have been the son of a Tamil Pariah woman by a Brahman
father, and to have been brought up by a Valluvan priest
of the Pariahs at Mylapore, now a suburb of Madras.
Though a Pariah, he was deemed worthy of election to
the Academy of Madura—an honour usually reserved
exclusively for Brahmans of learning. At times of census,
the Valluvans return Tiruvalluvan as one of their subdivisions.

The Hindu religion has been influenced by various
reformers, among whom Sankara Ācharya, Rāmānuja,
Vallabhācharya, and Chaitanya stand out conspicuously.
The reputed birthplace of Sankara Ācharya, a Malabar
Brahman who lived about the ninth century, is still shown
on the bank of the Alwaye river in Travancore. **Sankara**
developed the theory of pantheistic monism or Advaita,
and went to Badrināth in the Central Himalayas, where,
at the present day, a Nambutiri (west coast) Brahman
officiates as priest at the shrine of Vishnu. **Rāmānuja**,
who lived in the twelfth century, and is stated to have
been educated at Conjeeveram, was the founder of the
Vaishnava sect of Hindus. He lived at Trichinopoly,
and is said to have introduced the worship of Vishnu at

Tirupati, and to have founded 700 maths or monasteries. **Mādhva Ācharya**, who was born at the close of the twelfth century, was the founder of the Dvaita philosophy, and established temples at Udipi in South Canara, and other places. In the fifteenth century, **Vallabhācharya**, a Telugu Brahman, was the originator of the worship of Bala Gopala or the youthful Krishna. About the same time, **Chaitanya**, who was born at Nadiā in Bengal, extended the worship of Jagannāth at Puri, and his influence has had a lasting effect on the religion of the inhabitants of the Oriya country.

Of European divines, the most celebrated is **Francis Xavier** (1506–52), whose remains are buried at Goa. On the occasion of his visit to the south-east coast, he committed to memory Tamil translations of the Creed, Lord's Prayer, Ave Maria, and Decalogue, and baptised many thousands of converts, among whom large numbers of Paravas were included. The converts were known as Comorin Christians. Xavier was canonised by Pope Gregory XV in 1621. Fishermen are said, even at the present day, to call out "Xavier, Xavier," in times of storm and danger. **Robert de Nobili** (1606–56) founded a mission at Madura in 1624, in the reign of Tirumala Naik. The Lutheran missionaries **Ziegenbalg** and **Plütschau** were sent to India in 1706 by the King of Denmark, to found the Royal Danish Mission. Ziegenbalg was buried at the New Jerusalem church, Tranquebar. He was the author of a useful work on the Genealogy of the South Indian gods. The Jesuit missionary **Beschi**, who arrived at Goa in 1707, proceeded to Madura, and became Diwān to Chanda Sahib. He wrote many poems and religious works in Tamil. The Danish missionary **Schwartz** (1726–90) was sent by the Madras Government on a secret mission to Haidar Ali at Seringapatam. He settled at Trichinopoly, where he became army chaplain. His grave is in

St Peter's church, Tanjore, and his memory is perpetuated

Fig. 86. Abbé Dubois.

by a statue by Flaxman, representing the last visit of Rāja
Sarabhoji to him, in Christ Church, which he built. The

Danish missionary **Gericke** was a contemporary of Schwartz. **Abbé Dubois** (1765—1848), who was attached to the Pondicherry mission, proceeded to Mysore after the death of Tīpu Sultan in 1799, to reconvert the forced perverts to Islām. During his long sojourn in India, he made a close study of Native life, and his *Mœurs, Institutions, et Cérémonies des Peuples de l'Inde*, which has been translated into English, survives as a classic. His portrait, painted by Thomas Hickey, is now the property of the Madras Literary Society. **Claudius Buchanan** (1766—1815), who came to India as a chaplain on the Calcutta establishment, was the author of *Christian Researches in India*. He made tours in Southern India, and translated the Scriptures into Malayālam and other languages. **Reginald Heber** (1783—1826), Bishop of Calcutta, and author of many hymns and poems, died in a swimming-bath at Trichinopoly, after delivering an address from the steps of Schwartz's house. He was buried in the Church of St John. **Daniel Corrie** (1777—1836), who came to India as a Bengal chaplain, was consecrated as first Bishop of Madras in 1835. His memory is kept green by a statue in the Cathedral, and by Bishop Corrie's School. In quite recent times, **Robert Caldwell** was missionary Bishop of Tinnevelly (1877-91), and was the author of *The Comparative Grammar of the Dravidian Languages*, and other works.

Sir Thomas Strange was the first Chief Justice of Madras (1801-16), when the Recorder's Court was superseded by the Supreme Court. **Charles Philip Brown** (C. P. B.), at one time Judge of Masulipatam, where his house was known as Brown's College, was the author of a Telugu Dictionary and Grammar, which are recognised standard works. **Arthur Coke Burnell**, a former Judge of Tanjore, published a classified Index to the Sanskrit Manuscripts in the Tanjore Palace Library, and was the author of *A Hand-book of South Indian Palæography*, and other works. In collaboration with Sir Henry Yule, he compiled the invaluable *Hobson-Jobson: a Glossary of Anglo-Indian Words and Phrases*. Hobson-Jobson, it may be noted, is a corruption of the Mohurrum cry " Hasan, Husain." **John Dawson Mayne**, who practised at the Madras Bar from 1857–72, was the author of many works, which included *Commentaries on the Indian Penal Code*, *Treatise on Hindu Law and Usage*, and *The Criminal Law of India*. Thackeray dedicated *The Virginians* to **Sir Henry Davison**, who was Chief Justice of Madras (1859–60). Among lawyers of recent times, whose memory is held in esteem, are **Sir Charles Turner**, Chief Justice of Madras, **William Holloway** and **Sir T. Mutusawmy Aiyar**, Judges of the High Court, and **John Bruce Norton**, Advocate-General.

In the domain of Botany, **Hendrik van Rheede**, a Governor of the Malabar coast, published (1686—1703) a book on the flora of the west coast, entitled *Hortus Malabaricus* (the garden of Malabar), which was edited by Commelyn. The letter-press thereof was written under the superintendence of Casearius, and the drawings were mostly done by Mathæus. The French naturalist **Sonnerat**, who visited South India in the eighteenth century, made large botanical collections. He was followed by **Leschenault de la Tour, Perrottet,** and **Noton. Koenig,** the Danish physician to the Tranquebar Mission, with the missionaries **Rottler, Klein,** and **Heyne** ("the United Brothers"), made extensive collections during their tours in the south. The German missionaries **Bernard Schmid** and **Hohenacker** collected plants mainly on the Nīlgiris. During his journey through Mysore, Canara, and Malabar, **Francis Buchanan** (Hamilton) brought together a very considerable herbarium, and made many drawings and descriptions of the plants which he collected. **William Roxburgh**, keeper of the Calcutta Botanical Gardens, was the author (1795–98) of *Coromandel Plants*, of which he made a collection when surgeon at Sāmalkot in the Godāvari district, and *Flora Indica* (1820–32). **Robert Wight**, of the Madras Medical Service, made large botanical collections, and was the author of *Icones Plantarum Indiæ Orientalis* (1840–53), *Spicilegium Neilgherrense*, and, in conjunction with Arnott, of the *Prodromus Floræ Peninsulæ Indiæ Orientalis*. **Colonel R. H. Beddome**, head of the Madras Forest Department, was the author of *The Ferns of Southern India* (1863), *Flora Sylvatica* (1869), and other works. More recently, our knowledge of the flora of South India has been increased by the work of **M. A. Lawson** and **C. A. Barber**, Government Botanists, and **J. S. Gamble**, F.R.S.

Patrick Russell, who was Botanist to the East India Company, published *An Account of the Indian Snakes collected on the Coast of Coromandel* (1796), and *A Description of 200 Fishes collected at Vizagapatam* (1803). **T. C. Jerdon**, of the Madras Medical Service, was the author of *Illustrations of Indian Ornithology* (1847), *Birds of India* (1862), and *Mammals of India* (1867), which bear the impress of the born naturalist. **Edward Nicholson**, Assistant Surgeon, Royal Artillery, wrote an elementary treatise on Ophiology, entitled *Indian Snakes* (1870). **Francis Day**, of the Madras Medical Service, made a special study of Ichthyology, and published *Fishes of Malabar* (1865), *The Fishes of India* (1876–78), the volumes on fishes in the *Fauna of British India*, and numerous reports on the fishes of India and Great Britain.

In the field of Geology, **Francis Buchanan** made considerable geological and mineralogical collections during his South Indian travels. These he presented to the Marquess Wellesley, who had them placed in the library of the East India Company in London. **H. W. Voysey,** who wrote on various geological subjects between 1827 and 1833, gave an account of the native steel smelters in South India. **Captain J. T. Newbold**, F.R.S., published a large number of papers between 1833 and 1848. His work included references to the beryl mines of Padiyur; the nature of laterite, and of the black cotton soils; the magnesite and chromite of the Salem district; and various geological accounts of his journeys in South India, followed by a summary of the geology thereof, published in the *Journal of the Royal Asiatic Society* (1846, 1848, and 1850). **C. T. Kaye**, of the Madras Civil Service, who discovered the fossiliferous Cretaceous rocks of the Trichinopoly and Pondicherry areas, published various papers between 1840 and 1846. **H. F. Blanford** wrote the Geological Survey Memoirs on the Cretaceous rocks of the Trichinopoly area in 1863, and afterwards described some of the fossils. He also wrote a memoir on the Nīlgiris in 1858. In more recent times, geological work has been carried out in South India by **W. King, R. Bruce Foote**, and other members of the Geological Survey Department.

Norman Robert Pogson, who was Government Astronomer in Madras from 1861–91, was the discoverer of nine minor planets (Isis, Amphitrite, Ariadne, etc.) and twenty-one variable stars.

In the first rank of Indian administrators in recent times must be placed **Sir Sheshadri Aiyar**, the celebrated Dīwān of Mysore (1883–90). He is said to have "laboured assiduously to promote the economic and industrial development (gold-mining, railways, etc.) of the State, commencing with a deficit of 30 lakhs of rupees, and leaving with a surplus of 176 lakhs."

Rāvi Varma, the well-known artist, painted the portraits of many Indian Princes and others. He was a Koil Tampurān of Travancore, and connected by marriage with the Mahārāja of that State.

The **Rev. V. S. Azariah**, who was quite recently

consecrated as Assistant Bishop of Madras, is the first
Indian to be raised to the Anglican episcopate. The
Syrian Church on the west coast has had Indian bishops
for many centuries.

CHAPTER XXVII

THE CHIEF TOWNS AND VILLAGES

[The bracketed figures after each name give the population at the census,
1901.]

ADONI (30,416), in the Bellary district. The most
conspicuous building is the Jama Masjid, which is a fine
specimen of Muhammadan architecture, built with materials
from several Hindu temples by Sidi Masud Khān, a
Governor of Bijapur, who retired to Adoni in the seventeenth century. The town is at the present day an
important centre of the cotton trade. The population
is largely Muhammadan. Coins struck at Adoni by
several Moghul emperors bear the name Imtiyazgarh
(fort of distinction), which is said to have been given by
Aurangzīb.

ALWAYE (3,645), a village in Travancore, called by
the Portuguese Fiera d'Alva, which is a health resort for
residents at Cochin during the hot weather. At the
Sivarātri festival, a large gathering of Hindus collects
at the Siva temple in the bed of the Alwaye (Periyar)
river, on the banks of which the religious reformer Sankara
Ācharya is said to have been born.

ANANTAPUR (7,938). The administrative head-quarters
of the Anantapur district. When the Ceded Districts were
handed over to the English in 1800, Major (afterwards
Sir Thomas) Munro, who was appointed Collector thereof,

took up his abode here. Natives still name their children Munrol or Munrolappa.

ARCOT (10,734), in the North Arcot district, was formerly the capital of the Nawābs of the Carnatic, also known as the Nawābs of Arcot. Their palace is now in ruins, and the Delhi gate remains as the relic of the old rampart. The upkeep of the tomb of Nawāb Saādat-ullah

Fig. 87. Hill Fort, Anantapur.

Khān (1710—1732), in whose time the capital was transferred from Gingee to Arcot, is still provided for by Government.

BANGALORE (159,046). The seat of Government of the Mysore State and residence of the Mahārāja. The name, meaning city of beans (bengalu uru), is derived from a legend that a Hoysala king was once overtaken by night, and supped off beans and water provided by an old woman in a hut. The town is divided into two main quarters, the pettah or native town, and the civil and military station, under the control of the British Resident, in which the garrison is quartered. The Mysore Imperial Service Lancers and Mysore Bar Infantry are also quartered in the town. The Government Offices are located in the Cubbon Park, named after Sir Mark Cubbon, Commissioner of Mysore from 1834 to 1861, to whose memory an equestrian statue was erected. At the unveiling thereof the forehead was found daubed with Hindu sect-marks. Other buildings include the Central College, and the Indian Institute of Research, founded from Mr Tata's munificent bequest. The beautiful public garden, called the Lal Bāgh, dates from the time of Haidar Ali.

BELLARY (58,247). The administrative head-quarters of the Bellary district. It consists of several divisions, called the upper fort or fort hill, lower fort, cantonment for British and Indian troops, civil station, and several native quarters. The Cowl Bazar derives its name from the fact that it was originally occupied by followers and bazarmen attached to the troops, who had an agreement (cowl) that they should be free from taxes. During the Boer war deported prisoners were detained at Bellary.

BELUR, in Mysore. Celebrated for the temple of Chenna Kesava.

BEZWĀDA (24,224), in the Kistna district, where the great anicut (dam) has been constructed across the Kisna river.

BIMPLIPATAM (10,212), a sea-port town in the Godāvari district.

BOBBILI (17,837), a corruption of pedda puli, or great tiger. A town in the Vizagapatam district, where the Mahārāja of Bobbili resides. The title of Mahārāja was conferred on the Rāja in 1900. The place is celebrated in history for the attack on the fort by the French under

Fig. 88. Bēlur Temple.

Bussy and the army of Viziarām Rāzu in 1756. When Bussy entered the fort, he found every man of the garrison dead or mortally wounded. During the attack, in order to preserve the women and children from violation by the enemy, the habitations in the fort were set fire to, and those who attempted to escape were stabbed. The tragedy is commemorated by an obelisk erected by the Mahārāja, to whom the town owes the Victoria Market, Victoria Memorial Hall, a gosha hospital, and other buildings.

CALICUT (76,981). The administrative head-quarters of Malabar, which gives its name to the cotton cloth called calico. At West Hill are the barracks for British infantry. At the suburb of Kallāyi, where the Kallāyi river opens into the sea, there is a steam saw-mill for sawing timber, much of which is floated down the river.

CALINGAPATAM (5,019), a sea-port on the Ganjam coast.

CANNANORE (27,811), a sea-port town in Malabar, which was, in former times, an important military station, of which many evidences survive.

CHIDAMBARAM (19,909), in the South Arcot district, regarded by Saivites as one of the five most sacred places in South India, the others being Conjeeveram, Kālahasti, Tiruvanaikovil, and Tiruvannāmalai. At Chidambaram the emblem of the god is the ether linga, which has no actual existence, but is represented by an empty space in the holy of holies called the akasa or ether linga, wherein lies the so-called Chidambara rahasya, or secret of worship at Chidambaram. The deity worshipped is Natēsa or Natarāja, the lord or king of dancers. Of late years the Nāttukōttai Chettis (bankers and money-lenders) have spent very large sums on the restoration of the temple. The temple affairs are managed by a class of Brahmans called Dikshitars, who are also known as Thillai Muvayira-var, or the three thousand who started from Benares for

Thillai (now Chidambaram). They depend for their maintenance and the upkeep of the temple on public offerings,
and go about the country soliciting subscriptions. Like
various Malabar castes, the Dikshitars wear the kudumi
(top-knot) in the front of the head.

CHINGLEPUT (10,551), in the Chingleput district. The
town contains the Reformatory School, where the youthful
criminals of the Madras Presidency receive an excellent
industrial education. The old fort overlooks a picturesque
tank, two miles long by one mile broad. A cave outside
the town, originally constructed for a Buddhist hermit's
cell, has been converted into a Siva temple.

CHITTOOR (10,893). The administrative head-quarters
of the North Arcot district, situated 990 feet above the sea.
The locality is celebrated for its mangoes, which flourish in
topes (groves or orchards) in the neighbourhood.

COCANĀDA (48,096). The administrative head-quarters
of the Godāvari district, and the chief sea-port on the
Coromandel coast north of Madras.

COCHIN includes several distinct quarters. Of these,
British Cochin is situated on a strip of land between the
backwater and the sea, opposite the island of Vypeen.
The church, one of the oldest existing English churches
in India, contains many Portuguese and Dutch tombstones.
One of these bears the words VASCO DA..., but the armorial
bearings are not those of the Da Gama family. The native
quarter of Mattāncheri adjoins British Cochin, and contains
within it Jew's Town, occupied by the black and white Jews.
Across the water is Ernākulam, the capital of the Cochin
State, which has a durbar hall, public offices, and many
institutions. The British Residency is on the island of
Balghotty, close to Ernākulam.

COIMBATORE (53,080). The administrative head-
quarters of the Coimbatore district, situated 1300 feet
above the sea, between the Nīlgiri and Ānaimalai hills,

with a light rainfall and moderate mean temperature. The College of Agriculture has recently been transferred there from Madras, and a Forest School has been opened.

CONJEEVERAM (46,164), in the Chingleput district. The name is a corruption of Kānchipuram, meaning the shining or golden city. It is the most sacred town in South India, and, according to popular tradition, contains ten thousand lingams and a thousand temples. The great temple, at which the lingam is worshipped, is dedicated to Siva under the name of Yekambara Nādar, or lord of the one ether. The temple next in importance is dedicated to Vishnu under the name of Varatarājaswāmi. Yet another temple is dedicated to Kāmākshi, the wife of Siva. There are, in the town, many sacred tanks (ponds), by bathing in seven of which, corresponding to the days of the week, any human desire may be gratified and sins washed away. In the suburb of Tirupattikundram is a beautiful little Jain temple, with a cloistered court. It is a matter of history that Sir Hector Munro, who had retreated to Chingleput on hearing of Colonel Baillie's defeat a few miles off, threw his heavy guns and baggage into the tank of the Siva temple.

COONOOR (8,525), a favourite hot-weather resort on the Nīlgiri hills, 6000 feet above the sea, with a more temperate climate than Ootacamund. The climate is well adapted for fuchsias, roses, heliotrope, and tree-ferns, which grow luxuriantly. The place was visited by the Countess Canning, wife of the Viceroy, in 1858, and Lady Canning's Seat is named after her. The well laid-out public garden, known as Sim's Park, is named after Mr J. D. Sim, a former member of the Governor's Council, who initiated it in 1874. From Tiger's Hill, a magnificent view over the plains, extending as far as the Ānaimalai hills, is obtained. In the cemetery of All Saint's Church, Bishop Gell, who was Bishop of Madras from 1861 to 1898, lies buried. A

Pasteur Institute has been erected in recent years for the treatment of those who have been bitten by rabid dogs or jackals.

CUDDALORE (52,216). The administrative head-quarters of the South Arcot district. The name is said to be derived, not from kadal-ur, meaning sea-town, but from kūdal-ur, denoting a junction, or the place where the Ponnaiyar and Gadilam rivers meet. The town is divided into two main quarters, the Old Town, which is the business centre, and the New Town. The ruined Fort St David, with its subterranean passages, is situated within the municipal limits. The Collector's residence is the Garden House, which was formerly occupied by the local Governors.

CUDDAPAH (16,432). The administrative head-quarters of the Cuddapah district. It has a bad reputation for malaria. The English church, designed by Mr Chisholm when Government Architect, is one of the prettiest of the mofussil (up-country) churches.

DINDIGUL (25,182), in the Madura district, situated about 880 feet above the sea, and celebrated for the manufacture of cheroots.

GINGEE (524), a village in the South Arcot district, formerly the residence of a Viceroy of the Vijayanagar king. It is famous for its three forts, situated on three hills, named Kistnagiri, Rājagiri, and Chandrāya Drūg. The forts abound in relics of the past. Such, for example, are the Muhammadan building called the Audience Chamber, and granary, on Kistnagiri, and the building known as the Treasury, the masonry flagstaff, and cannon eleven feet long on Rājagiri. The Kalyāna Mahāl consists of a square court, with a tower of eight stories in the centre, surrounded by rooms, which is supposed to have been used by the ladies of the Governor's household. A long, smooth slab of rock is known as the Rāja's bathing-stone. The prisoner's well is a natural hole in a boulder about twenty feet long, down which prisoners are said to have been dropped, and left to die of starvation.

GOOTY (9,682), in the Anantapur district, celebrated for its hill fortress. On the top of a hill is a pavilion called Morāri Rao's seat, where the Marātha chieftain is said to have played chess and watched prisoners being hurled from the summit of a neighbouring rock. The body of Sir Thomas Munro, who died at Pattikanda in 1827, rested here for a short time, and a cenotaph was erected to his memory. His name is perpetuated by the Munro chattram for the accommodation of travellers. Coins were struck at Gooty by the Moghul Emperor Farrukhsiyar.

GOPALPUR (2,150). The chief sea-port of Ganjam. An iron pier was opened in 1887, but has proved useless for shipping, as, though 860 feet long, it does not extend beyond the line of surf.

GUNTUR (30,833). The administrative head-quarters of the Guntur district.

HALEBĪD (1,524). A village in Mysore on the site of the former capital of the Hoysala kings, called Dorasamudra or Dvarāvatipura. It is celebrated for the Hoysalesvara and Kedaresvara temples.

HAMPI, a small village in the Bellary district, which has given the name of the Hampi ruins to the magnificent remains of the city of Vijayanagar, the former capital of the Vijayanagar dynasty, which cover about nine square miles. The most beautiful of the ruins is the Vittalaswāmi temple near the bank of the Tungabhadra river. Other ruins include the Queen's bath, the elaborately carved platform called the Dasara Dibba, the mint, the temple of Hazāra Rāmaswāmi, the elephant stables, and the dancing-girls' street.

HOSUR (6,695), in the Salem district. The Remount Depôt, from which horses—mostly walers imported from Australia—are supplied to the cavalry and artillery, is

Fig. 89. Hazāra Rāmaswāmi temple, Hampi.

situated four miles from the town. The name waler is derived from New South Wales.

KĀLAHASTI (11,992), in the North Arcot district, where the Rāja of Kālahasti, one of the largest zamindāris in the Madras Presidency, has his residence. It is celebrated for its temple dedicated to Siva, where the vāya or wind linga is worshipped. The Sivarātri festival is celebrated in the month of Māsi (February—March) with great pomp.

KODAIKĀNAL (1,912). A hill-station, 7,000 feet above the sea, in the Madura district. Some of the first houses were built by American missionaries from Madura. A swamp was converted into a beautiful lake by Mr (afterwards Sir) Hugh Levinge, Collector of Madura, in 1863. Popular expeditions for hot-weather visitors include those to Pillar Rocks and the summit of Perumal hill (7,326 feet). At the Observatory, which was erected a few years ago, important investigations in solar physics have been carried out. At Shembaganur, below Kodaikānal, is a Jesuit Theological College.

KOTAGIRI (5,100). A hill-station on the eastern side of the Nīlgiri plateau, 6,500 feet above the sea, which is increasing in favour as a quiet hot-weather resort. It receives its name from the village of the Kotas, who are the artisans of the hills, and, in addition, cultivate food-grains, barley, potatoes, etc. Their two thatched temples are a conspicuous feature of the settlement. Kotagiri was visited by the Earl of Dalhousie, when he was Governor-General.

KOTTAYAM (17,522), in Travancore, is an important centre of the Syrian Christians, and possesses one of the oldest Syrian churches on the west coast. In the Syrian seminary are preserved two copper-plate charters, which have been deciphered by several epigraphists.

KUMBAKONAM (59,673), in the Tanjore district. The name is derived from ḱumbha, an earthen pot, and ghona, a nose or neck, and is connected with a legend of Brahma, whose pot, containing the essence of the sacred waters of the world, rested, after the deluge, at the spot now occupied by the Kumbheswara temple. The town is celebrated for the Mahāmakam tank, where orthodox Hiṇdus believe that the holy waters of the Ganges appear once in twelve years, when the planet Jupiter is in conjunction with the moon in the makha asterism of the constellation Leo. The event attracts enormous numbers of pilgrims, who bathe *en masse* in the tank. The depth of the water therein is said to be lowered by the municipal authorities, so that the pilgrims can bathe without fear of getting drowned.

KURNOOL (25,376). The administrative head-quarters of the Kurnool district, situated at the confluence of the Tungabhadra and Hindri rivers.

MADANAPALLE (14,084), in the Cuddapah district, at an altitude of 2,250 feet above the sea. A favourite resort of district officials during the hot weather.

MADRAS (509,346) is the third largest city of the Indian Empire, and the head-quarters of the Madras Government from October till April. In former days the official residence of the Governor was the Fort House, now occupied by the Government Secretariat. The existing Government House is on the site originally occupied by the Governor's Garden House, of which Government House, Guindy, or Guindy Lodge, acquired in the time of Sir Thomas Munro, has been described as the lineal successor. In the park-like grounds of Government House is the Banqueting Hall, built when Lord Clive was Governor in 1802. The battle of Plassey (1757), from which his father, Robert Clive, took the title of Baron Clive of Plassey, and the storming of Seringapatam (1799), at which Tīpu Sultan was slain, are commemorated on the north and south pediments thereof. The Fort and southern suburbs were formerly known as the White Town, as distinguished from the native quarter

to the north, called the Black Town, which is now the
commercial centre of the city. The name Black Town
was changed to George Town, to commemorate the visit of
the Prince of Wales to Madras in 1906. The most densely
populated native quarters at the present day are George
Town and Triplicane. The principal Hindu temples are
situated in Triplicane and Mylapore. A large proportion
of the Eurasian community lives in Vepery. The principal European quarters are in Egmore, Chetpat, Kilpauk,
Nungumbaukum, Teynampet, and on the north bank of

Fig. 90. Government House and Banqueting Hall, Madras.

the Adyar river. On the south side of the Adyar are the
head-quarters of the Theosophical Society, which is associated with the names of Madame Blavatsky, Colonel
Olcott, and Mrs Annie Besant. The open space, called
the Island, which is reserved by the military department
as part of the fire zone round the Fort, and is the home of
the Gymkhana Club, is formed by the Cooum river. Other
open spaces, or lungs, are the People's Park, the Napier
and Robinson Parks, named after the Governors during
whose period of office they were laid out, and the gardens

of the Agri-horticultural Society. The Marina, suggested
by that at Palermo, which owes its existence to Sir Mountstuart Grant Duff, runs along the sea-face from the Napier
Bridge southward to St Thomé. Along the Marina are
the Presidency College, Marine Aquarium, Chepauk Palace
built by Nawāb Walajah of Arcot, and now used as an
office by the Board of Revenue, the College of Engineering,
and the Senate House of the Madras University, created as
an examining corporation in 1857, where the Governor as

Fig. 91. Chepauk Palace, Madras.

Chancellor confers degrees. Further north are the Law
Courts, surmounted by the light-house 166 feet above sea-
level, and the Law College. The foundation-stone of the
Luz Church bears the date 1516, and the St Thomé
Cathedral contains memorials of the Portuguese, commencing from 1557. St Mary's Church in the Fort, which
is the earliest English church in India, was consecrated in
1680. There were buried, among others, Sir Thomas Munro
and Lord Pigot, Governors of Madras. The Roman Catholic
Cathedral in Armenian Street was erected by the Capuchins

in 1775. St George's Cathedral was consecrated in 1815, and St Andrew's (the Scotch Kirk) in 1821. The name of the old weavers' quarter of Chintadripett is said to be a corruption of St Andrew's pett. The new Portuguese Cathedral in St Thomé is reputed to occupy the site where, according to tradition, St Thomas was buried after he had been murdered. The Observatory, from which the weather reports and storm warnings are now issued, dates back to the end of the eighteenth century. The Memorial Hall was erected by public subscription, to commemorate the freedom from disturbance in Madras in the dark days of the Mutiny, during which Lord Harris, at that time Governor of Madras, allowed Madras to be denuded of troops for service in North India. The mutiny led to the raising of the Madras Volunteer Guards, which still survive. The present Museum was formerly the Pantheon, or Assembly Rooms, where banquets, balls, and theatricals were held. There, in 1793, the Marquis Cornwallis, and the hostage princes of Mysore, were entertained. There, too, in 1805, Sir Arthur Wellesley (afterwards Duke of Wellington) was entertained on his departure from India. Adjoining the Museum and Connemara Public Library is the Victoria Memorial Building, the foundation stone of which was laid by the Prince of Wales in 1906. The Madras Club was founded in 1831, and the Cosmopolitan Club in more recent years. A cenotaph near the Law Courts contains two tablets, one to the infant son of Elihu Yale, Governor of Madras (1687–92), and the other to Mrs Yale's first husband. The cenotaph originally erected to the memory of the Marquis Cornwallis in Teynampet was subsequently moved to the front of the old High Court, now the Post Office. A replica of Boehm's statue of Queen Victoria is situated near the Senate House, and one of King Edward VII by Wade outside the gates of Government House. The equestrian statue by Chantrey

Fig. 92. Statue of the Marquis Cornwallis.

of Sir Thomas Munro keeps green the memory of the celebrated Governor of Madras. According to a legend, Sir Thomas Munro seized upon all the rice depôts, and starved the people by selling rice in egg-shells at one shell for a rupee. To punish him, the Government erected the statue in an open place without a canopy, so that the birds of the air might pollute his face. The statue of the Marquis Cornwallis, Governor-General and Commander-in-Chief, was removed a few years ago from the Fort square to the Connemara Library. On the pedestal of the statue he is represented receiving the two youthful sons of Tīpu Sultan as hostages after the siege of Seringapatam in 1792. The statue of General Neill, of the Madras Fusiliers, in the Mount Road, opposite the entrance to the Madras Club, perpetuates the memory of one who, as recorded on his monument at Ayr, stemmed the torrent of rebellion in Bengal, and fell gloriously at the relief of Lucknow in 1857. A statue of the Rev. William Miller was erected in 1900 on the Esplanade opposite the Madras Christian College, of which he was Principal for many years. A statue in the Law Courts honours the memory of Sir T. Mutusawmy Aiyar, a former Judge of the High Court. The Presidency College contains a statue of Mr E. B. Powell, a former Principal thereof and Director of Public Instruction.

MADURA (105,984). The administrative head-quarters of the Madura district. The town, which is situated on the right bank of the Vaigai river, is celebrated for the great temple of Sundareswara and Mīnākshi, the palace of Tiru-mala Naik, and the Teppakulam (raft-tank) with a small temple on an island in the centre. The Vasanta or Pudu Mantapam, which is a hall 333 feet long by 105 feet wide, is said to have been built as a summer residence for the god Sundareswara. The chattram near the railway station is attributed to Mangammāl, the Queen-Regent of the

Fig. 93. Palace of Tirumala Naik, Madura.

Nāyakkan dynasty (1689—1704). The residence of the Collector, called the Tamakam, is referred to in old records as the choultry called Fort Defiance, which was an outpost during the siege of Madura in 1764. The presence of large numbers of small copper coins of the Roman Emperors (Tiberius, Honorius, etc.) in the bed of the Vaigai river seems to point to the existence of a Roman colony at Madura at one period of its history.

MALAPPURAM (9,216). A village situated in the centre of the area in which the Māppilla (Moplah) fanatical (fanum, a temple) outbreaks have disturbed the peace of Malabar from time to time. A detachment of European troops has been quartered there since 1873, and a special police force since 1885. During the outbreak at Manjeri in 1896, the fanatics, when advancing to attack, were mostly shot down at a distance of 700 to 800 yards, every man wounded having his throat cut by his nearest friend. Those who die fighting are regarded as martyrs or saints.

MANGALORE (44,108). The administrative head-quarters of the South Canara district, situated on the backwater formed by the Netrāvati and Gurpur rivers. About 25 per cent. of the population are Christians. The St Aloysius College was founded by the Jesuit Mission in 1880.

MASULIPATAM (39,507), a sea-port on the coast of the Kistna district, which is also called Bunder (sea-port). The name bunder-boat is sometimes used on the east coast for boats which communicate with ships lying at anchor. Coins struck at Masulipatam by the Moghul Emperor Aurangzīb bear the name Machlipatam (fish-town). It was formerly celebrated for its carpets and cotton fabrics (palempores, etc.).

MÉLUKOTE (3,129), a sacred town in Mysore, which is the seat of the Srivaishnava Yatirāja math, founded by the reformer Rāmānuja in the twelfth century. The principal temple is that of Cheluvapille-rāya or Krishna, and there is a further temple of Narasimha on the summit of a rock. The population is very largely composed of Brahmans. A fine white clay, said to have been discovered by Emberumānar or Rāmānuja, is used for making the nāmam or sect-mark on the forehead, and is even consigned to Benares for this purpose.

MERCĀRA (6,732), the chief town of the province of Coorg, situated about 4,000 feet above the sea. The native town is called Mahādēvapet or Mahādeopet. The fort was built by Tīpu Sultan, who, with his liking for new names, called it Jafarābād. Inside the fort is the palace, built by Linga Rāja in 1812. One of the Rājas is said to have amused himself by standing on a balcony with a rifle, and making prisoners run across the yard, while he fired at them, under the promise that, if they escaped as far as the life-size figure of an elephant in the corner of the yard, their lives would be spared. The tombs of the Rājas have been described as a combination of the Hindu and Saracenic styles.

MYSORE (68,111), a corruption of Mahisur, or buffalo town. The capital of the Mysore State, and residence of the Mahārāja, whose magnificent new palace, built to replace the old one, which was partially destroyed by fire in 1897, bears testimony to the skill of the modern artisans. The extensive new quarter of the city is called Chāmarāj, after the late Mahārāja. The city contains many public buildings, such as the Victoria Jubilee Institute, public offices, and law courts. The house occupied by Colonel Arthur Wellesley (afterwards Duke of Wellington) when Governor of Mysore after the battle of Seringapatam (1799) still exists. The Residency, now called Government House, was built when Major Wilks was British Resident, and added to a few years later by Sir John Malcolm. The Dasara festival is celebrated at Mysore with great pomp. Southeast of the town is Chāmundi hill, named after the goddess

Fig. 94. Colossal figure of the sacred bull on Châmundi hill.

Kāli or Chāmundi, who is worshipped in the temple at the summit. A flight of stone steps leads thereto, and, on the way, is the colossal recumbent figure of the sacred bull Nandi.

NĀGERCOIL (25,712), formerly the capital of Travancore. The name is derived from the temple dedicated to the snake-god (nāga kovil), where many stone images of snakes are deposited. There is a belief that snake-bite is not fatal within a mile of the temple. Native Christian women are employed in the manufacture of lace.

NANJANGŪD (5,991), in Mysore, celebrated for the temple of Nanjundēsvara. The annual car-festival attracts a number of devotees. Some Todas of the Nīlgiris have been known to make a pilgrimage to the temple, and sacrifice their locks as a thank-offering for the birth of male issue.

NELLORE (32,040). The administrative head-quarters of the Nellore district.

OOTACAMUND(18,596), a hill-station on the Nīlgiris, over 7,000 feet above the sea, which is the head-quarters of the Madras Government during the hot weather. The Government Offices are situated on Stonehouse hill, where the first house was built by Mr Sullivan, Collector of Coimbatore, in 1821. Government House, the building of which was commenced in 1876, when the Duke of Buckingham was Governor of Madras, stands above the beautiful Government Gardens, which started as a kitchen-garden in 1845. In the valley between the surrounding hills, an extensive lake has been formed by damming a stream which runs through the low-lying ground, part of which has been levelled to form the Hobart Park for the Gymkhana Club and race-course. The station is now overgrown with introduced Australian blue-gums (*Eucalyptus*), *Acacia melanoxylon* and golden wattle(*Acacia dealbata*). The great charm lies in the open downs, which are the home of the Ootacamund Hunt.

Fig. 95. Ootacamund, general view.

PALAMCOTTAH (39,545). The administrative head-quarters of the Tinnevelly district. It is an important centre of the Christian Missions, and the residence of the Bishop of Tinnevelly.

PALMANER (4,850). A village in the North Arcot district, 2,247 feet above the sea. Owing to its cool climate, it serves as a sanitarium for district officials.

PATTIKONDA (4,373). A village in the Kurnool district, where Sir Thomas Munro, when Governor of Madras, died of cholera in 1827. To his memory Government had a well constructed, and a mantapam or porch built, round which a grove of tamarind trees was planted.

PĪRMED, a small hill-station in Travancore, about 3,500 feet above the sea, surrounded by tea estates. Its name, meaning Pīr's hill, is said to be derived from a Muhammadan saint, named Pīr Muhammad, who lived there in retreat.

PONDICHERRY (27,448), the capital of the French Possessions in India. The town is divided into two quarters, the Ville Blanche and Ville Noire, corresponding to the White Town and Black Town of Madras. Some of the streets are named after Frenchmen celebrated in Indian history, e.g. Rue Dupleix, Rue Mahé de La Bourdonnais, etc. Facing the pier in the Place de la République or Place Dupleix is a statue of Dupleix, erected in 1870, which is mounted on a pedestal formed of Hindu sculptures. These sculptures, and others which may be seen in the town, are said to have been originally carried off by the French from the Venkatarāmaswāmi temple at Gingee. The town possesses a Government House, Hotel de Ville, Cathedral, Public Library, and various official buildings. The water-supply is derived from artesian wells. The vehicle commonly used by residents is a "push-push," which is dragged and pushed by coolies. The sepoys (or spáhis) are dressed in picturesque zouave uniform.

Fig. 96. Statue of Dupleix, Pondicherry.

PORTO NOVO (13,712), a sea-port in the South Arcot district, founded by the Portuguese in the latter part of the sixteenth century. The name means in Portuguese New Haven. The town is called in Tamil Parangi-pettai (European town), and by Muhammadans, Muhammad Bandar (port). A curious durga in the town is that of Araikāsu Nāchiyar, or the one pie lady, offerings to whom must on no account be worth more than one pie ($\frac{1}{192}$ of a rupee).

PUDUKKOTTAI (20,347). The chief town of the Pudukkottai State, where the Rāja has a palace, which is used on State occasions, e.g. at the Dasara festival. Many improvements were carried out in the town by Sir Seshayya Sāstri, K.C.S.I., who was Dīwān-Regent during the minority of the present Rāja.

PULICAT (5,448), in the Chingleput district, was formerly the principal settlement of the Dutch on the Coromandel coast. The Dutch cemetery, which is preserved by the Madras Government, contains many tombs elaborately carved with armorial bearings and lengthy inscriptions. The most imposing tomb is the mausoleum of one of the Governors. One of the entrances to the cemetery has a quaint Romanesque lich-gate, on each side of which is a carved skeleton, one holding an hour-glass, and the other supporting a skull on a column.

QUILON or Kollam (15,691), a sea-port on the Travancore coast, and the western terminus of the Tinnevelly-Quilon railway. The palace of the Mahārāja is on the border of the backwater, which was called by General Cullen the Loch Lomond of Travancore. There is, in Malabar, another Kollam or Quilon. The Malayālis (inhabitants of the west coast) compute the time by the Kollam or Malabar era (M.E.), which commenced on 25th August, 825 A.D. The commencement thereof is supposed to date either from the institution of the great Onam festival, or the departure of the last Perumāl

(Emperor) of Kērala for Arabia, whence he did not return.

RĀJAHMUNDRY (36,408), in the Godāvari district, on the Godāvari river.

RĀMNĀD (36,408), in the Rāmnād district, contains the palace of the Rāja of Rāmnād, who is the head of the Maravan caste. The Rājas bear the title of Sētupati, or lord of the bridge. According to tradition, the Sētupati line took its rise in the time of Rāma, who, on his return from Lanka (Ceylon), appointed seven guardians of the pass (Adam's bridge) connecting Ceylon with the Indian mainland. The Rājas formerly had the right of coinage, and the coins bear the word Sētu or Sētupati in Tamil characters.

RUSSELLKONDA (3,493) in Ganjam, named after Mr George Russell, who was deputed, between 1832 and 1836, to suppress the recalcitrant hill-chiefs called Bissoyis. Martial law was proclaimed, and some of the Bissoyis were hanged, and others transported. One result of Mr Russell's reports on the state of affairs in Ganjam was the suppression of the human (meriah) sacrifices practised by the hill Kondhs.

ST THOMAS' MOUNT (15,571), a military cantonment (pronounced cantoonment) about eight miles from Madras, called by natives Parangimalai or European's hill (Parangi or Firingi, Frank or European). On the summit of the mount, which is 220 feet above the sea, is a Portuguese church, built on the spot where the cross of St Thomas the apostle is supposed to have been found. St Thomas, according to tradition, came to Mylapore, now a suburb of Madras, and was stoned, and killed by Brahmans with a spear, near the mount. It is recorded, in connection with the disease called elephantiasis, that "the old Roman le-gendaries impute the cause of these great swelled legs to a curse St Thomas laid upon his murderers and their posterity."

SALEM (70,621). The administrative head-quarters of the Salem district.

SERINGAPATAM (8,584), a corruption of Srī Ranga patam, or the town of Srī Ranga. Situated, in Mysore, on an island in the Cauvery river, the east end of which is occupied by the suburb of Ganjam. At the storming of the fort in 1799, Tīpu Sultan was slain. The medal, struck in commemoration of the event, represents the fort, and the British lion jumping on the Mysore tiger. The tombs of Haidar Ali and Tīpu are within the mausoleum or Gumbaz, which was built by the latter. The doors of the inner entrance thereto, made of ebony inlaid with ivory, were presented by Lord Dalhousie, when he was Governor-General. The Darya Daulat Bāgh was the summer palace of Tīpu. The walls are decorated with an amusing series of grotesque pictures, illustrating the defeat of Colonel Baillie at Conjeeveram in 1780, Haidar and Tīpu in pro-cession, etc. The pictures were defaced by Tīpu before the siege, but restored by Lord Dalhousie. Near the Mysore gate is the large mosque erected by Tīpu. The Wellesley bridge over the Cauvery was built by Purniya, the Dīwān-Regent of Mysore, and named after the Marquess Wellesley, the Governor-General.

SOMNĀTHPUR (1,468). A village in Mysore, celebrated for the Chenna Kesava temple.

SRĀVANA BELGOLA (1,926). A village in Mysore, famed for its Jain bastis, and the colossal figure of Gum-matta or Gomata Rāya (p. 153).

SRINGERI (10,656), in Mysore. The math founded by the Hindu reformer Sankara Āchārya, who lived about the ninth century, is situated there. This math is the seat of the high-priest of the Smarta Brahmans. Sringeri is the traditional birthplace of Rishya Sringa, a celebrated cha-racter in the Rāmāyana, who grew up to manhood without having ever seen a woman. He was enticed away to the north, became the priest of Dasaratha, and performed the sacrifice which resulted in the birth of Rāma.

SRĪRANGAM (23,039), in the Trichinopoly district, on

Fig. 97. Carved pillars of portico, Srīrangam temple.

the island of Srīrangam in the Cauvery river. It is celebrated for the great Vishnu temple of Ranganātha. According to tradition, the Orloff diamond, which is one

T.   18

of the Russian crown jewels, was once the eye of the idol, and was stolen by a French deserter in the eighteenth century. The Siva temple is very sacred, as it contains the water lingam. The reformer Rāmānuja settled at Srīrangam in his latter years.

TANJORE (57,870). The administrative head-quarters of the Tanjore district, celebrated for the Brihatiswaraswāmi temple, with its colossal stone bull (Nandi). Among the

Fig. 98. Colossal stone bull, Tanjore temple.

Hindu figures on the tower, is that of a European, which, according to tradition, was prophetic of the advent of the British, or is the figure of a Dane, who helped to build the temple. A big iron cannon, nearly 30 feet long, is attributed to the same Dane. The Library contains a valuable collection of oriental manuscripts, brought together by the Nāyak and Marātha kings of Tanjore. The palace of the latter contains portraits of the various kings, and a statue of Rāja Sarabhoji by Chantrey. It is now occupied by the surviving Rānis of Rāja Sivaji, on whose death in 1855, the Rāj became extinct. Three years before his death, he married, in addition to his existing wives, seventeen girls.

TELLICHERRY (27,883). A sea-port on the Malabar coast, which was once the principal British trading station on the west coast. Silver coins struck by the English East India Company bear the initial letter T, the scales of justice, the figures 99, and date 1805.

TINNEVELLY (40,469). The chief town in the Tinnevelly district, on the Tambraparni river.

TIRUCHENDUR (26,056) in the Tinnevelly district. A great resort of pilgrims, who come there to visit the temple, which is built out into the sea.

TIRUPATI (15,485), in the North Arcot district, sometimes called Lower Tirupati, to distinguish it from Upper Tirupati or Tirumala, the sacred hill of pilgrimage. Many of those who resort thither do so in the performance of a vow made to the god Venkatēswaraswāmi in case of sickness, desire for male offspring, and for other reasons. Sometimes the devotees part with locks, or the entire hair of the head, and are shaved by barbers on the spot. In many families, offerings of money for the god are stored in boxes called undi, and eventually presented at the shrine. On the way leading up the hill, knots may be seen tied in the leaves of young date-palms. This is the work of virgins, who, by so doing, hope to ensure the tying of the marriage tāli on their necks. Men cause their names to be cut in the rocks on the wayside, or on the stones, with which the path leading to the temple is paved, in the belief that good luck will follow, if dust from the feet of some pious man falls on it. The summit of the hill, which is 2,500 feet high, is reached by a flight of stone steps. A paved road leads thence to Tirumala. The affairs of the temple are presided over by two religious heads, called Jiyengars, and a Mahant, or secular head and trustee.

TIRUVANNĀMALAI (17,069), in the South Arcot district. At the foot of Tiruvannāmala (the holy fire hill) is a celebrated temple. At one of its festivals a huge beacon is lighted in memory of a legend connected with Siva and Parvati, and the appearance of the former on the hill as a pillar of fire.

TRANQUEBAR (13,142), on the coast of the Tanjore district, formerly a Danish settlement. The town is entered by a gateway, bearing the monogram of the King of Denmark, and date 1792. The present English church was built by the Danes in 1620, and the New Jerusalem church by the Danish missionary Ziegenbalg in 1717. The former contains various Danish relics, such as a silver communion service, and a painting of the Last Supper.

TRICHINOPOLY (104,721). The administrative head-quarters of the Trichinopoly district, situated on the right bank of the Cauvery river. The town is celebrated for the rock, rising to a height of 273 feet, which is ascended by a flight of stone steps. The rock temple is dedicated to Māthubuthesvara or Tāyumānavar. A representation of the rock is sculptured on the monument in Westminster Abbey to Stringer Lawrence, who defeated the French at the battle of the Golden Rock in 1753. At the foot of the rock is the teppakulam tank, which, as well as the rock, is illuminated on great occasions.

TRICHUR (15,585) in the Cochin State, the origin of which is, by tradition, attributed to Parasu Rāma. The temple of Vadakunnāthan, reputed to be the oldest temple on the west coast, is situated on an eminence, and surrounded by a high wall. There are several maths, where Nambutiri Brahmans are fed, and instructed in the Vēdas. The town also possesses a palace, and two Syrian Christian churches

Fig. 99.   Rock Temple, Trichinopoly.

TRIVANDRUM (57,882), the capital of the Travancore State, and residence of the Mahārāja, whose palace, as well as the Padmanabhaswāmi temple, is situated within the town. The buildings include the British Residency, the Museum, designed by Mr Chisholm on the lines of Malayālam architecture, and situated in the public gardens, the Mahārāja's college, and the observatory. The Mahārāja's Nāyar Brigade is quartered in the town.

TUTICORIN (28,048). The southern terminus of the South India railway in Tinnevelly, and port of embarkation for Ceylon. It is famous for its pearl-fisheries, and is an important centre of the cotton industry. About 30 per cent. of the population are Paravas, whose forefathers were converted *en masse* to the Roman Catholic religion by Michael Vaz, Vicar-General of the Bishop of Goa, and Francis Xavier, in the sixteenth century.

UDIAMPERUR (5,327) in Travancore, where Alexis de Menezes, Roman Catholic Archbishop of Goa, held, in 1599, the celebrated synod of Diamper, which had an important bearing on the future of the Roman Catholic and Syrian churches. Menezes is said, like a second Omar, to have had all the books written in the Syrian or Chaldæan language, which he could collect, committed to the flames, not only at the synod, but during his subsequent visitation of the Syrian churches.

VELLORE (43,537) in the North Arcot district, celebrated for its temple and fort. In 1806, a mutiny broke out among the native troops, with the object of massacring the Europeans, and seizing the fort in the name of the sons of Tīpu Sultan, who had been detained at Vellore since their father's death in 1799. The exciting cause of discontent is said to have been the introduction of a new leather headgear bearing a faint resemblance to a European topi (hat), and of a new turnscrew in the shape of a cross, which was ordered to be worn next the heart.

Fig. 100. Vellore Fort.

VINUKONDA (7,266) in the Guntur district, situated under the Vinukonda hill. The name, meaning hill of hearing, is connected with a tradition that it was here that Rāma heard the news of the abduction of his wife Sīta.

VIZAGAPATAM (40,892). A sea-port town, and the administrative head-quarters of the Vizagapatam district, situated in the bay formed by the headland called Dolphin's Nose. Many of the officials live at the delightful suburb of Waltair, to the north of the town.

VIZIANAGRAM (37,270) in the Vizagapatam district. The name is a corruption of Vijaya-nagaram (city of victory), and is derived from Viziarāma Rāzu, who founded it. The palace of the Rāja of Vizianagram is situated within the fort, and in front of it are statues of the last Mahārāja and his father.

WELLINGTON (4,793). A military cantonment and convalescent depôt on the Nīlgiri hills, 6,100 feet above the sea. It was originally called Jakatala after a Badaga village in the neighbourhood, but was named Wellington, after the first Duke, by Sir Charles Trevelyan, Governor of Madras, in 1860. It is garrisoned by British Infantry. The race-course is situated in a hollow, within an amphitheatre of wooded hills, below the cantonment.

WHITEFIELD (968), a settlement in Mysore for Eurasians and Anglo-Indians, named after Mr D. S. White, the founder of the Eurasian and Anglo-Indian Association. The colonists are mainly occupied in the cultivation of fruit, vegetables, and food-grains, rearing fowls, etc.

YERCAUD (7,787), a corruption of Er-kād, meaning lake-wood. A hill-station in the Salem district, which finds favour as a quiet health-resort in the hot weather.

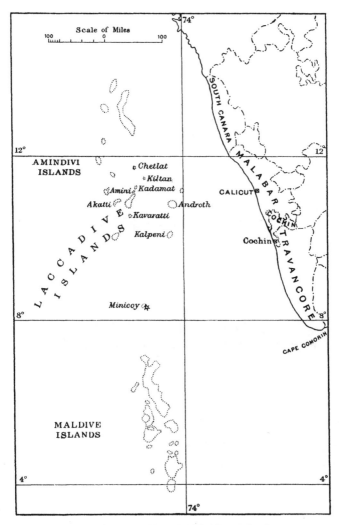

Map of the Laccadive and Maldive Islands.

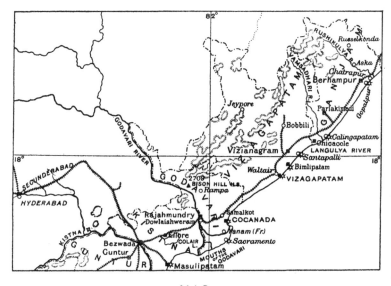

MAP

OF THE

MADRAS PRESIDENCY,

MYSORE, COORG, AND THE ASSOCIATED STATES.

Scale of Miles

50   0   50   100

⊠ TOWN	Municipality

| TINNEVELLY | Towns having 40,000 and more Inhabitants |

| Guntur | ,,   ,,   from 20 to 40,000   , |

| Hindupur | ,,   ,,   ,, 10 to 20,000   ,, |

| *Pamban* | ,,   ,,   below 10,000   ,, |

BANGALORE⎫ Towns outside the
Maddur ⎭   Presidency Administration.

—·—·—·—   District Boundary

▲
8642   G.T. Station and Height in feet above sea level

☆   Light house

▨ ▤   Native State

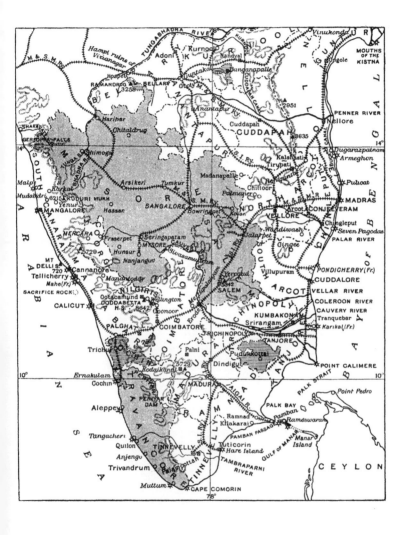

LIST OF BOOKS, ETC.,

PLACED UNDER CONTRIBUTION

BARNETT (L. D.), Hinduism [Religions : ancient and modern, 1906].

BLANFORD (W. T.), Mammalia [Fauna of British India, 1888–91].

BREEKS (J. W.), Account of the Primitive Tribes and Monuments of the Nīlagiris, 1873.

BRUCE (J.), Annals of the Honorable East India Company, 3 vols, 1810.

BUCKLAND (C. E.), Dictionary of Indian Biography, 1906.

CALDWELL (R.), Comparative Grammar of the Dravidian or South Indian Family of Languages, 1875.

Census Reports, Madras, Mysore, etc.

CHURCH (A. H.), Food-grains of India, 1886.

CROOKE (W.), The Rude Stone Monuments of India [Proc. Cotteswold Naturalists' Field Club, XV, part II, 1905].

    The Tribes and Castes of the North-western Provinces and Oudh, 4 vols, 1896.

DANVERS (F. C.), The Portuguese in India, 2 vols, 1894.

    The Dutch in Malabar [Selections from the Records of the Madras Government, 1911].

Encyclopædia Britannica, 11th ed., 1910–11.

FERGUSSON (J.), History of Indian and Eastern Architecture, ed. 1910, 2 vols.

FERMOR (L. L.), Manganese in India [Trans. Mining and Geological Institute of India, 1906].

    Manganese-ore Deposits of India [Mem. Geol. Survey of India, XXXVII, 1909].

FOOTE (R. B.), Catalogue of the Prehistoric Antiquities in the Government Museum, Madras, 1901.

    The Geology of Bellary district [Mem. Geol. Survey of India, XXV, 1896].

    Notes on some recent Neolithic and Palæolithic Finds in South India [Journ. Asiat. Soc. Bengal, LVI, part II, 1887].

GRIERSON (G. A.), Linguistic Survey of India, 1904–8.

HAVELL (E. B.), The Ideals of Indian Art, 1911.

HOLLAND (T. H.), Corundum [Geol. Survey of India, 1898].
  The Charnockite series [Mem. Geol. Survey of India, XXVIII, part 2, 1900].
  Mica Deposits in India [Mem. Geol. Survey of India, XXXIV, part 2, 1902].

IBN BATOUTAH, Voyages, 4 vols, Paris, 1853–8.

Imperial Gazetteer of India, 26 vols, 1907–9.

JACKSON (J. R.), Commercial Botany of the Nineteenth Century, 1890.

JONES (R. Ll.), A Discussion of Types of Weather in Madras [Mem. Indian Meteorological Department, XX, part 4, 1908].

LAKE (P.), Note on the Mud-banks of the Travancore Coast [Rec. Geol. Survey of India, XXIII, 1890].

Letters from Madras, By a Lady, 1843.

LOVE (H. D.), Descriptive List of Pictures in Government House and the Banqueting Hall, Madras, 1903.

Madras District Gazetteers and Manuals.

MARSDEN (W.), Travels of Marco Polo, 1818.

MAXWELL-LEFROY (H.), Indian Insect Life, 1909.

Meteorites, Introduction to the Study [British Museum, Natural History, 1908].

MIDDLEMISS (C. S.), Preliminary Notes on some Corundum Localities in the Salem and Coimbatore Districts [Rec. Geol. Survey of India, XXIX, 1896].

Minerals, Introduction to the Study [British Museum, Natural History, 1910].

ORME (R.), History of the Military Transactions of the British Nation in Indostan, 2 vols, 1861.

REA (A.), Monumental Remains of the Dutch East India Company in the Presidency of Madras [Arch. Survey of India, XXV, 1897].
  Pallava Architecture [Arch. Survey of India, XXXIV, 1909].
  Prehistoric Antiquities of Tinnevelly: Āditanallur [Annual Report, Arch. Survey of India, 1902–3].
  The Stupa of Bhattiprolu [Arch. Survey of India, XV, 1894].

REYNOLDS (B. O.), Irrigation Works, Madras, 1906.

RICE (L.), Mysore and Coorg Manual, 1878.

RISLEY (H. H.), Tribes and Castes of Bengal, 2 vols, 1891–2.

RIVERS (W. H. R.), The Todas, 1906.

Rubber Exhibition, Official Guide, 1911.

Statistical Abstract relating to British India, 1910.

Statistical Atlas of India, 2nd ed., 1895.

THOMPSON (E. W.), The last Siege of Seringapatam, 1907.

THOMSON (Sir J.), The City of Madras [Journ. Society of Arts, LV, No. 2836, 1907].

THURSTON (E.), The Castes and Tribes of Southern India, 7 vols, 1909.
    History of the Coinage of the Territories of the East India Company in the Indian Peninsula, 1890.
    Pearl and Chank Fisheries of the Gulf of Manaar [Bull. Madras Museum, No. 1, 1894].
    Sea Fisheries of Malabar and South Canara [Bull. Madras Museum, III, No. 2, 1900].

WARTH (H.), Quarrying of Granite in India by means of Wood Fire [Nature, LI, 1894–5].

WATT (Sir G.), The Commercial Products of India, 1908.

WHITEHEAD (Bishop), The Village Deities of Southern India [Bull. Madras Museum, V, No. 3, 1907].

WILSON (H. M.), Irrigation in India [U.S. Geological Survey, 2nd ed., 1903].

YULE (H.), and A. C. BURNELL, Hobson-Jobson, 2nd ed., 1903.

INDEX

INDEX

Erramala hills 21

Fasli year 194
Fire by friction 127
Fish-curing 220
Fish insect 97
Fish-maws 219
Fish oil 219–20
Fish, sacred 30
Fishery Department 225
Fishes 95–7
Flying-fox 87
Food-grains 195–6
Fort Defiance (Madura) 263
Fort St David 172, 176, 252
Fort St George 1, 169, 171, 174, 256
Foxcroft, George 237
Fraserpet 28
Freemasonry 10, 12, 237
French coins 7, 173
French Company 171, 172
French possessions 6–7
Frogs 95
Frost 46
Fruits, cultivated 197–200

Gandikota fort 27
Gangaikonda Cholapuram, temple 158
Ganges, legends 24, 27, 256
Gell, Bishop 251
Gentoo 171
Geologists, distinguished 243–4
Gersoppa falls 23
Ghāt, meaning of word 13
Ghāts, eastern 13, 20–22; vegetation 107–8
Ghāts, western 13, 17–20, 189; vegetation 104–5
Ghī 213
Gingee 246, 252, 268
Gingelly oil 197
Ginger 197
Gneiss 57, 62
Godāvari river 24, 35, 190, 205
Golconda, kings 70, 169
Gold-fields 61, 71–3
Gold-washers 73
Golden Firman 169
Golden Rock, battle 174, 276
Gomatēsvara, colossal stone figure 153
Gondi language 123
Gondwāna geological formation 62–3
Gondwānaland 63
Gooty 253
Gopalpur 37, 253

Gourami 97
Gram 195
Grāma Dēvata (village deities) 135–6
Granite 57, 59
Grant Duff, Sir Mountstuart 18, 258
Graphite 73
Ground-nut 197
Gudigar wood-carvers 230
Guntur 253
Gurpur river 23, 263

Hagari river 26
Haidar Ali 36, 50, 177, 239, 247, 272
Halebīd 162, 253
Hamadryad 94
Hamilton, see Buchanan-Hamilton
Hampi (Vijayanagar) 26, 253
Hare island 35
Harris, General (Lord Harris) 180, 259
Hastings, Warren 177
Heber, Reginald 241
High Range, Travancore 18
Hindu death rites, sacred bath 28
Hindu idols for settlers in Burma 43
Hinduism 130
Hindustani language 124
Hobart, Lord 238
Hobson-Jobson 242
Holeyas, privileges 130
Hook-swinging 129
Hope island 35
Hosur, remount depôt 253
Hulikal Drūg 13
Husain Dost Khān 173

"Ibex" (wild goat) 91
Ibn Batuta 11, 234
"Iguana" 95
Inām land 195
Indian corn 195
Indigo 212
Indo-Saracenic Architecture 164
Infanticide 127–8
Insectivora 87
Insects 97–102; mimicry 97, 100; season dimorphism 99
Iron smelting 74–5
Irrigation works 200–7
Irula 17, 127, 141
Ivory carving 231

Jackal 87, 211
Jack fruit 199
Jaggery 119, 210

INDEX 291

Pumping and Boring Department
   202-3
Purana geological formations 62
Purnaiya, Regent of Mysore 180, 272
Pushkaram festival 25
Pushpagiri 22
Python 94

Quilon 37, 270
Quinine, manufacture 218

Rāgi 195
Railways, Bengal-Nagpur 187; Great
   India Peninsula 186; Madras and
   South Mahratta 186-7; Nīlgiri
   187; Partakimedi 187; Shoranur-
   Cochin 187; South Indian 187-90
Rainfall, statistics 47, 49, 52
Rājahmundry 25, 271
Rāma, legends 8-9, 24, 153, 271,
   272-3, 280
Rāmandrūg 5; manganese 75
Rāmānuja 130, 131, 238, 263, 264,
   274
Rāmēsvaram 33, 161, 224
Rāmnād 271
Rampa rebellion 21
Rangaswāmi pillar 15
Rat 32, 87-8
Rat-flea and plague 88
Rat-snake 32
Rattan 114
Rāvi Varma 244
Red Hills tank 201
Red sanders tree 108, 113
Reformatory school 250
Regent diamond 71
Rēgur 208
Religion, statistics 137
Remount depôt 253
Rheede, Hendrik van 242
Rice 195
Richelieu, Cardinal 171
Roberts, Earl 236
Rodents 87
Roman coins 67, 263
Rosewood 105; carving 231
Roxburgh, William 243-4
Rubber, cultivation 218
Rumbold, Sir Thomas 238
Ruminants 90
Rushikulya river 193, 205
Russellkonda 271
Ryat 193
Ryatwāri land revenue system 194
Ryswick, treaty 172

Sacramento shoal 25
Sacrifice rock 36
Sago palm 114; spirit distilled 119
St Mary's island 36
St Thomas 259, 271
St Thomas' Mount 59, 271
Sāl tree 108, 109, 113
Salem 209, 272
Saltpetre, manufacture 79
Sāmalkot, sugar-cane station 210
Samarskite 79
Sandalwood 108, 110, 113; carving
   230, 231
Sandstone 61, 62, 80
Sandur State 5, 184; manganese 75
Sankara Āchārya 131, 238, 245, 272
Sankaridrūg 57
"Sardines" 219-20
Saurāshtra 123
Saw-fish 96
Schist 57, 62
Schwartz 239
Sea fisheries, statistics 220
Sea-snakes 94
Seaports, principal 37
Seasons 44-53
Sedimentary rocks 54
Sericulture 100
Seringapatam 164, 272; history, 178,
   180, 256
Servile classes, privileges 129-30
Sētupati, coins 271
Seven Pagodas, see Mahābalipuram
Seven, sacred number 24, 271
Shale 61, 62
Shānar 117
Shānbōg 183
Shark-charmer 223
Sharks 95-6; fins 219
Shembaganur, Jesuit college 255
Sheshadri Aiyar, Sir 244
Shevaroy hills 22, 59; rubber culti-
   vation 218
Shiyāli, mats 234
Shola 106, 113
Sholingur, battle 177
Shoranur 187
Silk-moths 100
Silpa Sastras 161
Singarāzu peak 20
Sivagaṅga, metal-ware 230
Sivarātri festival 245, 255
Sivasamudram island, 28
Snakes 94
Soils, classification 194
Somnāthpur, temple 162, 272

For EU product safety concerns, contact us at Calle de José Abascal, 56–1°,
28003 Madrid, Spain or eugpsr@cambridge.org.

www.ingramcontent.com/pod-product-compliance
Ingram Content Group UK Ltd.
Pitfield, Milton Keynes, MK11 3LW, UK
UKHW012329130625
459647UK00009B/168